THE ECONOMIC TRIBULATION

How to Survive & Prosper!

LARRY BALLARD

ISBN: 978-0-9844733-0-4

Published by

BRIDGER HOUSE PUBLISHERS, INC.

P.O. Box 2208, Carson City, NV 89702, 1-800-729-4131

Larry Ballard

www.GeopoliticalAffairs.net

email: larryballard1@yahoo.com

Printed in the United States of America

Layout / Typesetting:
Julie Melton, The Right Type Graphics, USA

10 9 8 7 6 5 4 3 2 1

Contents

Introduction

I am not a politician like President Obama, or a real estate mogul, like Donald Trump, or a captain of industry, like Bill Gates. I have no agenda or vested interest in writing this book other than to try to help as many people as possible get their financial house in order, so they will be in a position to survive the economic melt down of the U.S. economy and possibly even prosper from it. My motivation comes from the fact that I grew up in the ghetto, in the inner city of St. Louis. As a matter of fact, I lived in a burrow by the name of Wellstone, which had the distinction of being the second poorest burrow in St. Louis. I was one of only four white kids in my elementary school. When I was in third grade, by an unbelievable twist of fate, I was bussed to the white suburbs, where the *"poor white boy"* was utterly shunned by his fellow white students because, well just because.

The experiences of my early childhood taught me that poverty is a thief that comes in the night. It steels your self-respect, your hope and your dreams and leaves you feeling demoralized, angry and disillusioned. Worse, it paralyzes you with fear. Poverty has no respect for age, gender, race or education. It treats all people equally disrespectful.

From another perspective, I want to help save as many marriages as possible. I am divorced and, in large part, the reasons for my divorce originated in my early childhood and the fear that resulted from poverty. It made me into a workaholic. Today, most Americans are workaholics, although the cause of their affliction originates from a different source than mine. Mine originated from fear of poverty, while theirs originates from the fact that they have been brainwashed by Madison Avenue advertisers into believing that their happiness depends on having material possessions. Their battle cry is *"I want that, and I want it now."* Moreover, in order to get it, they are willing to sell their souls to the money changers. In effect, they become indentured servants who have to work like slaves to pay for goods and services they were falsely convinced they couldn't live without. The net result of this pursuit of materialism has been to estrange husbands and wives and leave children to fend for themselves, as both Mom and Dad leave them alone in order to pursue the all mighty dollar. The American family, indeed the entire society, is estranged, and divorce is sweeping the nation like a plague. There is nothing that can put strain on a marriage or for that matter a family faster than having money problems. This strain is all the more serious when the family was estranged to begin with.

Regrets, I have a few, and I sincerely would like to see as many of you as possible not have to learn the hard way, like I did, that getting money man's way is an invitation to disaster. It doesn't cost a thing to stop and smell a rose, look at a sunset, play with your children or hug your wife. The truth is that the best things in life are free. God is in the beauty and fragrance of the flower, the power and majesty of the ocean, the grace of a swan, the beauty of an eagle. Indeed, he is in all that is beautiful and good and worthwhile. He wants us to take the time to get to know our family and neighbors even more, He wants us to take the time to get to know Him, so:

He can take away our fear and show us the beauty and love that is the essence of His kingdom. God is love, and love is worth more than any material possession you could ever own. It is time we came to our senses and stopped chasing things and started loving one another.

Best Wishes,
Larry Ballard

PART I

America's Economic Outlook

Chapter 1: THE AMERICAN FAMILY IN CRISIS!

Chapter 2: ADDICTED TO CREDIT!
What Happens When the Credit Runs Out?

Chapter 3: COLLAPSE OF THEIR U.S. ECONOMY!
An Historic Prospective!

Chapter 4: THE GREAT DEPRESSION (1929-1941)
Is History Repeating Itself?

Despite what you might think from looking at the chapter headings above, this is a book of hope and inspiration!

I believe that we are in what will prove to be the Second Great Depression. We need to know that, so we will be motivated to get our financial houses in order so we can protect our financial assets and our families from experiencing unnecessary hardship. If we are properly positioned, it is even possible to financially prosper in hard economic times.

This book will arm people with a realistic seven-step plan for how to live within their means, get out of debt, protect their assets from economic upheaval, and develop a realistic retirement program that will see them retire well off and have the life they always wanted. It will show them how to take control of their lives and truly enjoy themselves.

CHAPTER 1

THE AMERICAN FAMILY IN CRISIS

If you have not read the introduction to this book, please do so now before you read any further. This book is ultimately about *"empowering people to take control of their lives and their finances."* However, before I can get to the good news, I have to give you a compelling reason to change, which means I have to walk you through the economic problems that I believe make it compulsory that we Americans must learn to be more financially self-sufficient. I also want to give you a chance to get to know me, so you can determine whether my advice is credible. The first three chapters of this book are intended to make us reevaluate some of our financial decisions and consider the possibility that we might need to change our spending habits. This book makes some predictions most people won't want to hear. Nevertheless, the *Bible* says, *"know the truth, and the truth will set you free."* The truth contained in the pages of this book will not only set people free, but also protect us and our families from hardship and show us how to be both prosperous and happy! This is a book of hope, not a book of despair. Unfortunately, people are resistant to change and often the only way to bring about meaningful change is to present the consequences of not changing. Again, I say please read the introduction before going any further. If ever there was a book you need to read, this is it!

Welcome back! Hopefully, you have read the introduction and have some insight into who I am and exactly what has motivated me to write this book. My story and your story might not be the same. My reality and yours might be different, colored as they have been by different circumstances. Nevertheless, it is very important for you to understand where I am coming from so that, as you read this book, you grow to trust me and view me as a friend. Although I may be telling you something you don't want to hear, you will listen, because you know I have your best interest at heart. You see, there are some topics like the ones in this book that we would just rather not even think about, because, heaven help us, if we believe what we read, our world will never be the same. Life will never again be as simple. We can never again go through life oblivious to what is going on around us. Once our eyes are open, like it or not, we see the truth. My purpose for writing this book is precisely to open your eyes and, as it says in the *Bible*, *"let those with eyes see, and those with ears hear."* The message in this book is too important to stand on social propriety. I have to tell the truth and hope that this book gets in the hands of those with eyes to see and ears to hear. Our financial future depends on it. Our happiness depends on it and, perhaps most important, the future of our sons and daughters depends on it.

Consider the following, and ask yourself if it in any way applies to you, and if it does what are you prepared to do about it?

The average American has approximately $10,000 in credit card debt. Assuming a minimum monthly payment and an interest rate of 18 percent, it will take approximately 30 years to pay off the credit card debt at a total cost of over $20,000. If invested with an annual return of 10 percent, that $20,000 would result in savings of $400,000 over 30 years.

It is hard to believe, but:

- ■ Half of all Americans have less than $25,000 in savings.

- ■ One fifth of all Americans have nothing, zero, nada in savings.

- ■ According to a study done by the American Association of Retired Persons (AARP), the average baby boomer that is approaching retirement has approximately $1,000 in savings.

Most Americans are on the 40/40 program. That is to say, they work 40 hours a week, spend what they make, work some more, spend what they make, and repeat this cycle over and over again for 40 years and end up with nothing to show for all their hard work.

Did you see yourself or any of your family or friends in these statistics? If so, my goal in this book is to provide you with two life-altering things: the necessary knowledge to change your circumstances and the will to change! This book contends that the events that led up to The Great Depression of 1929 are being repeated, resulting in a second Great Depression. But, let me ask you a question. What if I present my case for why I believe there we are headed for a total economic collapse and you don't buy into it? In that event, is there any reason for you to keep reading? Yes, there is, and here it is! Ask yourself what the difference is between a recession and a depression. When you correctly understand the difference, you will know why you need to be armed with the information in this book. I don't think there can be much question that the American economy is being impacted by globalization and that, as a result, our financial security is not on as sound a footing as it was a few years ago. That means that America has for the last several years been experiencing a chronic recession. Likewise, I believe it is reasonable to say that as we go forward the effects of globalization will continue to negatively impact our financial security, as we are impacted by mergers and acquisitions, downsizing, outsourcing and the governments out of control spending. So, again I ask what is the difference between a recession and a depression? On a personal level, a recession becomes a depression the second we and our families are impacted. If your manager calls you into his office on a Friday at 4p.m., asks you to sit down and proceeds to tell you that he is terribly sorry but sales are down and the company is forced to lay you off; that is the very instance at which the recession becomes a depression for you and your family!

This book effectively asks if some unforeseen economic hardship were to befall you and your family would you be able to survive it. Would it be an inconvenience, or would it be a catastrophe that could thrust you and your family into economic hardship and create your personal version of the Great Depression?

I guess I should fess up and admit that I am a Christian, but those of you who aren't need not panic. My primary purpose in this book is not to extol the virtues of religion. I quote verses from the *Bible* occasionally when they help get my point across. Your religious beliefs are not my concern, and I will not be trying to convert you to my religion.

However, all religions have certain guiding principles that help us in attaining prosperity and finding that elusive phantom known as happiness. It is important to get these two topics across in this book. I contend that, contrary to what we would like to admit, most of our lives are out of control. Modern society puts us under pressure to perform. It gives us precious little time to ourselves. It pits faction against faction. It extols the virtues of wealth as a status symbol without stopping to consider the cost associated with attaining that wealth and whether or not it does us more harm than good.

Throughout this book I will repeatedly refer to the fact that there are two ways to get rich: **man's way and God's way. God's way adds happiness, and man's way adds sorrow.**

One of my primary reasons for writing this book is that I am very concerned about America and her future as a nation. I am equally concerned about the unhappiness and stress that is becoming an ever-present part of the daily lives of more and more Americans. I see that—despite our wealth, or more appropriately because of our pursuit of wealth—we are at our core, at the center of our beings, unhappy. What joy can life really hold, if we cannot smile, laugh, stop and smell the roses, and see the beauty in the simple pleasures of life, in the beauty that God gave us for free? What happiness can life possibly hold if we go through life constantly worried about finances? Will we have a job tomorrow? Can we pay our bills next month? What peace can we have if we are constantly stressed, because we have purchased material possessions for which we are worried about paying? In this instance, we have to ask ourselves whether we own the possessions or whether they, in some ironic twist of irony, own us?

I contend that much, if not most, of our stress and unhappiness stems from the fact that we have been brainwashed by Madison Avenue advertisers, who have convinced us that the pursuit of material possessions is the key to happiness. They have impressed this on our psyches to such a degree that our social and economic status defines our perceptions of our self-worth. Our self-esteem is literally defined by how big a house we live in, how fancy a car we drive, how much money we make. Unfortunately, little thought is given to defining our self-worth based on how good a citizen we are, how good a friend we are, how good a mother or father we are, or what values we demonstrate. No consideration is given to the personal freedoms that we give up in order to pursue these material possessions. No consideration is given to the damage that is done to our relationships, especially relationships with our loved ones. How can we have quality relationships if we are working all the time and have no time to share the pleasures of life with those we love?

Believe me I know what I am talking about here, because pursuit of money cost me my marriage. Because I had grown up in poverty, I was afraid of being poor, so I spent most of my adult life chasing the almighty dollar. Now I have learned the hard way just how unimportant money is when measured against the loss of intimacy with those we love. I learned the hard way that those who choose the pursuit of money, or *"man's way,"* because they think it will make them happy are in fact on a collision course with a greater sorrow than they can imagine. We mistakenly think that if we have money it will make us happy, but it won't. What makes us happy is to connect at some core level with other human beings and experience the love that God intended for us to experience. By experiencing carnal love we begin to understand what God's purpose is for us here on this earth. He is love incarnate and He wants us to grow to a point where we can gain some measure of the fact that LOVE IS THE MOST IMPORTANT THING IN THE WORLD! It is love, not money that brings us happiness. It is love, not money that makes life worth living. Also it is giving that makes us rich and taking that makes us poor. I finally understand why it is more blessed to give than to receive. I finally understand what is wrong with getting rich man's way and have compassion for all those who, by virtue of their circumstances, are headed for a personal tragedy that is designed to teach them the hard way that the pursuit of riches man's way brings sorrow.

America is like a Mack Truck carrying a load of nitroglycerin going down the highway at 70 miles per hour: the brakes are out and just ahead is a cliff, and it's just a matter of time before it goes careening off the cliff to plunge to certain destruction on the rocks below! The impact will be so explosive that there will not be any fragments left large enough to identify. The America we know will forever be changed and our lives will be shattered. I hope to warn as many people as possible and help as many as possible to get their lives in order so they will be able to stand against the winds of change that are surely blowing across this great nation.

Our imminent downfall stems from greed. We refuse to recognize that we are no longer the captain of industry we once were. With the industrialization of China and India and recent events in Europe, we have lost our strangle hold on world trade. As a result, our economic life-force, like the blood coursing through our veins, is ebbing away one drop at a time as the economic blood of our great nation flows abroad to strengthen those in far away lands.

We no longer control world trade. We no longer control the wealth of nations. We no longer wield the economic clout we once did. For these reasons, economic balance will be restored to the world economic system. We will be diminished as other countries are enlarged, and there is precious little we can do to prevent it. The harsh reality is that as America continues to consume more products from overseas than it produces domestically, our labor force will be negatively impacted. We will incur declining salaries, downsizing, outsourcing, mergers and acquisitions, and the wholesale elimination of our manufacturing sector as America becomes increasingly a service-oriented country.

The destabilization of our labor force has collided with the economic forces of banking, the stock market, and real estate and the economic imbalance has brought the economic engine that propels our economy to a grinding halt. As bad as it looks now the worst is yet to come as other countries eventually abandon the U.S. dollar plunging the U.S. into hyper-inflation. The result will be an economic collapse of unimaginable proportion. All that remains is for each of us to set our individual financial houses in order so we can weather the consequences as well as possible. If we bury our heads in the sand like an ostrich, we will suffer all the more. At the same time if we face economic reality there are things we can do. That is why I have written this book. It is a warning designed to help those who will listen and take action to protect themselves and their families. The seven keys to financial security and happiness will go a long way toward showing you how to put your financial house in order, so that you can escape the worst of the financial hardships that surely await us.

I would like to ask you to read the next few pages with a thought toward whether you might now, or at some point in the future, see yourself or your family experiencing events similar to those depicted in these true-life stories of people I have met along my journey through life. If you do see yourself in one of these stories, I urge you to ask yourself the following question. If my family were to encounter this problem, could we weather it and come out the other side both financially solvent and with our family in tact? Regardless of how you answer that question now, I hope that by the time you finish this book you will have the will to make the changes necessary to safeguard your future! I also hope you will, from the pages of this book, be able to formulate a plan that can substantially protect your family from the hardships that threaten this great nation as it transitions into a new role in the world economy.

God never brings anything on a nation without warning, so His people might be spared. He warned Noah of the flood. He warned Abraham of the destruction of Sodom and Gomorra. He warned Joseph of the seven-year famine in Egypt, and now he is warning America. Please heed the warning and be prepared to make the necessary changes so that, like God's people in Egypt, you will be able to get through the hard times ahead with as little suffering as possible!

It was a warm summer day, the birds were singing, butterflies were flitting from flower to flower, fish were biting in the lakes, and people were hiking along the beautiful trails that meandered through the trees that lined the slops of Mt. Saint Helen. Miles away in a geological monitoring station a seismograph recorded a minor earth tremor. Over the ensuing days, weeks and months, the tremors got increasingly frequent, and they grew stronger and stronger. To the scientist, this was a clear indication that at some point the mountain might explode in a volcanic eruption. Over time a bulge developed in the side of the mountain. Now to the scientist the warning signs were clear. There was no longer any question but when the mountain would blow her top. *I urge you to heed the warning signs lest you be caught off guard. This is no normal recession. America's declining job market has collided with the forces of banking, real estate, and the stock market, resulting in the inevitable implosion of the American economy. The America we once knew is gone for ever and we have to face that reality!*

The lives of the people depicted in the stories to follow provide the same kind of warning signs that the seismograph provided scientists about Mt. Saint Helens. I hope you, like the scientist, will pay attention and take action. The stories in this chapter represent the warning signs of an economy in trouble, but the story of the cause of the Great

Depression, depicted in the Chapter 3, like the bulge on the side of Mt. Saint Helens, signals that the end is in sight. The mountain is about to explode. The economy is about to melt down, and it's time to head for shelter. It's time to get your financial house in order, get out from under as much debt as possible and store up provisions for the long famine ahead.

Ryan's Stock Market Lesson: Our first story opened in the fall of 2002. Ryan, a 65 year-old executive calls me and wants me to come over to talk to him about listing his home. I immediately assume he is selling in order to downsize or perhaps to move to a warmer climate for retirement. When I arrive at his home, I quickly get the impression that something is wrong. There seems to be a sense of urgency in Ryan's voice and demeanor. Sensing a problem, I tell him I can't help if I don't know what is going on. He gets a grimace on his face and invites me to join him for a cup of coffee over which he promises to tell me his situation. He proceeds to confide that he has lost almost everything he has in the recent stock market crash. He had mortgaged his home and taken much of his retirement fund and invested the money in the stock market, confident that he would make a killing by investing in the Internet. He felt the dot-com stocks represented the next technological breakthrough and that there was no way he could lose. He expected to make a killing, retire and live the good life. Instead, the market had a $6.9 trillion crash, and he lost everything he had. He would probably never be able to retire. To make matters worse, he was behind on his taxes, and he was about to lose his home. Elaine, his wife, was so upset she couldn't stay in the room when he told me what had happened. This was surely a tragedy, but one that could have been avoided by a little restraint. There is a saying, *"Hogs get slaughtered, but pigs get fat."* Look at your investment portfolio and ask yourself these questions. Am I over leveraged? Am I in high-growth, high-risk investments that could get wiped out in a sudden downturn of the economy? Is the financial future of my family at risk?

Norman's 9/11 Lesson: I met Norman and his wife, Lucie, when they called me to give them a market analysis of their home. They had a modest three-bedroom home with a crawl space, instead of an actual basement. They had two children and a third on the way, and they needed a four-bedroom home with a basement, so the kids would have a place to play in the cold Chicago winters. Norm was working for an entrepreneurial start-up company, and he was excited because, after three years of hard work, the company had been sold. He was about to get a sizeable sum of money from his stock options. I listed his home, and it sold almost immediately. To be honest, I had told Norman and Lucie that the home might take a while to sell because it was one of the few homes in the subdivision without a basement. Their buyers wanted a quick close, so we had only 30 days to get Norman's family into a new home. They found a home almost immediately, and it looked like things were working out perfectly. The only problem was that Norm wasn't going to get the money from the sale of the company until after the closing. It made him a little nervous, but he was okay, because in almost no time he would have the money from the stocks. One week after they closed, we turned on our TVs and were shocked and horrified to see the footage of the planes crashing into the Twin Towers. Little did Norm know that the tragedy in New York would shortly affect him and his family. As we all know, the economy went into a serious recession following 9/11. The company that was buying Norm's company had a serious financial setback in the aftermath of 9/11 and the deal fell through. The company would eventually sell, but not for three long years. This left Norm in a bind. He had his new dream home and a baby on the way, and he didn't know how he was going to be able to make ends meet. Every month he had a shortfall and had to dip into savings. The problem was that in order to buy the new home he had seriously depleted his savings so things were extremely tight. They were able to keep the house, but it was a real hardship. They had creditors harassing them for three years, and it almost goes without saying that their credit was shot. You could say that Norm should have waited until he had his money in hand. I am sure in hindsight, he would agree, but at the time he had no reason not to wear rose-colored glasses and extend himself. The lesson is that it is okay to take calculated risks, but we need to have the resources to cover us if things don't go the way we hope. We should always have at least six months and preferably a year of living expenses in liquid assets in case of emergency. Ask yourself if what happened to Norm had happened to you, how would you have fared?

Craig's Merger Lesson: Craig was a top executive making almost $250,000 a year plus approximately $100,000 in bonuses. You could say he had made it. He lived in a beautiful home and belonged to the country club. He drove a BMW, and his wife drove a Lexus. They had a house full of beautiful furniture, and they went on two lavish vacations every year. They had surely realized the American dream. One day Craig went into work and found out his company was going to be acquired. He didn't think much of it because he felt he was sufficiently high up in the company to be okay. As it turned out, he wasn't quite high up enough. The merger agreement did provide so-called golden parachutes for the President, the Director of Operations, and the Director of Marketing, but Craig was Vice President of Sales, and the new company wanted their own man in that position. So Craig was out. Even when they laid Craig off, he wasn't too worried, because he had gotten six months' salary as severance pay. Craig immediately put his resume on the market confident that he would get a new job almost immediately. As a matter of fact, he did get three job offers in no time flat. However there was a problem. They were all for considerably less than he had been making. As it turned out, Craig had been in his old job for several years. In that time he had not been watching what was happening in the job market. Because of overseas competition American companies had been cutting back the salaries in middle management, and now they were capping salaries of top management as well. The simple reality that was about to befall Craig was that he was not going to get another job making what he had been making. After about six months Craig took a job out of desperation, but he discretely kept his resume on the market. After two years, he still had not been able to land another killer job, and he finally called me, because he was being forced to sell his house and downsize. As it turned out, Craig was what I call a *"penny millionaire."* From the outside he looked rich, but it was an illusion. I recently saw a commercial on TV that reminds me of Craig's situation. There is a man mowing the lawn, and as he cuts the grass he is thinking, *"I have a beautiful house, expensive cars, my kids are going to top-notch colleges, and I have absolutely no idea how I am going to pay my bills at the end of the month."* Are you, or is anyone you know, overextended? Have you, or has anyone you know, experienced a cut in salary? If the answer to either of these questions is yes, you know first-hand how much stress being in debt can cause! If we learn to live within our means, these types of problems are inconveniences not catastrophes. But when we allow ourselves to go too far into debt we trade our freedom for a pair of **golden hand cuffs** and we become **indentured servants** instead of **free men!**

Mike, John and Kith's Age-Discrimination Lesson: This next story is actually a trilogy. It's the story of three men, Mike, John and Kith, all beset by a similar set of circumstances. They were all forced out of corporate America before they were ready to retire.

I met Mike at a coffee shop. I was standing behind him and over-heard him telling the clerk that he had just been forced out of corporate America. He was lamenting that he didn't know what he was going to do with the rest of his life. I approached him and told him I had made the transition some years earlier and suggested that perhaps we should meet for a cup of coffee the following day to discuss his options. As it turned out Mike was very conservative and lived well within his means. He had a side business, so he had some income aside from his former job. He had a sizeable 401K plan, but he was not sure how to tap into it. I referred him to some people I knew, and he did some networking of his own. Within a few months he had his life back together and was happier than he had ever been. He restructured his 401K plan and was able to access his money in order to invest it the way he wanted, and he had taken a low-pressure job. It didn't pay that kind of salary to which he was accustomed, but he was able to pay his bills with no worries. Life was good. In his mind being forced out of corporate America was the best thing that had ever happened to him. Mike's happy ending wasn't accidental. **He had a plan and he worked it. He made saving a MUST, and he made sure he was an informed investor. He sought advice from others, but in the end he took his own counsel.**

John's story was not as rosy as Mike's. When I met him he had lost his job nearly two years previously. He had found a job, but unfortunately it didn't pay anywhere near as much as he had been used to making in corporate America. For two years he had continually had to tap into his savings. Now the savings were depleted, and he was forced to face the harsh reality that he was going to have to sell his home and downsize. This was particularly hard on him, because he still had small children, and he didn't want to uproot them and take them away from their friends. Perhaps even more upsetting was the fear that his children would lose respect for him. I helped him get situated in a new home, but they still struggled to make ends meet. Nearly two more years passed, and he finally got a job in his field. Though it paid considerably more than his previous job, it still paid less than he had originally made. By now his wife Katie had to go to work, and she was stressed out trying to work full time and be a mother and home maker, or as they are called *"super moms."* It's okay to be a super mom in your 20s or 30s, but, try it in your 50s, and you will find it is a completely different matter. The stress finally got to be too much for her, and she developed some health problems, which further added to their difficulties. Another year passed and John got a promotion and a substantial raise. However, even then, he wasn't making as much as he had been at his original job. What had happened was that over the five-year period of his tribulation, salaries had slowly declined. The reality finally set in that the good-old days were gone, never to return. John and Katie are doing okay now, but they live in fear of the day that the demon called age discrimination may once again come knocking at their door. I hasten to interject, that although they are okay now, their savings have been seriously depleted, so they live in fear and wonder how they will ever retire. The problem here was that like many Americans John had not been aggressive with his 401K plan, and he simply had inadequate savings. If we are not regularly putting 10 percent of our income into our retirement programs, we simply will not accrue adequate savings for retirement. More on this later.

Kith's Story is heart breaking. He was a very senior executive, and to a substantial degree, he defined himself by what he did for a living. At 59, he was older than Mike and John. His children were grown so it was just him and his wife, Ruth. Although he had made good money, he lived high on the hog. He had a reasonable retirement program, but was no where near adequate for him to retire and maintain that same lifestyle as before. After a year of trying to get another job, he resigned himself to the fact that his career was over. Simply put, he was a casualty of age discrimination even though we all know there is no such thing. It wasn't long after that, that he had to sell his gorgeous house and move into a town home. This, coupled with the loss of his career, put him over the edge. He got severely depressed, started drinking, and withdrew further and further from his wife, Ruth. The marriage was effectively on the rocks. Because Kith and Ruth couldn't afford to get divorced they just coexisted and went about their drab unhappy lives. Another year passed. Then one night as Ruth got ready for bed she called for Kith to come up from the basement and his self imposed isolation, but he didn't answer. She went to check on him and found him on the floor dead. The death certificate read heart attack, but a more accurate diagnosis would have been heart break. To this day Ruth lives by herself and asks God, *"Why me? Why did things have to turn out so badly?"*

As you reflect on these three stories ask yourself these questions. What would you do if your career were to be cut short by ten to fifteen years? Could you survive financially? Do you have an identity outside of what you do for a living or is what you do who you are? Have you thought about what you want to do when you retire, and do you have plans that will give your life purpose and meaning? Life is about more than money!

Mark and Jane's First-Home Lesson. I met Mark and Jane when they called me about a rental property. They are an extremely nice young couple in their early 30s with two children. They both work, but they never seem to be able to get ahead. They had a lot of credit card debt, and their credit wasn't very good. They were extremely discouraged because they thought they would never own a home. They confided in me and asked if there was anything I could do to help them. I told them that they would have to continue to rent for a while, but, if they did what I told them to do they would probably be able to get a home in a year. They agreed to rent an apartment that was smaller than the one they really wanted, but it was considerably less expensive. I referred them to someone who helped them get their credit cards paid down and their credit score up. They saved as much as they could, which wasn't much. Nevertheless a year later they were able to buy a small home. Three years later they sold that home and bought a larger home that better met the needs of their family. They are not rich, but they are doing okay! They learned their lesson about credit cards. They live within their means and have a forced savings plan through work. They are building a future. I put this story in here because I know how hard it is these days for young people to get started. Just as in the story of Mark and Jane the first step to financial security is to get out from under credit card debt and to start a forced savings program. I will tell you how to build wealth in part III of this book. There is hope.

Brian's Business Lesson: I could go on with these stories almost indefinitely because unfortunately there are a lot of people out there who are being negatively impacted by the winds of change that are blowing across America. Lest I risk boring you, I will end with just one more story. I met Brian nearly ten years ago. His father had founded a successful tool and dye company in the 1940s. When he died he left the business to Brian. Brian had been raised in the business, so he was more astute than most. He also had contracts with a number of large corporations, so by all accounts he had a very successful business. Nevertheless his company was in trouble. He was losing business right and left to firms in China that drastically undercut his prices. Slowly the corporate clients that had been established over a lifetime slipped away like sand through an hourglass. Brian could see that time was running out for his business. The end was in sight. What could he do? Who would buy his company when he was losing business and was clearly headed down the tubes? As I said, Brian was more astute than most. He analyzed the situation and came up with a brilliant solution. He went to all his corporate clients and made a proposal to them. He proposed to take his company in a new direction. He knew he could not compete with the cheap labor from China, but he also knew that the first step in the tool and dye business was to make working proto-types and that step involved close coordination with the manufacturers' design engineers which make frequent changes that have to be turned around quickly. This task required close proximity to the engineers. Brian had found a business model that placed more value on service than price and, thus, a way to save his business. Unfortunately, most of his competitors didn't have his vision and didn't react fast enough to the market shift, and an entire industry became virtually extinct. If you go into Brian's plant today you will find that nearly half of his employ-ees once owned their own tool and dye companies, but they were now employees. Even so, they are glad to have a job, because they know that many of their colleagues were not as fortunate. I used Brian as my example here, but the bigger picture is that across America millions of people are being negatively affected as America loses global market share. As a result, people either lose their jobs or are forced to take jobs at substantially lower salaries.

     As you think about Brian's situation, ask yourself what you would do if you found yourself in a situation where your vocation was threatened by competition from cheap foreign labor or was becom-ing obsolescent owing to advances in technology? Do you have any supplemental income to soften the financial strain? Do you have an alternate skill that would enable you to easily change vocations? Should the situation require it, are you financially able to go back to school and get the necessary education to switch vocations? In a word, how well equipped are you to weather the hardships imposed by change?

If you think you are safe in your industry, don't be so sure. There are more vulnerable industries than you would ever imagine. For example, the graphics arts field has been severely impacted by software from Microsoft that is so user-friendly it has allowed many companies to do their graphic design work in house for less money. How many accountants do you think have lost tax business due to software like TurboTax? As hard as it may be to believe, much of the legal research for large litigation cases is done in India as is much of our pharmaceutical research. You might be surprised to know how many movies are being made in India and Budapest, where production companies can build the set for a fraction of the cost in Hollywood. If you need computer support, chances are you will be talking to someone in India or Ireland. How much of our electronic industry has gone to Japan? The Chinese are now getting into the auto business. Ask yourself where all the shoe factories went. How many of your designer clothes do you think were made in America versus China?

On any given day, we could wake up and find that our vocation is being threatened by technology or foreign competition. There are no safe havens. Are you prepared? Do you have a plan?

At the risk of repeating myself, please reflect on this. America has lost its stranglehold on world trade, and as a result, economic balance will be restored to the world economic system. We will be diminished as other countries are enlarged, and there is precious little we can do to prevent it. America's imminent downfall stems from our greed. For precisely that reason, our economic life-force, like the blood coursing through our veins, is ebbing away one drop at a time as the economic blood of our great nation flows abroad to strengthen those in far away lands. Think about the words you just read and ask yourself if in your heart of hearts they don't in fact resonate with truth! Things may sound bleak and scary, and it may make you want to throw your hands up in the air and give up, but it is not hopeless. If I thought it was hopeless I would not have written this book. **Think of this book in the context**

of the midnight ride of Paul Revere, except instead of saying "the British are coming," I am saying "our money is going."

If we will just face economic reality and stop our mad pursuit of materialism, we can restore balance and, along with it, we can regain the happiness we lost.

Speaking of happiness, I found an excellent poem to end this chapter. It is at once soft and poetic and harsh and eye opening. It perfectly depicts what we as Americans have lost in our mad scramble for wealth man's way. This poem is from the most unexpected of sources. In an ironic way it is from the perfect source, because if George Carlin the gross, insensitive comedian from the 1970s can see America the way he does, maybe, just maybe there is hope that the rest of us can wake up and come to our senses.

"The paradox of our time in history is that we have taller buildings but shorter tempers; wider freeways, but narrower viewpoints. We spend more, but have less; we buy more, but enjoy less. We have bigger houses and smaller families; more conveniences, but less time.

We have more degrees, but less sense, more knowledge, but less judgment; more experts, yet more problems; more medicine, but less wellness.

We drink too much, smoke too much, spend too much recklessly, laugh too little, drive too fast, get too angry, stay up too late, get up too tired, read too little, watch TV too much, and pray too seldom. We have multiplied our possessions, but reduced our values. We talk too much, love too seldom, and hate too often.

We've learned how to make a living, but not a life. We've added years to life, not life to years.

We've been all the way to the moon and back, but have trouble crossing the street to meet a new neighbor. We conquered outer space, but not inner space. We've done large things, but not better things.

We've cleaned up the air, but polluted the soil. We've conquered the atom, but not our prejudice. We write more, but learn less. We plan more, but accomplish less. We've learned to rush, but not to wait. We build more computers to hold more information, to produce more copies than ever, but we communicate less and less.

These are the times of fast foods and slow digestion, big men and small character, steep profits and shallow relationships. These are the days of two incomes but more divorces, fancier houses, but broken homes.

These are the days of quick tips, disposable diapers, throw away morality, one-night stands, overweight bodies, and pills that do everything from cheer, to quiet, to kill. It is a time when there is much in the showroom window and nothing in the stockroom. A time when technology can bring this letter to you, and a time when you can choose either to share this insight, or just hit delete...

Remember spend some time with your loved ones because they are not going to be around forever. Remember, say a kind word to someone who looks up to you in awe because that little person will soon grow up and leave your side. Remember, to give a warm hug to the one next to you because that is the only treasure you can give with your heart, and it doesn't cost a cent.

Remember, to say "I love you" to your partner, and your loved ones, but most of all mean it. A kiss and an embrace will mend hurt when it comes from deep inside you. Remember to hold hands and cherish the moment for some day that person will not be there.

Give time to love, give time to speak, and give time to share the precious thoughts in your mind.

AND ALWAYS REMEMBER: "Life is not measured by the number of breaths we take, but by the moments that take our breath away."

George Carlin wrote this in memory of his wife. It gives us a lot to think about regarding where our life is headed and whether it's a journey worth taking, if we are a people who can yet stop and smell the sweet nectar of life and share it with someone we love. In moments of grief we realize that love, not money is the most important thing in the world. That is what George Carlin is telling us here, and it is what I am saying as well. I am not saying that money isn't important, because it is. We live in a material world, and we need a certain amount of money just to exist, but we need more than that in order to chase away the demon of fear. Here is the interesting thing, **there is a point where our pursuit of money and our enjoyment of life are at BALANCE and at that precise point is where happiness is found**. If we have too little, we are stressed out and fear haunts our thoughts and gives us no peace. On the other hand, if we go into debt and spend money we don't have fear, once again takes control of our lives and takes our peace away. Only at the point where we are at "balance" are we able to find peace and happiness.

As we get into Chapter 3 and my prediction of a second Great Depression, it doesn't make one bit of difference if I am right or not, because the depression, if and when it comes, will just be the final chapter of a story that is playing out in America each and every day.

If today we get up and we have a job, there is no depression, but if at the end of the day we get laid off the depression will have just started.

The extent to which that depression affects us will depend on:

- How prepared were we?

- Whether we were in debt or debt free?

- Did we live well within our means or were we over extended?

- Did we have an alternate source of income or was our job our only source?

- Did we have a well-funded retirement plan or did we opt out because saving wasn't a **must**?

- Were our assets diversified so they were protected or were we invested in a lot of high-risk speculative investments?

- Did we have liquidity, or was all of our money tied up where we couldn't get at it when we needed it?

- Was our economic house built on a rock or was it built on a shaky foundation supported by debt?

Like the three little pigs, we have to ask ourselves if our house is built of brick or straw and will it withstand the winds of change or will the big bad wolf "huff and puff and blow our house down?"

As I close this chapter I want to disclose something personal to you. Before my divorce I was semi-retired and was looking forward to a comfortable retirement. Now, I will have to work for years to rebuild. However, I know this: things happen; that's just life! What is important is not so much what happens to us as it is how we react to it!

Do we let circumstances defeat us, or do we get up, brush off and get on with life? We have to get up because we have no other choice and, hopefully when we do get up, we are wiser for the experience. I have learned a lot from my mistakes and hopefully after reading this chapter you will reflect on your personal situation and, unlike me, you will make the necessary changes before your house gets blown down, and you find out the hard way what the difference is between a recession and a depression. If we take action, there is still time, but I hope that we as a nation, and we as individuals, will heed the warning signs and take the appropriate actions. May God Bless you, and may you learn to build wealth God's way, which adds no sorrow!"

CHAPTER 2

ADDICTED TO CREDIT!

What Happens When the Credit Runs Out?

The pilgrims who founded this country understood the basis of financial prosperity. To them it was simple. They took their guidance from
the *Bible*, which says neither a borrower nor a lender be and admon-
ishes, *"The rich ruleth over the poor and the borrower is servant to
the lender"* (Matthew 6:11). If more of us would heed this sage advice
we would discover the peace and joy that God intends for those who
walk in His ways. Unfortunately, the vast majority of the population
has been snared by the allure of material possessions, and in order to
get what we want and to get it now we have become credit junkies.

The very title of this chapter, "Addicted to Credit," makes me
cringe. An addiction is an insidious disease that starts out by giving
the user a rush, a sense of euphoria and a sense of empowerment and
invincibility. Then, ever so slowly it takes control of the user until
eventually life as he knew it is over. Without realizing it, and certainly without being able to control it, the addiction has taken control
to the point that everything the addict does is centered on his addiction. What once was a recreational drug that gave him a rush is now
the master of his life!

Credit is no less insidious and addictive than drugs. It has all the
attributes of a narcotic or a hallucinogen. At first it makes you feel
good, gives you a rush and a sense of empowerment. Having that
new car is good for your EGO; but, you need some new threads to go
with it. While you're at it how about a new house, complete with all
new furniture? And, for good measure don't you think you deserve

a vacation? There you go, you have arrived. You have achieved the American dream. The Jones' have nothing on you. You are the man. The only question now is how in the world you are going to pay for all that stuff? Suddenly, the realization hits that you eventually have to pay the piper, and pay him, and pay him and pay him. What started out to be fun has all the sudden become drudgery. No, it's worse than that. It is a life sentence of indentured servitude. Welcome to the world of the addict. You have lost control of your life. You can now look forward to spending your future working for things that you consumed in the past, many of which have long since lost their luster and many of which are just plain worn out or obsolete. In real terms so much of what you make goes to pay your debt service that you have precious little left for the true necessities of life, mush less the luxuries. Maybe you won't go on that vacation this year. "No, I have to go on the vacation; the wife and kids will be disappointed if we don't go. But somehow I have to get out from under these high interest payments. I know I will refinance and lower my monthly payments. Then I will be okay." Yep, credit is just like a narcotic, and you are just like a drug addict. All you need is another fix of cocaine or in this instance another round of credit and everything will be okay; that is, until the next time.

While the credit addict is busy being stressed out about how he is going to pay his bills at the end of the month, his life is speeding past. His children are growing up and somehow he never got around to setting up that college fund. He intended to do it tomorrow; but tomorrow never came. Then one day he looks in the mirror, and he sees his first gray hair and realizes that he is no longer a spring chicken. As a matter fact he is on the verge of becoming a senior citizen. Then it dawns on him that another one of those things he intended to get around to was saving for retirement. Now it is too late, he is a statistic. He is one of the 25 percent of Americans over 65 who still have a mortgage. Guess he never stopped to realize that every time he refinanced, his 30-year loan started over. Yes, his payment was lower, but his sentence was longer. What a shame. You can't avoid the inevitable. What happens when you are 70 and can't work anymore, but still have 20 years left on your mortgage and can't make the payments? The devil always gets his due.

Why is it they call retirement, *"the golden years?"* The term engenders a vision of a life of leisure, coming and going as you please, spending time with the grand kids, taking that second honeymoon you never had time to take, and in general enjoying life and stopping to smell the roses. This sounds pretty good to me. Unfortunately our credit junkie will never see retirement because once again he is a sad statistic. He is among the one-fifth of Americans who will retire with no savings—nada, nothing! Or, maybe he managed to save a little and is one of the one-half of Americans who will retire with less than $25,000. Nonetheless, he is in deep donkey dung, and that is the price a credit junkie pays for his quick fix.

What happens if one day the unexpected happens. He loses his job, gets in a car accident, gets divorced or encounters any of a host of life's little surprises? He has no safety net, and his house of cards comes crashing down. The illusion is no longer valid. With no financial reserves, foreclosure and or bankruptcy may well be his bed fellows. Addiction does not have a happy ending. Eventually, one way or another, you have to pay the piper.

Amid all this doom and gloom, I almost forgot about his kids. They may wish they had skipped some of those fancy vacations when they find out how much those student loans are going to cost them. What choice do they have: a high school education and a minimum wage job, or a college education with the promise of the good life, but at the cost of starting out deep in debt and behind the eight ball? Not much of a choice is it? What a shame!

None of this is what I think of when I hear the words *"the American dream."* America is supposed to be the land of opportunity. When I think of America, I envision a uniquely proud, hard-working, industrious nation of immigrants who came to this country in pursuit of a better life. They worked hard, saved their money, lived within their means and pulled together to help one another in hard times. What ever happened to the nation forged by the sweat of our forefathers? What ever happened to the once proud America that was the world's undisputed economic superpower?

THE EMERGENCE OF CONSUMER LENDING

As a subsequent chapter will elaborate, the root cause of America's credit addiction and its insidious economic decline were born out of the desperation of the Great Depression. Americans suffered unparalleled unemployment and horrible economic hardship. The government and big business concluded that, in order to keep the engine of commerce strong, they had to aggressively encourage spending. The outgrowth of that decision was the birth of consumer credit pioneered by General Motors. The key to consumer credit was to convince consumers that they didn't just *"want"* the products of mass production they *"needed"* them. Out of this endeavor the Madison Avenue Advertising industry was born, and America embarked on the largest propaganda blitz the world has ever seen. Americans were absolutely convinced that who they were was defined by what they had and how they looked. With this belief ingrained in their psyches it wasn't difficult to hook an entire generation of Americans on credit.

THE EVOLUTION OF THE CREDIT CARD INDUSTRY

In the beginning the concept of consumer credit was actually well intended. It made the products of mass production more readily available to the middle class, and credit was given responsibly to those who could demonstrate that they were good credit risks: those who would make their payments on time and pay their loans off as scheduled. This credit thing seemed to be a good deal for everyone. The corporations were happy because they could sell more products. The public was happy because people could buy new cars and other important items they were struggling to be able to purchase. The government was happy because the economy was strong, employment was high and the American public was content. Unfortunately, it didn't take the CEOs of the banks long to realize that they were sitting on one of the largest fortunes the world would ever see.

There is a saying:

"Power corrupts and absolute power corrupts absolutely."

With this in mind, I want you to ask yourself what you would do if you were the CEO of a large bank and one day you realized that you could borrow money at a low rate and lend it out at a higher rate. What if, in addition you could charge a late fee if the customer didn't pay on time? What if you could also charge an over-limit fee if the customer charged more than his available credit line? To top it off, what if you could double, triple or quadruple the interest rate if the client had a history of late payments? Welcome to the world of predatory lending. It's big business, and it is obscenely profitable. That is why they call it predatory lending. It turns honest Americans like you and me into slaves who live on the ragged edge of financial ruin.

If you want to hook someone on something you generally have to ease them into it. Then, as they become addicted you gradually increase the cost and the pain. It is no different with credit cards. According to Bud Hibbs, consumer advocate, in the 1980s late fees averaged $15 and over-limit fees were another $15, so if you took a double whammy you might get hit with a $30 penalty on top of your normal monthly fee. Fast forward to the present, and late and over-limit fees have increased by a horrendous 160 percent, from $15 each to $43 each, so a double whammy now costs you a whopping $86, plus your regular monthly payment. That isn't all that has changed. When you initially get your credit card, the interest rate will probably run anywhere from 0 percent to 10 percent. Make a few late payments and your rate might go to 30 percent, 35 percent, 40 percent, 45 percent or more. That credit card just became a huge ball and chain. It has made you an indentured servant, slaving to make the credit card company executives rich at your expense. The average American has nearly $10,000 in credit card debt, if he makes only the minimum monthly payment; it will take him 30 years to pay it off. One of the keys to accumulating wealth is to create an *"annuity revenue stream"* that pays you year after year with little to no effort on your part. I guess the credit card executives have found the mother lode of annuity revenue streams. Is it any wonder they bombard us with over 4 billion credit card offers per year? According to Stephen Brobek of the Federation of Consumer Credit, the credit card companies have made an astounding $3 trillion of credit available to consumers.

Somehow being wealthy automatically engenders a certain degree of respect or, in the case of a corporation, a better term is respectability. But unfortunately that respect and trust is often misplaced. This is definitely the case with the banks and credit card companies. They put forth the public persona of being respectable corporations, when in fact many of them are involved in the worst type of predatory lending. You might be surprised to know that many of those *"Pay Day Loan Stores"* that you see in seedy lower socioeconomic neighborhoods are owned by some of the biggest, most prestigious banks in the country.

For example, according to Bud Hibbs, consumer advocate, the largest check-cashing chain in the United States is owned by Wells Fargo, the nation's fourth largest bank. Given their *"usury rates,"* I see the Pay Day Loan Stores as analogous to *"loan sharks."* The only difference is that one is run by a guy named Guido and the other is run by a college graduate in a $1000 suit. In either case, a fleecing is still a fleecing. In a similar vein, investigative reporter, Mike Hudson, did an exposé on why it is so difficult for poor people to get out of poverty. He discovered to his surprise that the bottom feeders taking advantage of poor people, helping to trap them in their cycle of poverty were some of the most respected companies in the nation, such as Citibank, Chase Manhattan and Household Finance.

Now that we have established who we are actually dealing with, let's take a look at who gets those 4 billion credit card offers each year. Last year, Tom Smurf lost his job. He and his wife Samantha got behind on their bills and had to declare bankruptcy. Do you think they could get a credit card, or do you think they would be too high a risk? My son, Brett, went away to college. As a full-time student living away from home and working a part time job, do you think he would qualify for a credit card? If he did get one, do you think it would require my signature as his parent? Nancy is a single mom who has a history of late payments and a low credit score. She feels she needs a credit card to cover her in case of emergencies. Do you think she would be able to get a credit card?

Believe it or not, in all likelihood all of these people would be able to get a credit card. As a matter of fact, the credit card companies would rather have these people than an executive with a 750 credit score, making $200,000 a year, with his house and car paid for and a ton of money in the bank. I know it sounds crazy, but it actually makes sense. It used to be that banks were very careful about the risk of default, because it only took a few bad loans to seriously impact their profitability. But, now in the age of super credit card profits, the banks can afford a substantial number of bad loans and still make loads of money. Take for example the Smurfs, who are just out of bankruptcy. The credit card companies actually target people just out of bankruptcy, because they know they **cannot declare bankruptcy again. In addition, they know these people are addicted to credit and, more important, they know they are willing to make minimum payments literally forever.** What about that 18 year-old college student with a part-time job? He is one of their favorite targets as well. And, by the way, he can get the credit card without parental approval. What they know about him is that if he gets in over his head, there is a good chance mom and dad will step in and bail him out; after all he is their son. It's like McDonalds, who targets kids and refers to clients as users. They want to get that college student hooked on credit for life. What about Nancy, our single mom struggling to make ends meet? She is a target too, because they know that she probably can't pay off her balance each month, and if she has to use her card for an emergency she will most likely only make the minimum payment. Do you see now why I said that the credit card czars are sitting on the mother lode of all annuity programs? **All they have to do is target those least able to pay and hook them on credit**. Then, they can sit back and collect their late fees and over-limit fees. When people don't pay on time, the banks raise the interest rates through the ceiling almost certainly assuring that the consumer will be able to make only the minimum payment. There you have it. The credit card czars have an indentured servant who will spend the rest of her life giving them hard-earned money so they can live in the lap of luxury while their victims languish in despair teetering on the brink of poverty.

It is no accident that I call these people victims. That is exactly what they are. Consider the human suffering that these predators bring about. For example, divorce rates in this country are in excess of 50 percent, and experts say that financial trouble is the number one cause of divorce.

Consider those college kids. We all know that college can be stressful and the pressure is bad enough without adding to it by having some unscrupulous credit collectors calling a student and playing mind games with him. The credit card executives will tell you they are offering a valuable service to the public and at one level, they are, but because of the exorbitant fees and practice of targeting those least able to pay, they are vicious predators trafficking in human misery. Imagine if you can what it must have felt like to be Trisha or Jane from Norman, Oklahoma when they were informed that their daughters had hung themselves distraught over credit card debt. In 1999, Trisha and Jane testified in support of a bill that would have banned credit card companies from college campuses. Imagine two housewives from Oklahoma, sitting in a U.S. Senate hearing across from a panel of powerful banking executives all lobbying against a bill that could potentially save the lives of college kids across the country and in some small way give the deaths of their daughters some measure of meaning. Now imagine the pain and indignation those women must have felt when it came time for the banking executives to testify and they found the executives didn't have to answer a single question. You see the hearings were running late, and there just wasn't time for questions. My comment, somewhat sarcastic though it may be, is: *"How convenient for those bankers not to have to justify their predatory practices. As they say something stinks in Denmark?"* Needless to say, the bill did not pass. What a shame.

Again in 2005 the question of giving credit cards to college students was up for debate. At that Senate hearing on consumer credit, Senator Jack Reed, a democrat from Rhode Island asked, *"How do banks determine the credit worthiness of an 18 year-old college student?"* Julie Williams, Comptroller of the Currency (OCC), **(the federal government's top regulator)** responded, *"The credit card companies use a variety of models to try to model the risk of certain populations that they would offer cards to. They can look at their experience with individuals that attend particular types of schools, particular schools. What their credit performance has been."* I can appreciate Miss Williams's lofty position. Perhaps I am just a little slow, but I don't think she answered Senator Reed's question, so I will pose it again:

"How do banks determine the credit worthiness of an 18 year-old college student?"

Were I present in the hearing and had I been allowed to ask a question, I would have been a little more blunt than Senator Reed. My question would have gone something like this: *"How in the world could you possibly expect a college student with no income, or at most a part-time minimum wage job, to possibly pay his credit card bill when it comes in? Is it conceivable that in fact you are not profiling credit worthiness, but rather targeting college kids because you know they fit the profile of your most profitable client, which is a slow payer who generally makes the minimum payment and gets hit with late fees and over-balance fees?"*

Looking at the plight of these millions of Americans, one might well ask what the government will do to help them. Surely, the government will come to their aid and do something to protect the American people from these predators who force millions of hard-working Americans into bankruptcy and/or foreclosure each year.

- **_Bankruptcy Bill_**: Former President George W. Bush signed a new bankruptcy bill that makes it much harder for people to get out from under collection predators.

  - The Bankruptcy Bill was written by NBNA, the nation's second-largest credit card company.

  - In 2005, NBNA was President Bush's largest campaign contributor.

- **_2001: Providian Law Suit:_** Providian paid $40 million to settle charges that it defrauded its customers.

  - In 2004, President Bush appointed Deputy Attorney General, Larry Thompson, who had been questioned about ties to Providian, to head a swat team on crime.

- **_2004: 30 states sue banks for predatory and discriminatory practices:_**

  - Once again the federal government's top regulator, Julie Williams, OCC, rushed to the aid of the credit card companies, saying:

  "If we had a basis for concluding that a bank had a practice that was unfair or deceptive, if it violated protection standards that apply to them, then we can tell them to stop immediately."

Are you somewhat baffled as to why the federal government seems to be siding with the predatory lenders to the detriment of the American people? Campaign contributions aside, there is a very plausible reason the government doesn't do something to tighten credit and stop what are obviously predatory lending practices. **It goes back to 1941 when the government and big business concluded that in order to keep the engine of commerce strong they had to aggressively encourage spending.**

And nothing encourages spending more than credit, and lots and lots of it; $3 trillion to be precise. Yes, that should be enough to keep the economy strong at least until the credit runs out.

"When the credit is over, the game will stop."
(Marrimer Ecclus, Chairman Federal Reserve, 1931-1934)

I don't know about you, but to me it looks like the credit is just about over. Consider the following:

- The average American has approximately **$10,000 in credit card debt** that, with minimum payments, will take over 30 years to pay off.

- In 1994, the U.S. average savings rate was 6 percent and in 2008 it was -1 percent.

- One-half of Americans have less than $5,000 in savings.

- One-fifth of Americans have $0—zero, nada—in savings.

If taking 30 years to pay off a $10,000 debt isn't indentured servitude, then I don't know what is. When you can't save, it is a pretty good indicator that you are living paycheck to paycheck, and you are maxed out. Ask yourself why Americans used to save, and now we don't. To me it is a clear indication that we are drowning financially and are at the end of our financial rope.

THE CREDIT COLLECTION BUSINESS

The credit card companies know that a substantial number of these high-risk clients will not be able to pay and that, by federal law, they will have to charge off their debt after 180 days. So, if they know this, why in the world would they ever loan these people money? Isn't that financially unsound business practice? No, as we have been discussing, it is highly profitable, even if it is unethical. I am sure we all agree that ethical practices are the hallmark of good business, but apparently when there are trillions of dollars at stake ethics are expendable.

As bad as it is to be an indentured servant to the credit card companies, it is nothing compared with what happens to you if you move from "**slow pay**" to "**no pay**" status, and the credit card companies write off your bad debt and sell it for pennies on the dollar to the "**collection buzzards**." Here is what happens and how it works. It isn't pretty. From the time you stop paying, the credit card companies have 180 days to write off the bad debt. During that time they are tacking on late fees, over-limit fees and additional credit fees like mad. According to Elizabeth Warren of Harvard Law School, there was a bankruptcy judge in Virginia who asked the credit card companies how much of what they were asking for was principal and how much was interest and fees? The response was that, on average, for every dollar they were asking for in principal, they were asking for $2 dollars in interest and fees.

I want you to put yourself in the shoes of a single mother who can barely get by as it is. She has a string of problems: her car breaks down, her child gets sick and her child support payments are in arrears. What in the world is she going to do? This is not one of the YUP-PIES of the NOW GENERATION who is addicted to consumer credit and indulges her every whim with another credit card purchase until she becomes a credit card addict. It may be hard to feel sorry for the spoiled brat who says, *"I want that and I want it now."* But, my heart goes out to the single mom who is living a life of quiet desperation already; because if she gets in trouble with the credit card companies, her despair becomes almost unbearable. Now, consider the two college students we discussed earlier. How desperate do you have to be to actually take your life?

This same scenario can be expanded to millions of low-income families across the nation who can barely afford the basics. There is an entire segment of the American population that survives paycheck to paycheck. They are worrying about how they are going to pay their bills, struggling to make ends meet and fretting about how they will pay their medical bills. Then one day the inevitable happens, and one of the kids get seriously ill or dad loses his job, and there is no safety net. The slow spiral begins. They turn to the credit cards to cover the emergency, and soon they can't make the payments and are drowning in debt. The next thing you know they default on their credit cards and the collection buzzards start pecking on their carcasses while they are still alive and kicking. Just when they think things can't get any worse, they receive a notice in the mail that foreclosure proceedings are being started. They rush out to talk to a real estate agent to see if they can salvage something by selling their home before it is foreclosed, but again they get bad news. Over the years they have refinanced a couple of times in order to consolidate their bills into lower monthly payments. That debt consolidation came at a cost, which was that they pulled much of the equity out of their home in order to pay other bills. The rational they were given by the mortgage company was that it was okay, because their home was going up in value, so they still had a lot of equity left. Then comes the final blow. The real estate agent does a competitive market analysis (CMA) to find that in the current depressed real estate market their home has lost 20-40 percent of its value. But, that still isn't all the bad news: sales commissions are another 6 percent and closing cost are an additional 3 percent. When they did the refinances they thought they still had equity, so they were okay. The grim reality is that they are upside-down on their mortgage, so foreclosure is probably inevitable. Not only is foreclosure inevitable, but so is bankruptcy. They just went from living on the fringe of the middle class to officially becoming a member of the ever-increasing segment of the American population that is truly impoverished and may well languish in the throes of poverty and despair for the rest of their lives.

By the way, debt collection is one of the fastest growing businesses on Wall Street. All you have to do is buy $1-2 million of bad debt for pennies on the dollar, rent an office, hire some young thugs to browbeat and intimidate people, and you are in the credit buzzard business.

From 1945 to 2009, the United States has gone from being the world's number one economic superpower to being the world's number one debtor nation. How did that happen? What was born out of the desperation of the Great Depression of 1929-1941 has now gone full cycle. America has gone from being a cash-and-carry society, to a society that used credit responsibly, to a nation of credit junkies whose credo is:

"I want that and I want it now."

It is made of people who are willing to go deep in debt to get what they want. When all this started, little did we know that what looked like the road to prosperity was actually the road to poverty and desperation. There is a limit to how long a person can spend more than he or she makes before the inevitable happens and he or she goes broke.

At this point, it is pretty clear how debt has eroded the financial security of millions of Americans, but the government is still financially strong, or is it? What holds true for a family holds true for a nation. You cannot indeterminately spend more than you make and avoid the inevitability of financial collapse. As I write this there is a real threat that very soon the U.S. dollar will cease to be the exclusive currency for all oil purchases. There are talks of going to a basket of foreign currencies excluding the dollar. The outcome of such a decision would be hyperinflation leading eventually to total economic collapse.

In my opinion, credit and debt are two sides of the same coin, and both represent serious, potentially fatal problems. Debt has been called the # 1 issue in America today. It threatens the very fabric of our society and threatens to rob us of our future. Consider the following:

ECONOMIC UPDATE 2009
U.S. WORLD'S #1 DEBTOR NATION

- **U.S. government spends more on interest than on:**
  - Homeland Security, education and healthcare combined.
- **Social Security Raided:**
  - 1983-88 Reagan takes $300 billion.
  - 1989 Bush takes $350 billion.
  - **OUTCOME:** As of 2005, the federal government had spent every penny of the social security fund just to make **minimum payments on the national debt.**
- **The government runs out of cash:**
  - In 1995, the government ran out of money and shut down for three days.
  - President Clinton had to borrow from the pension fund and social security to avoid default on the national debt.
  - In November 2004, the government ran out of money again, and President Bush raised debt limit by $800 billion.

Have you ever wondered why America can't support its troops overseas and why parents have to buy flack jackets for their sons and daughters in the military? Have you ever wondered why funding for school programs has been drastically cut or why we do not have affordable healthcare. Now you know.

"The government spends more on interest on the national debt than on homeland security, education and healthcare combined." The bottom line is there simply isn't enough money to pay the national debt and appropriately fund the essential services that previous generations took for granted. By my definition that means the government is broke or dangerously close to it.

Two additional barometers that are indicative of the nation's financial strength are the number of bankruptcies and foreclosures. Here again there is reason for alarm. Consider the following:

■ *Bankruptcies:*
  • 1994-2004 10 million Americans declared bankruptcy.

  • In 2008 more Americans will declare bankruptcy than divorce, graduate from college or get cancer.

    Comment: That sounds like an epidemic to me. What do you think?

■ *Housing Foreclosures:*
  • We are currently experiencing the highest foreclosure rate in the *37 years* records have been kept. Source: James Scurlock author of *Maxed Out* in *Nightline* interview with Elizabeth Warren.

  • The collapse of the sub-prime mortgage market resulted in the infamous Stimulus Plan which is nothing more than a taxpayer subsidized bail out of an irresponsible government.

    Comment: Sounds to me like the American Dream is no longer attainable or sustainable for millions of disenfranchised Americans. What do you think?

There seem to be a lot of theories about why there are so many foreclosures, so I guess one more won't hurt. To me, it seems really quite simple. In real terms, Americans' disposable incomes have been declining for nearly 20 years. However, during that time, the cost of housing has continued to go up, causing a gap between housing prices and affordability. Following the events of September 11, 2001, the economy went in the tank, so the government lowered interest rates to all-time lows, and a super-hot housing market ensued. Prices were driven up to unrealistic levels, because Americans have become accustomed to looking at cost not in real terms, but in terms of monthly payments. They view housing just like they do credit cards. They are willing to make the minimum monthly payments for 30 or more years. When interest rates went back to more normal and adjustable rates adjusted the true cost of those homes hit home, and the housing market tanked. I should note that this problem, as bad as it is, was compounded by the banks that made money available to people who simply were not creditworthy. Sound familiar? To make matters even worse, the banks made loans to people who were "poor credit risks" that amounted to 90-100 percent of the value of the over-inflated homes. Is it any wonder home prices are going through an inevitable market correction?

"What goes up must come down."

Foreclosures are at an all-time high and people seem surprised. Why? It was inevitable.

By the way, those upper-echelon corporate bankers and government officials are all scrambling to dodge the bullet. Meanwhile, who gets tagged with the blame? The government blames the mortgage companies, saying the appraisers were in cahoots with the real estate companies and overvalued the home appraisals. All that may be true, but let's not forget that at the heart of the entire debacle was a government in collusion with big business to keep the engine of the economy running. As bad as all this was the straw that broke the Camel's back was the predatory practice of bundling sub-prime loans in with conventional loans in what is called a (CDO) Collateralized Debt Obligation giving them unwarranted AAA ratings and selling these toxic assets to countries around the world. In so doing the U.S. not only damaged its economy but it damages the economy on a global scale. It is any wonder other nations are not thrilled about propping up the U.S. dollar? In my mind, it doesn't much matter who gets tagged with the blame, because I know who will foot the bill and take the brunt of the human suffering: the American people.

In a subsequent chapter, I will share with you a practical, easy-to-follow strategy to pay off your home in as little as one third to one half the normal time.

As I close this chapter, I would like to summarize how the United States went from being the world's #1 economic superpower to being the world's #1 debtor nation.

If you are a history buff like me, you know they say that; *"Most great nations fall from within from complacency and decadent over-indulgence,"* or in other words they die from the good life. They die from gluttony. Let's see if that isn't what is happening to America today. Below is my version of the seven deadly sins that are destined to lead to the destruction of America, unless we wake up, come to our senses and start acting responsibly.

THE SEVEN DEADLY SINS

1. ***Excessive Credit and Debt:*** We have the Madison Avenue advertising executives to thank for creating "THE NOW GENERATION" whose motto is:

   "I Want That and I Want It Now."

2. ***Over Consumption:*** We suffer from unwillingness to live within our means. We have to keep up with those Jones' no matter the cost. Who are the Jones' anyway, aren't we the Jones'?

3. ***Massive Budget Deficit:*** As the little boy lamented to his mom as she gave him a bath, *"Mommy, mommy my boat sank!"* Mom responded calmly, *"Well, Johnny, didn't I tell you not to poke a hole in the bottom of the boat?"* I think our economic boat has a hole in its bottom. What do you think? Simply put you can't indefinitely spend more than you make.

4. ***Massive Trade Deficits:*** You can't indefinitely import more than you export and not expect your wealth to be depleted. That is the stuff of Economics 101, but I guess our government officials missed that class.

5. *Failure to Save:* We could take a lesson from the lowly squirrel who knows enough to put food supplies away for a the harsh winter months.

6. *Budget Deficits Caused By Unfunded Entitlement Programs:* In the face of massive deficit spending caused in large part by Social Security, Medicare, Medicaid and other entitlement programs the Government is pushing a Healthcare Reform program that we clearly can not afford.

7. *Failure to Face Emerging Political and Economic Power Shift Caused by Globalization:* When the labor forces in China and India get pay that is a fraction of what our workers get, the handwriting is on the wall. A global shift of wealth and associated power is inevitable.

Let's just suppose for a second that I am wrong and the 2008 collapse isn't heralding the advent of the Second Great Depression, ask yourself:

■ Depression aside, could you survive a personal financial set back?

■ If not, are you teetering on the brink of poverty?

■ How much debt do you have?

■ How much savings do you have?

■ What are you prepared to do to protect your family from the effects of economic hardship?

America has consumed itself into a debt and credit crisis that threatens the very fabric of our society, but we are a strong and resilient people, and there is still time to wake up, smell the roses and put our financial house in order. There is time, but precious little of it. I urge you to take action before it is too late!

By the way, I urge you to Google "Maxed Out" and view an online video or get the book, written by James Scurlock. Much of my data for this chapter came from his excellent research.

CHAPTER 3

COLLAPSE OF THE U.S. ECONOMY!

An Historic Perspective!

Our fate is in our hands. The decisions we make now will determine our future. If things get out of kilter, circumstances will eventually and inevitably restore the balance. Understand this simple truth and you can predict the future with relative accuracy. Though you won't be able to pinpoint the time, or place or the exact events, you will be able to predict the inevitable outcome. In this case, the imbalance that will inevitably be corrected is that America will not be able to continue indefinitely to consume more material goods and natural resources per capita than any other country on the planet. So, the inevitable outcome is that America will eventually be brought to its knees! It will be stripped of much of its power and wealth, and its material consumption will be brought into line with its population relative to the world's population!

In other words, we are in for a lot of changes. Any time change occurs you always have two choices: hide your head in the sand like an ostrich and do nothing, or take appropriate action to minimize the damage to yourself and those you love. It's time to choose! There's no place to hide. The only way you can protect yourself is by taking steps to protect your wealth.

There is a generation of Americans who only know about the Vietnam War from movies and history books. There are even fewer Americans who were alive during World War II. And, there are just a few Americans who lived through the fear, desperation and hopelessness that described America during the 12 agonizing and demoralizing years of the Great Depression!

To most of us, America is the nation that emerged from World War II as the world's preeminent superpower. Separated from Europe by a vast ocean, America was spared the decimation of having a war fought on her soil. As a result, America emerged from the war in 1945 with all of its manufacturing might intact, while Europe lay in ruin with long, agonizing years of reconstruction ahead. At the time, China and India were third-world countries, so as fate would have it America had a stranglehold on world trade and for the next two decades virtually dominated the global economy. America was truly the world's preeminent economic superpower. From 1945 till the 2008 sub-prime collapse, America enjoyed a relatively uninterrupted period of economic prosperity. Succeeding generations have enjoyed the good life, and each generation has come to expect to have a better standard of living than the one before, but all that is about to change.

UNDERSTANDING THE EFFECTS OF GLOBALIZATION AND AN AGING POPULATION!

Europe: Europe has fully recovered from the destruction of World War II. Manufacturing has been rebuilt and modernized. More importantly, ancient trade barriers have been substantially reduced, making the European Union a far more formidable economic force than ever before. This means the United States not only has to contend with emerging third-world countries, but also with increased economic competition from the European Union. Also the events of 9/11 have clearly demonstrated that the U.S. is no longer exempt from the horrors of war.

Japan: Japan was quickly rebuilt from the ashes of Hiroshima and Nagasaki. This tiny island nation has actually taught mighty America a few hard lessons about long-term planning, constant quality improvement and global marketing. Just ask anyone in the automobile or electronic industries whether Japan is a formidable competitor.

To illustrate just how quickly things can change, consider this:

between the end of World War II and the end of the 1980s, Japan emerged as the number two economic superpower, but, in 2007, Japan found itself teetering on the brink of financial collapse. How in the world could a nation as strong as Japan get itself into such a predicament? Interestingly enough the problem that Japan faced is very similar to what America faced in 1986 and again in 2008. Specifically in 1986, America faced the collapse of the savings and loan industry due to trillions of dollars of unsecured real estate debt. In 2007 Japan faced that same problem, but the difference was that America acted quickly and passed the 1986 Tax Reform Act, effectively declaring trillions of dollars of American real estate to be worthless. A federal agency called the Resolution Trust Corporation (RTC) stepped in and sold off trillions of dollars of real estate for pennies on the dollar. Japan failed to act as decisively as America did; therefore, its banking crisis become even more serious than that America faced in 1986. But these economic cresses pail in comparison to the 2008 sub-prime collapse precipitated by predatory lending practices in the U.S. By bundling high risk sub-prime loans with conventional mortgages in what is called a (CDO) Collateralized Debt Obligation, and then giving them unwarranted AAA ratings, and selling these toxic assets to countries around the world the U.S. is responsible for perhaps the worst economic crisis of modern times. The U.S. not only damaged its economy but it damaged the economy on a global scale. Time will tell but this event may well cause the collapse to the U.S. Dollar and turn the U.S. into a third world country. Greed exacts its price!

America, Germany, France and Japan are all facing **problems caused by an aging population**, but Japan's population hit retirement age in the late 1980s and early 1990s, while the American population will not hit retirement age until 2010. Why is this important? By looking at what is happening in Japan, we can get an idea of what America may be facing after 2010.

Elderly Japanese, fearful about their financial security, have banded together to support legislation to make sure their financial needs are taken care of during their retirement years. The AARP is doing the same thing here in America, but there is a problem. When Social Security was founded in the 1930s, there were 42 workers for every recipient. By 2000, that number had dropped to 3.4 workers per recipient. The youth of America can plainly see that Social Security isn't going to be there when they retire, so continuing to pay into a doomed Social Security program will only raise their taxes with no benefits to them. It's another instance of passing a problem from one generation to the next. But, in this case, the youth of America know up front that they will never see Social Security, and they're going to fight tax increases to support the elderly. This will lead us straight into social chaos, as one generation fights for survival at the expense of another.

The governments proposed Healthcare Legislation reflects the opposite side of that coin as the government endeavors to take heal care benefits away from the elderly in order to spend those dollars on what they consider to be younger more productive people. We are engaged in a life and death struggle which is pitting the young against the old, mothers and fathers against their children and it has been caused by the government irresponsibly spending the money in the Social Security Fund. The government has sold us down the river pure and simple!

China, once an isolationist nation, has joined the World Trade Organization (WTO). China began this century with almost no modern manufacturing capability. But, the Chinese used what they had. They had abundant natural resources and an enormously huge labor force that has an extremely low standard of living. They were motivated to work long and hard for extremely low wages, because it gave them slowly, ever so slowly, a better standard of living. Underwritten by government subsidies, the Chinese targeted the tool and dye industry and the manufacturing sector. America found itself virtually unable to compete. Tooling moved to China at an alarming rate. Likewise, Chinese factories have taken over much of the manufacturing that was once done in the United States. The only way America could fight back was by increasing productivity, downsizing and initiating a variety of cost-cutting measures. What America couldn't do was lower wages to a point that would be competitive with China. All we have been able to do is slow the rate of hemorrhage in the loss of manufacturing, because we have not been able to remove the cause, which is the fact that factories in China can substantially undercut our labor costs! It's a vicious cycle. America buys cheap products from China, and this creates a trade deficit! The point is that our highly paid unionized labor force can't compete against China's low-cost labor. China will continue to take market share away from countries with higher labor costs. It's a simple fact, and if we are smart we will accept it and adjust our material consumption in accordance with our declining market share and resulting economic instability. Put simply, America can't keep all the economic marbles any longer. As a result, our standard of living is declining and will continue to do so for some time.

This means our wealth is going to China, where it is used to build modern plants, so that soon the United States will not only be unable to compete with its labor force and low wages, but also with its modern manufacturing plants. The net result is that America will be put at a further disadvantage and the downward spiral will continue.

It sounds like there is nothing which can be done to curve the U.S. trade deficit, but that isn't true! Though China has lower production cost it still has to ship its goods across the ocean to the U.S. As discussed in my other book <u>Modern Slavery</u> the U.S. government did everything it could to make China's shipping cost as low as possible. This degraded the U.S. manufacturing base and made the trade deficit worse.

Even worse the U.S. is the only major industrialized nation with no trade protection: According to Auggie Tantillo, Executive Director at the American Manufacturing Trade Action Coalition (AMTAC): **Of 138 major manufacturing nations the U.S. is the only nation that does not take advantage of a "Value Added Tax" (VAT) in order to protect its manufacturing base and maintain a favorable balance of trade.** The VAT was created by a French Economist Maurice Laure in the 1950's. At each stage of production the manufacturer adds a "Value Added Tax" which is assessed by the government as a percentage of the final value of the good or service and is passed on to the consumer as an indirect tax much like sales tax. Though the VAT varies from country to country the average is 15%. When a product is sold domestically the government retains the VAT, however if the same product is exported the government rebates the VAT to the manufacturer as a **(government subsidy).** Since the U.S. imposes no VAT its products incur on average a 15% export penalty when competing with "Free Trade Countries" which subsidize their manufacturers by rebating the VAT. It gets worse! U.S. imports into VAT countries are hit with the VAT a second time, this time in the form of a (Tariff). **Since the U.S. Government neither subsidizes exports nor charges a tariff at the border on imports U.S. products incur on average a 30% tax disadvantage.** This is not by accident. As I discuss in my book <u>Modern Slavery</u> it is by design and as far as I am concerned it is nothing short of criminal. Is it any wonder the U.S. has the largest trade deficit in the world?

As Tantillo, explains:

> *"...the VAT differential is a core driving aspect as to why U.S. companies find themselves continually at a disadvantage. If you extrapolate to the next step the VAT differential is a core reason for why we see the escalating growth in the U.S. trade deficit on an annual Basis."*

India, a matriarchal society, which has long valued spiritual pursuits over material pursuits, is becoming increasingly capitalistic. India, like China, has an enormous population that is willing to work for a fraction of the wages that American workers are either willing or able to accept. The difference between India and China is that, as a former English colony, India has a large English-speaking population. India targeted America's intellectual property and computer markets. India has been a dominant cause of the outsourcing that has taken place in much of America's market for computer programming and support. Just like China, Indian companies are using the money they get from American companies to increase their competitive edge.

It's a simple fact that China, and India are systematically taking global market share away from America. They are benefiting from

America's high labor costs and trade deficit, but tragically we make matters worse by not having a VAT and by not imposing import quotas, like other countries, in order to limit foreign imports and help reduce the trade deficit. As I discuss in <u>Modern Slavery</u>, the U.S. Government has made it blatantly clear that **The U.S. Is For Sale!**

Superpowers in Decline: I'd like to take you back to the early period of colonialism. England, France, Spain and Portugal used their superior naval fleets to colonize the globe. They dominated trade and assimilated the wealth of many subservient nations. They did this by controlling all of the vital sea ways through which ships had to pass in order to circumnavigate the globe. As long as they controlled the seas they had a choke hold on global trade. Control trade and you control the wealth of nations. Control the wealth of nations and you control world power. It's a footnote in history that none of these superpowers are still superpowers. They are economically strong countries, but not superpowers.

What happened to these countries and what does it have to do with America? They lost their control over the seas and in so doing lost their stranglehold on trade and with it their power. As to why this happened, let's take a quick glance back at colonial England. This tiny island nation tried to colonize mighty India, one of the most populous countries in the world and for a long time it was successful. But, eventually the Indian people revolted and took back their country and their wealth. Similarly, American Colonies under the cry *"No taxation without representation,"* claimed their independence and took control over this country. So, what is the point? The point is that those colonizing nations were simply too small to indefinitely control larger nations that wanted economic freedom. Likewise, America—as large and powerful as it may be cannot keep all the economic marbles indefinitely. The rest of the world is demanding its fair share of material wealth. The simple fact is that, like the colonizing nations that preceded us, America cannot indefinitely keep the rest of the world from claiming its fair share of the world's wealth. **So, what America needs to do is stop its excessive material consumption! Ironically, our excessive material consumption is hastening the <u>redistribution of wealth</u>.** America finds itself in a position where it can't compete with the labor cost of developing countries, so America is increasingly importing more than it exports. The resulting imbalance of trade effectively redistributes the world's wealth by taking dollars from the United States and redistributing them to other countries with the net effect being that **America has become the world's largest debtor nation!**

The privilege of being the world's largest debtor nation is accorded us due to our position as global peacekeepers and our still dominant economic presence. However, America will not be able to stave off the inevitable indefinitely. Day by day we get poorer while other countries get richer. The end is in sight! The outcome is inevitable! **It's just a matter of time before America loses its economic stranglehold on the world and the balance of wealth is restored! Wealth is being redistributed, and America is powerless to stop it!**

So, what's the likely outcome? It's difficult to say exactly. But, it is clear that America will, like England, France, Spain and Portugal before it, cease to be the world's undisputed economic superpower. In all likelihood, America, which is currently the number one economic superpower, will decline in the rankings. Now that China has joined the WTO, it is poised to expand markets worldwide and emerge as the world's number one economic superpower. **The U.S. economy is becoming increasingly unstable due to our government's unwillingness to stop the huge budget deficits! Economic collapse is inevitable unless we stop spending immediately and start acting responsibly.**

Russia, until recently was America's chief rival in its role as superpower. If Russia can fall, who is to say it can't happen to America? Russia fell from within, because its political system failed to support entrepreneurialism or capitalism and, without it, Russia was unable to compete in the ever-increasing technologically oriented global economy. Though Russia's problem was on the surface different from that of America, the root cause of the problem was essentially the same: **inabilities to compete against the emerging countries, which together are establishing a new world order that will see the redistribution of wealth and the restoration of balance!**

PUTTING IT ALL TOGETHER — WHAT THE FUTURE HOLDS!

To put it all in perspective we live in, as George Orwell called it, a *"brave new world"* in which people have given over responsibility for their financial well-being to the government and the corporations, which have broken their promises to take care of us. We live in a world where we have to learn to take responsibility for ourselves. We live in a world where we go to bed wondering if we will have a job tomorrow and, if we do, whether we will be asked to do more work for less pay. We live in a world where we have become estranged from our families and friends, a world where it's every man for himself. All in all we live in a world where we are constantly ***ANXIOUS*** *about job security,* ***STRESSED*** *by the pace of change,* ***UNTRUSTING*** *of our leaders,* ***WORRIED*** *about our future and even more worried about our children's future,* ***FEARFUL*** *of terrorism,* ***ESTRANGED*** *from our families and friends,* ***ISOLATED*** *from society,* ***LONELY*** *with no one to turn to,* ***AFRAID TO THE POINT OF PARALYSIS!***

IN SUMMARY WE CAN EXPECT:

- *A worsening trade deficit* as America continues to import more than it exports and deliberately encourages trade deficits by not imposing a VAT or import restrictions.

- *Continuing erosion of our job market* as America continues to lose jobs, owing to competition from emerging countries, particularly China and India.

- **Worsening corporate stability** as corporations attempt to adjust to the new global economy. This will be seen in the form of mergers, acquisitions, outsourcing, downsizing, layoffs and corporate bankruptcies.

- **Increasing tendency for people to have multiple careers in their lifetimes** as society struggles to adapt to corporate instability caused by the global economy and rapid technological changes.

- **Declining or no health-care coverage** as the government struggles to cope with the issues brought on by an aging society.

- **Collapse of the social security system,** as 75 million Americans reach retirement age and rely on a dangerously under-funded social security program.

- **Increasing financial hardship among the elderly** as fewer members of this group have sufficient income to pay living—and health-care costs during retirement years, the government and corporations fail to provide expected levels of benefits and many of this group is unprepared for the changes ahead.

- **Declining standards of living compared with previous generations** brought about by increased global competition from emerging countries and the social and political issues caused by an aging society.

- **Worsening job satisfaction** as corporations place more demands on employees and provide lower salaries, less security and fewer benefits.

- **Increasing social unrest** as an exploding population competes for limited jobs and natural resources and the young and old fight over who is, or is not, going to take care of whom?

- **Collapsing stock market** as 75,000,000 retirees consistently withdraw their money from their 401k's in order to cover living expenses.

- **Collapse of U.S. currency** as the strain of globalization coupled with the demands of caring for an aging population brings the nation to its knees. **Even worse if we don't stop printing money we can expect hyperinflation and a complete collapse of the dollar and the U.S. economy!**

Due to globalization all the nations of the world are tied together as never before. Much of Europe is experiencing economic crisis. As the U.S. and Europe experience financial crisis they import fewer goods from China and China's economy is likewise negatively impacted. Russia depends heavily on export of natural resources, but as economies around the world experience financial crisis they need less of Russia's natural resources and the Russian economy is negatively impacted. We are interdependent and unless we start cooperating the entire global economic system is going to collapse. We need a New Briton Wood fixed exchange system in order to stabilize international commerce and the U.S. China, Russia and India as the four largest economies on the planet need to start working together. In a later chapter we will discuss The American System, which was the economic system which was responsible for America's rise to economic super power at the beginning of the industrial revolution. It holds the key to developing infrastructure around the world and infrastructure is the essential component to economic growth and expansion. Additionally we need to become less interdependent which means we need to move away from globalization, not toward it. The American System demonstrated that nations are stronger when they function as sovereign Nation States which are more or less self-sufficient. We have to stop going around the world in search of slave labor and cheap natural resources and help nations around the world build their infrastructures so they can join the 21st century. Our current system of economic oppression simply will not work in the future, that is not unless we are all willing to live under the oppression of a One World suppressive Communist Government.

In the next chapter, we will explore the causes of the Great Depression of 1929-1941 and ponder the question of whether or not history is repeating itself. What I want to leave you with, however, is that we are not powerless. There are things we can do; and I do believe we still have time to prepare if we are willing to adjust our lifestyles. Hang in with me and keep reading, and I promise I will leave you with a practical plan for protecting your assets and achieving financial security and happiness.

CHAPTER 4

THE GREAT DEPRESSION (1929-1941)

Is History Repeating Itself?

I want to warn you in advance this chapter is strong medicine, but I believe that it is crucial to our financial security and to our overall well-being that we understand:

- What caused the Great Depression!

- Why history will almost certainly repeat itself!

- How the Federal Government is intentionally bankrupting America.

- Just how bad things could get!

- How quickly things can happen!

- What we need to do to protect ourselves!

In 1918, America emerged from World War I as a super power and was about to embark on a period of unparalleled prosperity. As 1929 approached few Americans had any idea that their world was about to change in unimaginable fashion or that America and the rest of the world was about to be plunged into an economic abyss of unimaginable proportion. America had enjoyed nearly three decades of almost unhindered economic growth and prosperity, capped by the lavish spending and high living of the Roaring 1920s. Virtually no one was prepared for what was about to transpire. It was simply unimaginable at the time.

THE PLIGHT OF THE AMERICAN PEOPLE
DURING THE DEPRESSION!

The Great Depression created an America hitherto unimagined. This great nation had represented the hopes and dreams of millions of immigrants who had left their homes to come to this country to forge new lives. This was a nation built on the hopes and dreams of people who believed in rugged individualism. This was the land of opportunity and eternal optimism, and now it had become a nation of people numbed by the reality of unbelievable financial hardship. It was a nation of people in disbelief, a nation of people who were almost too dazed to know what to do. In order to give even a small measure of the severity of the Great Depression, we need to take a look at how it impacted the lives of a generation of Americans who would forever have their lives defined by the bleak reality that they had lived through the Great Depression!

By 1932 the depression was in its fourth year, and no matter what the government did it didn't seem to work. Over 10 million people, or approximately 20 percent of the population, were unemployed and were locked in the grips of depression, despair, gloom and the inevitable loss of self esteem that besets a person when he has no hope or when his nightly companion is fear of starvation. Cities like Chicago, Detroit and Minneapolis/St. Paul, once shinning examples of capitalism, were hit especially hard, because they represented the industrial might of a nation that had very little use for their products. Only one third as many automobiles rolled off the assembly lines in 1933 as in 1929. Accordingly, steel and iron production fell approximately 60 percent, and residential and commercial construction fell to one fifth of pre-depression levels. Fewer automobiles and houses meant fewer jobs for lumberjacks; steel workers; ore miners; factory workers who made appliances; engineers; architects; carpenters; plumbers; roofers; plasters; painters and electricians. It wasn't just the uneducated or unskilled laborers who were affected. The depression had no respect for age, race, gender or education; some people were just luckier than others. In aggregate the unemployment rate in these cities neared 50 percent.

No matter where you turned, the outlook was bleak. There was not only an army of unemployed, but also an army of underemployed, as nationwide the combined effects of unemployment and involuntary part-time employment left 50 percent of the American workforce unutilized for a decade.

Social workers consistently reported that, despite the fact that people had lost jobs through no fault of their own, unemployed men experienced not only depression, but also feelings of guilt and self-recrimination. They felt that in some indeterminable way they had let their families down; they had failed their children and they were somehow *"less of a man,"* because they didn't have a job. If their wives worked and they didn't, the situation was even worse as a role reversal occurred, and the husbands became subservient and submissive to their wives, the bread winners. The entire family structure was turned upside down, and it often resulted in separation or divorce, with the husband eventually leaving. Tens of thousands of unemployed men, labeled *"hobos,"* hit the highways and railways, looking for work. With heads bowed in shame, they stood in soup lines; they huddled in box cars and around camp fires, their clothes tattered, their shoes lined with newspaper to plug the holes. They anguished and lamented and prayed for relief from their torment, but their prayers went unanswered. Those who stayed put scrimped and scraped. Often families would move in together to share expenses. Every penny was precious. Food was basic, no frills; socks were darned; clothes were patched; nothing went to waste. People went about the business of survival, and it was a harsh business, which nightly visited them with feelings of despair and hopelessness.

I found this quote by Frank Walker, President of the National Emergency Council (1934) to be especially heart wrenching. He reports, *"I saw old friends of mine—men, I had gone to school with—digging ditches and laying sewer pipe. They were wearing their regular business suits as they worked, because they couldn't afford overalls and rubber boots. If I ever thought, 'there but for the grace of God go I,' it was right then."*

There was a certain irony to the depression. In Oregon, apples fell to the ground and rotted for want of buyers. In the breadbasket, wheat also went unsold. Striking farmers overturned milk trucks and blocked deliveries of cattle and hogs to the stock yards in Omaha. This was contrasted by visions of tens of thousands of men standing in soup lines. In the cities, people scrounged in trash cans for scraps of food. The pity of it, such want in a sea of plenty.

Across the country, family farms encumbered by debt went on auction blocks by the thousands, as banks first foreclosed and then tried to recoup some of their losses by turning around and auctioning them to the highest bidders. Throughout the Midwest, groups of neighbors gathered to intimidate would-be buyers. This tactic frequently resulted in the original owner being able to buy back his or her farm, sometimes for as little as one cent.

Much of the tragedy of the American people was reported by Loretta Hickock. While working for the Associated Press, Hickock was assigned to cover Eleanor Roosevelt during the presidential campaign. She and Eleanor became close friends, and Eleanor was influential in convincing her to resign from her position (in June of 1933) and take an assignment from the White House to travel across America and record the plight of Americans in the depression.

In a summary report written on New Year's Day 1935, Hickock recounted her worries about a *"stranded generation,"* men over 40 with half-grown families who might never get their jobs back. Through loss of skill and through mental and physical deterioration, owing to long periods of enforced idleness, the relief clients—the people who had been longest without work—were gradually forced into the class of *"unemployables,"* like rusty tools, abandoned, not worth using any more. And, so they go on—the gaunt, ragged legion of the industrially damned, bewildered and apathetic, many of them terrifyingly patient (Lowitt and Beaslen. *One Third of a Nation*. 361-63).

Hopkins concluded: *"The elderly through hardship, discouragement and sickness as well as advanced years, have gone into an occupational oblivion from which they will never be rescued by private industry."* (Hopkins, *Spending to Save*. 161).

In Oct. 1933, Hickock wrote Eleanor Roosevelt from North Dakota, *"These plains are beautiful, but oh the terrible, crushing dumbness of life here. And the suffering, for both people and animals... Most of the farm buildings haven't been painted in God knows how long! If I had to live here I'd just quietly call it a day and commit suicide... The people up here... are in a daze. A sort of nameless dread hangs over the people."* (Richard Lowett and Maurine, eds. *One Third of A Nation*).

"As winter closed its grip over the northern plains, farmers were burning cow manure (buffalo chips) and rushes cut from dried lakes for fuel. Even the animals suffered. The plight of the livestock is pitiable. Milk cows are drying up for lack of feed. Farmers eligible for relief road work did not have teams healthy enough to pull road scrapers. Half-starved horses have dropped in the harness right on the road job..." (Davis 3:55 – 91-96).

By any measure of human suffering, the Great Depression was an event never experienced by any generation of Americans before or since. Unfortunately, I have to tell you that a convergence of events makes it highly likely that history will soon repeat itself and possibly reap even greater vengeance on us than the Great Depression. Before this chapter is over, we will discover just how this could come about and just how bad *"bad"* could be!

CAUSES OF THE GREAT DEPRESSION AND CORRELATIONS TO THE PRESENT!

The Significance of the Stock Market Crash of 1929

The cartoon on the next page represents the common stereotype that the 1929 stock market crash caused the Great Depression and vanquished the life savings of most Americans. In actuality the 1929 depression was generally agreed not to have been caused by the stock market crash. That was certainly a contributing factor, but the causes were many. In 1929, the stock market fell 42 percent, and it took 25 years, until 1955, for it to recover to pre-1929 levels, however few American's owned stock. In fact, only about 3 million Americans, or approximately 2.5 percent of the population owned securities. So, myths aside, 97.5 percent of the population owned no stock in 1929. Even indirect ownership of stock was minimal until the formation of pension funds gave millions of Americans a stake in capitalism.

"NOT ALL THE KINGS' HORSES OR ALL THE KINGS' MEN COULD PUT HUMPTY DUMPTY BACK TOGETHER AGAIN."

How the 1929 crash figures in as a cause of the Great Depression was that Germany depended on loans from American banks to make its $33 billion War reparation payments to Britain and France. Britain and France, in turn, used the money to pay War loans owed to the U.S. Treasury. **The stock market crash dried up the well of American _credit_ and severely disrupted international cash flows.** This interruption of funds ultimately resulted in Germany defaulting on its reparation payments, and France retaliated by occupying the Ruhr, Germany's industrial heartland. This act touched off **hyperinflation** and triggered a cascade of events, which turned the American depression of 1929 into the worldwide Great Depression, which for a decade defined the lives of a generation of Americans and Europeans. Their lives would be defined by the fear that is a certain outgrowth of economic uncertainty! Out of this despair and sense of hopelessness, Adolph Hitler rose to power and was installed as Chancellor of Germany. A constantly repeating theme in history is that fear and desperation caused by economic hardship often topples governments and leads to tyranny; such was the case in Germany.

Under Consumption Caused by the Greed of the Robber Barons

Since the onset of the industrial revolution, the so-called robber barons of industry had operated virtually unencumbered by the government or anything else. However, a new era was about to dawn. In his campaign speech at the Common Wealth Club of San Francisco (Sept. 23, 1932), President Roosevelt announced a new era: *"A mere builder of more industrial plants, organizer of more corporations, is as likely to be a danger as a help. The day of the great promoter or the financial titan, to whom we granted everything if only he would build, or develop, is over. Our task now is not discovery or exploitation of natural resources, or necessarily producing more goods. It is the sober, less dramatic business of administrating resources and plants already in hand, of seeking to reestablish foreign markets for our surplus production, of meeting the problems of under consumption, of adjusting production to consumption, of distributing wealth and products more equitably."* (PPA (1929 -32) 751-52).

The belief intoned in this speech was that the imbalance that resulted in **under consumption** originated with the owners of industry and their failure to pass on a fair share of the spectacular profits of the 1920s to laborers in the form of higher wages and to consumers in the form of lower prices. As a result, the productivity gains of mass production had created a serious imbalance in the economic fabric of capitalism. Mass production by its very definition demands mass purchasing power in order to consume its fruits. On account of their greed, the robber barons of industry had left the American population with insufficient discretionary income to buy their products. As a result, **inventories rose, production slowed, unemployment ensued** and buying power dropped even further, creating a problem that would not be resolved until massive government spending in response to World War II stimulated adequate buying power to consume the goods of mass production and put people back to work.

Weak Banking System

President Hoover believed the banking system was the **weakest link in the economic chain.** He described it as, *"The element sensitive to fear… the worst part of the dismal tragedy with which I had to deal."* (Hoover. *Memoirs: The Great Depression*: 21, 84).

The American banking system was inherently unstable and subject to fear. Even during the good times of the 1920s, banks failed at a rate of approximately 500 per year. Then, in 1933, after suffering over 5000 bank failures, Americans converged on banks across the nation in a massive bank run. On the day of Roosevelt's inauguration as President, the government responded by proclaiming a nationwide shut down of the banking industry. Underlying the weakness of the American banking system was the sheer number of banks. There were some 25,000 banks operating, or failing to operate, under the confines of 52 different regulatory agencies. In addition, confidence was easily shaken, owing to the lack of any structure to guarantee the safety of depositors' savings.

As we shall shortly see, the events that combined to cause the Great Depression have substantial corollaries in today's economy, and history is poised to repeat itself. If a Great Depression befalls America are you be prepared? The answer for most Americans is no, and that is precisely why I have written this book. I want to warn those who will listen and arm them with strategies to protect themselves, as much as possible, from the ravages that befall the people of a nation when the economic system falters.

CORRELATIONS TO THE PRESENT!

Thanks to the advent of the 401K, unlike in 1929 when less than 3% of the population owned stock now most Americans have most of their retirement funds invested in the stock market so a collapse of the stock market would be truly devastating.

Just like in 1929 we are facing a **credit crisis**. Americans have maxed out their credit lines. In 1994, the average savings rate was

6 percent and in 2008 it was -1 percent. This translates into reduced buying power and economic slow down. Even more calamitous is the 2008 sub-prime collapse which according to our politicians threatened to completely dry up the credit markets and literally cause an economic collapse unless we bailed out the banks by giving them a $700 billion bail out in the form of the now infamous Stimulus Bill. This of course started the printing presses and we are dangerously close to going into **hyperinflation**. If as looks likely, international markets decide to no longer transact oil purchases in U.S. dollars the outcome will almost certainly be hyperinflation leading to the **collapse of not only the dollar but a total collapse of the U.S. economy leaving the U.S. relegated to the status of a third world country!** Given Obama's agenda of the Redistribution of Wealth and given the instability brought about by an economic collapse I can even foresee the possibility of the collapse of the Republic to be replaced by a Socialist/Communist Government and possibly even the rise of a strong man like Hitler.

As bad as the Great Depression was all indications are that what we are facing now is much worse. We better wake up before it is too late.

PROBABLE CAUSES OF THE SECOND GREAT DEPRESSION!

There is no question that President Roosevelt's New Deal legislation did, for a substantial period, provide the American people with the security he strove to provide. However, his plan had an unfortunate flaw: you cannot legislate against greed. So, as we are about to see, once again there are imbalances precipitated by greed that threaten to plunge us into a second Great Depression, but this time I fear it will be even worse!

Route Cause of Second Great Depression: There is once again an imbalance between production and consumption, resulting in an inadequate supply of discretionary money **(credit)** to purchase goods in a sufficient quantity to keep the engine of mass production operating at a sufficient level.

The Four Cylinders of the Economic Engine: In order to provide a framework for comparison, I will draw my comparisons from events related to the four cylinders of the economic engine.

1. **Banking**
2. **Real Estate**
3. **The Stock Market**
4. **The Job Market**

I will analyze them one at a time in order to develop the lattice work that underpins my prediction of a second Great Depression. Though there are a myriad of possible events that could trigger the second Great Depression, they all have one thing in common: they are in some way the result of economic imbalances created by greed.

1. ***Banking***: (Historic Perspective) As a result of the New Deal legislation, bank runs, which had customarily occurred at the rate of hundreds per year, dropped to less than ten per year in the decade following 1933. Despite the fact that the legislation removed the fear associated with the banking industry, it could not remove the propensity for greed and, therefore, the likelihood that history would repeat itself.

    Once again, a privileged few have gotten rich off of the hard work of the masses. They have gotten rich man's way, and we are about to pay the consequences for their greed. The money lenders and robber barons have once again gotten control of other people's money and created an imbalance that is poised to plunge America into the second Great Depression. Follow along as we explore why the money supply (credit) has ostensibly dried up!

    Credit Card Debt: (Historic Perspective) In 1919, General Motors pioneered *"consumer credit"* or *"installment buying"* in order to stimulate automobile sales. They also embarked on a massive advertising campaign designed to convince people that they didn't just want an automobile, they needed one. Add to this President Roosevelt's comments in his Commonwealth Club address stating *"...that the private sector left to its own devises would never again be capable of generating sufficient investment or employment to sustain even 1920's levels of economic output"* and you can see why the government made it so easy for people to get credit and lots of it.

Basically, what happened was that the government, fearful of unemployment and wanting to keep the engine of production running, allowed the credit card companies to proliferate in order to keep people buying. The materialistic feeding frenzy that resulted was further proliferated by the billions that were spent by Madison Avenue advertising companies in order to, as General Motors had done before them, convince consumers that they didn't just want, but **they needed the products of industry. They took it a step further and convinced us that our image was tied to our external projection of perceived wealth. They defined our egos our very self-image based on material consumption and in the process made the masses indentured servants. The masses became indentured to the credit card companies and indentured to the debt they had incurred to buy material goods they couldn't afford. So, in reality their possessions owned them rather than them owning their possessions.**

Make no mistake this is a very serious problem. It has created a death spiral just as lethal as the one created by the robber barons of the 1920s. It started with mothers going to work so the family could have *"a better standard of living."* Then came the house mortgage, the car payment and the credit card payments. Then, when the bills got too high they were rolled into a home equity loan. Many Americans are in debt up to their eyeballs and have no more available credit, which means their mad frenzy of buying has likewise come to an end. As this happens, the cylinders of the economic engine seize up. In pursuit of the *"good life,"* America has become the world's largest debtor nation. In 2005, for the first time since 1941, America had ZERO SAVINGS. That is nada, zilch, zero, not one dime and as of 2008 the savings rate was -1%.

THE GOVERNMENT IS CORRUPT!

Not only did the government in conjunction with Madison Avenue brainwash us and turn us into Credit Junkies it also rigged the system so we could never get out of debt! In a landmark case the Supreme Court ruled that the legal rate a credit card company could charge was based on the state in which it was incorporated. With the stroke of a pen the sovereign rights of the states had once again been usurped by the Federal Government, "With that decision the government had effectively legalized Loan sharking/Predatory Lending." Banks rushed to incorporate in New Hampshire, Delaware, Virginia, South Dakota, Utah, Nevada and Arizona none of which had usury laws. Rates quickly jumped to as high as 30% or more resulting in a situation where the average American now owes $10,000 in credit card debt and if they pay the minimum, because that is all they can afford, it will take them 30 years to pay off their debt. If that isn't slavery I don't know what is. And it's all thanks to the crooks in Washington! Wake up America! This subject is covered in detail in my book Modern Slavery.

Insolvency of Social Security: Social Security isn't exactly a banking issue, but it will affect the banks. To put into perspective the severity of the problem, consider these facts:

- In 1930, when the Social Security system was founded, only 8 percent of the population was over 65.

- By 2012-2016, as the 75 million baby boomers retire, over 25 percent of the population will be over 65.

- In 1930, there were 42 workers for every recipient.

- By 2000, there were 3.4 workers per recipient.

It doesn't take a genius to figure out that Social Security is in a death spiral. Former President Bush knew younger Americans were skeptical about whether they would ever receive any Social Security benefits, so he proposed legislation to allow them to put a portion of their Social Security contribution into the stock market. To my mind, it's not a solution at all, because the number of younger Americans potentially contributing is a much smaller group than the baby boomer generation, which will be withdrawing funds. In reality, the problem is worse than the numbers above would suggest. The number of people needing assistance from Social Security goes well beyond the 75 million baby boomers. By 2020, the number of people needing financial assistance from the government, in one form or another, is estimated to be 150 million, or roughly 50 percent of our current population of 300 million. This number includes the 75 million baby boomers, plus immigrants, the poor and the disabled. As large as this number is, it doesn't include the millions of federal and state employees who have government pensions. How in the world can the government possibly take care of that many people?

THE GOVERNMENT IS CORRUPT!

Remember Social Security was originally designed to pay recipients from dividends, and with 23 people paying in for every recipient there were enormous surpluses which were supposed to collect interest so that as the population aged there would be plenty of money to keep the fund solvent. Make no mistake the only reason Social Security is bankrupt is because **the crooks in Washington stole the money** and they ought to be going to jail instead of setting in their plush offices waiting to collect their pensions which by the way are fully funded outside the Social Security System. Wake up America! Washington is corrupt, and that means both the Republicans and the Democrats. It's time to take back the reins of power! This subject is covered in detail in my book Modern Slavery.

2. *Real Estate:* (Historic Perspective) The establishment of standardized appraisal methodologies and building codes removed much of the risk involved in home buying. However, as we will see, it opened the door to the type of over leveraging that triggered the 1929 stock market crash. So, once again, greed is pivotal in bringing about the second Great Depression.

Following the events of September 11, 2001, the stock market fell and the economy went into a major slump. In order to avoid a full-blown depression, the government lowered the interest rate to one basis point, which was the lowest it had been since 1941. The availability of cheap money resulted in a real-estate boom that restarted the economic engine. The problem was that, out of greed, mortgage companies, wanting to take advantage of the availability of cheap money from the government, made loans they had no business making. Zero-down loans and interest-only loans became common. Then in 2008 came the inevitable collapse of the housing bubble in what came to be called the Sub-prime collapse. The net result was an economic crash resulting in trillions of dollars in defaulted mortgages and record foreclosures causing the greatest economic crisis in the history of the U.S. At the end of this section I will disclose how none of this could have happened without the intervention of the crooks in Washington!

I predict that the real estate collapse is not over. If unemployment remains high and consumer sales remain down we can expect that somewhere between 2010 & 2012 that we will experience a 2nd real estate collapse, this time in the commercial market. It will likely be precipitated by wholesale failure of retail businesses resulting in the closing of malls all across the country.

Referring back to the aftermath of 9/11, millions of Americans took advantage of the low interest rates to refinance their homes. Frequently, they not only refinanced their homes but also rolled in their high-interest credit card debt, their car payments, and children's college loans. They could borrow up to 125% of their homes value. If that isn't over leveraging, I can't imagine what is.

Many people, especially the baby boomers at the peak of their income-earning potential, took advantage of the situation by selling their homes and up sizing to larger more expensive homes, which they thought they could afford because of the lower interest rates. There is a problem, however, that they had failed to anticipate. On account of globalization and the resulting trade deficit, salaries have been stable or declining since roughly the 1980s. Housing prices have, however, increased steadily during this same period. I purchased my first investment property in 1970 for $17,500. It was a 10-room duplex. At the peak of the market that property was valued at $165,000 which is a nearly 10 fold increase in price. But, in the period between then and now, salaries have not gone up at rates anywhere near that. As a matter of fact, actual buying power has gone down appreciably. This disparity between salaries and housing cost is in large part what triggered the nationwide bursting of the real-estate bubble. The economic collapse is going to be particularly hard on the retiring baby boomers because many of them were counting on huge profits from the sale of their homes to pay cash for smaller homes and fund their retirement programs. They failed to notice that the generation coming up behind them is not only smaller than their generation, but also is experiencing a decline in adjusted income. As a result, there is not going to be demand for big, expensive houses. In addition, if President Obama's Cap & Trade Legislation is passed we can expect energy costs to, as Obama said, *"Skyrocket"* making those big houses even more of a white elephant. This may result in a 3rd real estate bubble a few years from now as the baby boomers begin to retire in mass.

The intersection of falling salaries and rising home prices created a situation in which many Americans could no longer afford to purchase a home contributing to the 2008 housing bubble.

THE GOVERNMENT IS CORRUPT!

The real estate collapses wasn't caused by collapse of the sub-prime real estate market as most believe. That was certainly a factor, but the real culprit was that Wall Street got in on the feeding frenzy when they introduced something called a Collateralized Debt Obligation (CDO) which is a scam where by high risk sub-prime mortgages were bundled together with conventional mortgages, given inappropriately high AAA ratings and sold to unsuspecting securities investors around the world. This could never have happened if it had not been for the Federal Governments dismantling of the Glass-Steagall Act which *"prohibited commercial banks from owning or being owned by full service brokerage firms."* This set the stage for the predatory lending practices which led to the sub-prime collapse of 2008, but even so the crisis could have been avoided if it wasn't for even more intervention by the Federal Government. Many governors saw what was happening and moved to pass anti-predatory lending laws, but the Bush administration blocked their efforts at every turn. **The Bush administration used the Office of the Controller of the Currency (OCC) to nullify all the state mandates.** According to Eliot Spencer Former New York Governor: *"In 2003, during the height of the predatory lending crisis, the OCC invoked a clause from the 1863 National Bank Act to issue formal opinion* **preempting all state predatory lending laws, thereby rendering them inoperative.** *The OCC also promulgated new rules that prevented states from enforcing any of their own consumer protection laws against national banks. The federal governments' actions were so egregious and so unprecedented that all 50 states attorneys general, and all 50 state banking superintendents, actively fought the new rules."* If we want to save America we have to get the crooks out of Washington and that means both parties. They are both bought and paid for by the banking concerns. This subject is covered in more detail in my book Modern Slavery.

3. *The Stock Market:* In a word, the cause of the 1929 crash was GREED, pure and simple, unabridged greed! In a feeding frenzy, investors borrowed money from banks to buy stocks on the margin, sometimes with as little as 10 percent down. The New Deal legislation made the stock market safer by making such transactions

illegal, but once again we see that you cannot legislate against greed. This time around instead of stocks on margin it was homes on adjustable rate mortgages bought with zero down. Different scam same result.

Recent Stock Market Crashes: Over the years legislators have systematically dismantled the safeguards of the New Deal which were put into effect to protect the banking and securities markets. As a result we had another crash in the 1980s. (This topic is covered in detail in my book <u>Modern Slavery</u>.) Things were so bad that on Black Friday the markets were closed. When they opened on Monday the banks were planning to call in all of their loans, effectively causing a catastrophic collapse of the market. This catastrophe was barely averted because over the weekend the Federal Reserve, headed by then newly appointed Chairman Alan Greenspan, contacted all the banks and guaranteed coverage of their loans.

Most recently, between March of 2000 and the summer of 2002, the stock market lost a staggering $6.9 trillion. As a result, millions of people have been forced out of retirement and back to work and millions of others who were planning to retire soon are wondering if they will ever be able to retire. They are left scratching their heads, asking themselves what went wrong. This hardly sounds like the security that President Roosevelt envisioned, but it certainly gives us a warning about the vulnerability of the stock market in years to come!

The 1929 stock market crash was caused by massive speculative buying. By contrast, the bull market of 2000-2002 was driven by speculation on dot-com stocks and was funded by money coming from the 75 million baby boomers who were experiencing their peak income earning years and were putting their considerable discretionary income into the stock market as part of their retirement plan. The market couldn't sustain the speculative bull market and crashed, and millions of people lost their life savings. Doesn't this sound remarkably similar to what caused the 1929 crash? Again, I say you cannot legislate against greed!

Should a catastrophic stock market crash occur in the future, its impact would be far more devastating to the nation than the 1929 crash. This is because, as of 1974, the U.S. government passed the Employee Retirement Income Security Act (ERISA), which paved the way for 401(k)s and other similar retirement vehicles. The significance of this legislation is that in 1929 only 2.5 percent of the population owned stock, but now because of the creation of 401(k)s as America's primary retirement vehicle, most of the population has its money in the stock market. This means that the effects of a stock market crash like the one that occurred in 1929 would be much more devastating. Remember, it took 25 years for the stock market to recover back to pre-1929 levels.

A 25-year recovery is no big deal when only 2.5 percent of the population is affected, but when the vast majority of the population has its life savings in the stock market, and it has a catastrophic collapse there are no words to describe the human suffering that will result! The hardest hit will be the elderly, simply because they don't have enough time to recover like a younger person could.

Do you remember the Enron scandal precipitated by energy deregulation? President Obama's Cap & Trade Legislation creates an unprecedented opportunity for speculation and for the Wall Street crowd to once again scam the American people. Over time as CO_2 emission are ratcheted down CO_2 certificates will become the object of speculative bidding which could lead to a stock market crash.

Sell off of stocks by baby boomers: The vast majority of the baby boomers have most of their retirement invested in tax-deferred, 401(k)s, primarily in, non-dividend or low-dividend paying mutual funds. In 2012-2016 the first wave of baby boomers will hit 70, and at the age of 70 ½ they must start paying the federal government the taxes owed on their tax-deferred stock purchases. To make matters even worse, most of the baby boomers won't be able to live on the meager dividends from their 401(k)s, so they will have to regularly sell their stocks. To put the gravity of this situation into perspective, consider that the total American population is approximately 300 million. That means that based on current statistics, 25 percent of the population will be regularly selling their stocks. According to the law of supply and demand the only direction prices can go in an instance like this is down. To give you an idea of just how serious this problem is if we assumed that the 75 million baby boomers pulled $2,000 per month out of the stock market to live on, that would be $150 billion per month being pulled out of the engine that drives economic growth and stability. Moreover, I believe that as retirees see this flight of money from the stock market and the resulting fall of stock prices they will do what the Japanese did in the 1980s and 1990s, which is pull much of their money out of the stock market and put it in banks where they think it is safer. (That is if the dollar has not already collapsed due to hyperinflation) The problem is two fold: this will not only further drive down stock prices, but it will also create a glut of money in the banks, which will drive down interest rates. This will leave the retirees unable to live off the low interest rates they are paid on their savings. This scenario is tantamount to a time bomb waiting to go off with catastrophic economic consequences.

The pre-1974 Defined Benefit Programs (DBP), or company-funded pension funds, generally included cost-of-living escalators and health-care benefits. The post-1974 Defined Contribution Programs (DCP) and 401(k)s don't have cost-of-living escalators or any provision to provide for health-care costs. The retiree is 100 percent dependent on his or her retirement program to cover cost-of-living increases and medical expenses. In a nutshell, this means that if his pension program doesn't provide enough cash flow to live, he will have no choice other than to sell stocks. This further compounds the situation described above and hastens the withdrawal of money from the stock market, thus, putting further downward pressure on stock prices.

THE GOVERNMENT IS CORRUPT!

As covered in the last section most of the instability we see in the Stock Market exists because the government dismantled New Deal Legislation, including the Glass-Steagall Act which prohibited commercial banks from owning or being owned by full service brokerage firms. Additionally the government blocked efforts by governors to prevent predatory lending practices in their states.

The U.S. is being intentionally bankrupt by the puppet Federal Government and their handlers the corrupt private banking elite of the Federal Reserve and The World Bank. See my book Modern Slavery to learn why the Federal Reserve is at the heart of America's economic woes and why according to the 16th Amendment the Federal Income Tax is an illegal tax imposed on the American people by private banking concerns.

4. *The Job Market:* Though the New Deal passed legislation to provide workers unemployment insurance, no legislation can assure workers a job. As always, jobs depend on the availability of disposable income to purchase the goods of mass production and fuel the engine of the economy. Between 1945 and the mid-1970s America had a strangle hold on world trade. Then the tide shifted and we began buying more and more products from Japan, Europe, China and India until, thanks to our deficit spending and trade deficits, America allowed her wealth to be siphoned off, resulting in a situation where the nation that just a few decades earlier was the world's wealthiest nation is now the world's largest debtor nation.

Some may argue that in a global economy the interdependency between countries is so great that one superpower cannot afford to allow another to have an economic collapse. This line of thinking is supported by history and how the collapse of the German economy contributed to the Great Depression. It is precisely because of this type of fear that China and Japan have invested so heavily in American Treasury Notes, Corporations and Real Estate. They know it would not be in their best interest to see the American economy collapse. There are however indications that they are becoming unwilling to continue backing the U.S. Dollar in light of the massive deficit spending of the Obama Administration. **We are rapidly approaching the point where cutting The U.S. dollar loose makes more sense than continuing to prop it up.** If this occurs the **U.S. will almost certainly experience hyperinflation resulting in the destruction of the U.S. dollar and U.S. economy!**

THE GOVERNMENT IS CORRUPT!

The Stimulus: was sold to the American public based on the contention that without it there would be *"No Credit and the Economy Would Collapse."* But the day after the Stimulus was passed the Bush Administration sent Henry Paulson of The Treasury Department to give billions in bail out money to select banks to buy other banks *creating a banking monopoly structured and designed by the Federal Government! This was completely contrary to the promises of the Federal Government that the money would be used to provide credit to stimulate the economy and create jobs.* The government saw to it that the corrupt bankers got billions but Main Street was hung out to dry. Small businesses which account for ¾ of all new jobs got virtually nothing. It is no accident unemployment is where it is.

Intentional Loosing Trade Policies and the Gutting of U.S. Manufacturing: According to Auggie Tantillo, Executive Director at the American Manufacturing Trade Action Coalition (AMTAC): Of 138 major manufacturing nations the U.S. is the only nation that does not take advantage of a "Value Added Tax" (VAT) in order to protect it's manufacturing base and maintain a favorable balance of trade. A VAT is assessed by the government as a percentage of the final value of a good or service and is passed on to the consumer as an indirect tax. When a product is sold domestically the government retains the VAT, however if the same product is exported the government rebates the VAT as a **(government subsidy)**. U.S. imports into VAT countries are hit with the VAT a second time, this time in the form of a **(Tariff). Since the U.S. Government neither subsidizes exports nor charges a tariff at the border on imports U.S. products incur on average a 30% tax disadvantage.** As I discuss in my book <u>Modern Slavery</u> this is by design, and it is a major cause of the gutting of the U.S. Manufacturing Sector and resulting loss of jobs. The crooks belong in Jail!

A TIME TO REFLECT!

It's time we stopped and reflected on the consequences our decisions have wrought. We need to ask: Are we still the invincible economic and military superpower that emerged victorious from World War II? Are we the land of opportunity, as we were for so many immigrants who came to our shores in search of a better life? Or, are we a nation in the twilight of her power? Are we a nation of indentured servants? Are we a nation of people who daily become more and more *"necessitous,"* a nation that teeter on the brink of economic, political, social and personal oblivion? Are we a nation of God-fearing people who worship God, like the pilgrims who founded this country? Or, have we been perverted by the pursuit of money, power, and what we call the good life? Have our actions brought us the happiness we dreamt about? Are we a nation to whom much was given and who has blessed others by giving much back? Or, are we a nation that has taken and taken until our bank account with God has been depleted, and He is about to foreclose on our prosperity and purify us until our suffering resounds in the heavens, and we repent, and through God's grace get a chance to once again become the great nation of our forefathers, a nation dedicated to God, a nation that God blesses and that, in turn, is a blessing to others, a nation of people who have found wealth *"God's way,"* and in the process have found true happiness and the understanding of what *"TRUE WEALTH"* really is? Whatever your view is of who we are as a nation, one thing is almost certain. **We are a nation that has a rendezvous with destiny!** The question is will we choose God's way or man's way? Will we choose God or Mammon? Will our pursuit of wealth be our downfall or will it be a blessing to others? The choice is ours.

God's Way to Riches: Matthew 6:33 clearly shows us *"God's way!" But seek first the kingdom of God and his righteousness: and all these things shall be added unto you."* Proverbs 10:22: *The blessing of the Lord it maketh rich, and he addeth no sorrow.*

Man's Way to Riches: God warns those that put the pursuit of money and power ahead of the pursuit of God: *"... they that will be rich fall into temptation and a snare, and into many foolish and hurtful lusts, which drown men in destruction and perdition. For the love* *of money is the root of all evil: which while some coveted after, they have erred from the faith, and pierced themselves through with many sorrows.* (1 Timothy 6:9-10)

It's not too late! If we turn away from our pursuit of materialism and selfish greed, we can find the wealth that addeth no sorrow. However, if we continue our present course, God will have no choice but to loosen the hounds of war and the four horsemen of the apocalypse to wreak havoc on us until we repent and turn to him! Our future is in our hands!

Jesus said to them, "Watch out!
Be on your guard against all kinds of greed;
a man's life does not consist in the abundance of his possessions. "
(Luke 12:15)

Take Back America From The Crooks In Washington!

Part II

God's Plan for Your Life!

Chapter 5:   PROSPERITY CONSCIOUSNESS!
            The Spiritual Basis of Wealth

Part III of this book provides a tangible seven-step program on how to build wealth so that you can retire well off. Here, in Part II, we are looking at the spiritual aspects of wealth building and examining how the definition of material wealth and spiritual wealth differ.

Material wealth is about the process of accumulating money. By contrast, spiritual wealth examines how the pursuit of money can either lead to happiness or unhappiness. I contend that just having money isn't enough. It benefits a man very little if he has money and is unhappy. Spiritual wealth gives us both financial prosperity and happiness and that after all is the quintessential definition of true wealth!

> *The blessing of the Lord it maketh rich,*
> *and he addeth no sorrow.* (Proverbs 10:22)

> *And it shall be given unto you; good measure, pressed down,*
> *and shaken together. And running over, shall men give unto*
> *your bosom. For with the same measure that ye met withal*
> *it shall be measured to you again.* (Luke 6:30)

God has a plan for your life and it is a good one!

CHAPTER 5

PROSPERITY CONSCIOUSNESS

The Spiritual Basis of Wealth!

WHAT IS PROSPERITY TO YOU?

To some people, it is knowing that at the end of the month they can pay their bills without having to worry about where the money is coming from, while for others it's about having a big house and a fancy car. For still others, it's the security that comes from having their home, no matter how modest, paid for, and having money in the bank for a rainy day.

To me prosperity has a broader definition. It's about whether I am happy! It has to do with my personal freedoms: my freedom from fear and my ability to manage my time, so I can spend my time with those I love, as opposed to having to spend an inordinate amount of my time working to pay for things that own me rather than me owning them. Given this perspective, I define prosperity as being debt free. If I'm debt free, regardless of how big a house I have or how fancy a car I drive, I am free to do the things that I want to do, and I am in control of my life. I am not a slave to my possessions, because I truly own them rather than them owning me.

To put this in perspective, I want to ask you a question. Suppose you could have two of the following, but only two. No cheating! You cannot under any circumstances have all three. Your choices are:

1. _____ You can be rich beyond your wildest dreams!

2. _____ You can be the epitome of picture-perfect health and beauty!

3. _____ You can be euphorically happy and in love with life!

Would I be right if I guessed you chose happiness and health and not money? That should be an eye opener for most of us. You see, we know that life has very little meaning, unless we are happy and have our health, but when we get right down to it, we want it all. No compromises for us; we want it all. This type of thinking leads to a major fallacy, which is the belief that our health is a given and that if we have money happiness will automatically follow. Nothing could be further from the truth, especially if we are willing to go into debt in order to get the things we want! The *Bible* tells us...

Wait, before I tell you what the *Bible* says, let me say this. I know that not everyone reading this book is a Christian. Regardless of what religious beliefs you have the *Bible* has proven to be a reliable historic document as well as a practical guide to prosperity, diet, hygiene and the basic principles of physics. This said I hope you will consider what I have to say from that perspective without getting hung up on any religious beliefs. Okay, the *Bible* says:

> *The rich ruleth over the poor and the*
> *borrower is servant to the lender.* (Matthew 6:11-12)

This simple little statement is really quite profound. Let's dissect it and see what we come up with. "The rich ruleth over the poor." I am sure we can all agree with that statement. The question is why do the rich ruleth over the poor? The answer is: because the rich get the fruits of the labor of the poor! The poor work for the rich; they pay them rent; they borrow money from them and pay them interest on the money they borrow. The poor put in a day's labor and receive a day's pay, which they use to buy the necessities of life, while the rich sit back and collect money from the poor. The rich are therefore able to "leverage" the fruits of their labor, because their incomes are not dependent on their labor alone; they receive payments from the poor, who increase their wealth, and as they say, "the rich get richer and the poor get poorer." If we accept this as being true, the next question is what if anything can you do to end your dependency on the rich? In the broadest sense that is what this entire book is about, but in this specific context, the simple answer is that "you can stop paying your hard-earned money to the rich." I know that is easier said than done, but all excuses aside it can be done. If you are willing to live within your means, which means you have to lose all those nice little credit cards, you can slowly but surely get out of debt and stop allowing the rich to get rich off the fruits of your labor. We will get into specifics of exactly how to accomplish this later in this book. For now, all I want you to do is answer this question:

Do you want to be debt free, and are you willing to make some sacrifices in order to realize that objective?

If the answer is yes, I can give you a roadmap that will guide you, step by step down the yellow brick road. All you have to do is follow the trail of bread crumbs that I leave for you. What do you say? Are you willing to take the trip with me? I promise I won't let you get lost. I will hold your hand every step of the way. In truth, it is an exciting, life-altering journey, which takes you down the road, around the bend, across the creek to the rainbow and that elusive pot of gold that we have all heard about in fairy tales. Well, I am here to tell you not all fairy tales are fables. Some are true, but there is a bit of magic involved. You see, whether your dream comes true depends on whether or not you believe your dream can come true. So, are you willing to be like a child and believe, just believe! For now, we don't have to know how the magic works, all we have to do is believe. If you believe, you have faith and with faith miracles are possible!

Now faith is the substance of things hoped for,
the evidence of things not seen. (Hebrews 11:1)

I am sure some of you are saying what is up with all these *Bible* quotes? I bought this book because I wanted practical financial advice, not a bunch of religious rhetoric. I ask you to indulge me. The information in the *Bible* is practical. You see there are two ways to get rich, the "world's way," which leads to unhappiness and "God's way," which leads to happiness. The world's way, the most common way, the way which is most prevalent in the United States and most countries in the world, is based on the precept that there is an insufficient supply of wealth, so wealth is accumulated at the expense of someone else. It's the concept that **"the borrower is servant to the lender."** The lender gets rich off the sweat of the borrower. That is why debt is tantamount to indentured servitude and the borrower is bound by invisible chains that are every bit as hard to break as those forged from the hardest steel.

> *The blessing of the Lord it maketh rich,*
> *and <u>he addeth no sorrow</u>.* (Proverbs 10:22)

My goal in this book is to teach you how to break those chains and find financial freedom. Even more important, my goal is to show you how to be happy, which means I have to tell you about God's way. At first God's way seems impractical and unlikely, yet once you truly understand the beauty of its simplicity, it becomes every bit as tangible as the world's way. In fact, I believe I can show you that God's way makes more sense than the world's way. I invite you to come along on a journey of discovery!

This next part is for all those Christians who right about now are saying this guy doesn't know what he is talking about. God doesn't want his people chasing after money. I can just see them getting out their *Bibles* and quoting scriptures like these.

> *But they that will be rich fall into temptation and a snare, and into*
> *many foolish and hurtful lusts, which drown men in destruction*
> *and perdition. For <u>the love of money is the root of all evil:</u>*
> *which <u>while some coveted after, they have erred from the faith</u>,*
> *and pierced themselves through with many sorrows.*
> (1 Timothy 6:9-10)

> *And Jesus looked around about, and said unto his disciples.*
> *How hardly shall they that have riches enter into the kingdom of God.*
> *And the disciples were astonished at his words, But Jesus answereth*
> *again and said unto them, children, how <u>hard it is for them that trust in</u>*
> *<u>riches to enter into the kingdom</u> of God.*
> (Mark 10:23-24)

> *And they were astonished out of measure, saying among themselves,*
> *who then can be saved?* (Mark 10:26)

He that <u>loveth silver</u> shall not be satisfied with silver; nor he that <u>loveth abundance</u> with increase. This is also vanity. (Ecclesiastes 5:10)

<u>No man can serve two masters,</u> for either he will hate the one and love the other, or else he will hold to the one, and despise the other. <u>Ye cannot serve God and mammon.</u> (Matthew 6:24)

Let's take another look at Proverbs 10:2: "The blessing of the Lord it maketh rich, and he addeth no sorrow." This scripture is in direct contradiction to those above, so which is right? They are both right! The distinction is that Proverbs 10:22 is talking about God's way and the other scriptures are talking about man's way. God is very clear that he wants to bless us and prosper us. It's our wrong thinking about money that is the problem, not money itself. If we covet money, which is the world's way, it will make us unhappy and enslave us. We cut off God's promise of prosperity: if we get money we hoard it and use it for selfish ends, rather than giving of it so that it may be a blessing to others. Our selfish hoarding cuts us off from the blessings and brings problems of all sorts, problems that we foolishly bring on ourselves and for which we have only ourselves to blame. On the other hand, if we seek first the Kingdom of Heaven and give freely of that which has been given to us, God will make us not only wealthy, but also happy. Notice in Mark 10:23.24 when Jesus said, "How hardly shall they that have riches enter into the kingdom of God." And the disciples responded in Mark 10:26: "And they were astonished out of measure, saying among themselves, who then can be saved?" Their confusion arose from the fact that they knew the scripture, and they knew that God always blessed those who were obedient to him. For example, God told Abraham I'll bless you, and I will make you a blessing (Genesis 12:2). Abraham was one of the richest men in the *Bible*. Likewise, Job who God greatly favored was also exceedingly wealthy. Since God favored these men with wealth it must not be money that is evil but how a person views the money and if he covets it or not. Look back at 1 Timothy 6:9-10, Mark 10:23-24 and Ecclesiastes 5:10. I have underlined the portions of the scriptures that make them about man's way as opposed to God's way. By contrast Matthew 6:33 clearly shows us God's way.

"But seek first the kingdom of God and his righteousness: and all these things shall be added unto you. "

God's Promise of Prosperity!

God wants man to prosper, and he wants us to grow into the understanding that, like him, we are spiritual beings who have power— power beyond our comprehension!

And God said, Let us make man in our image, after our likeness: and let them have dominion over the fish of the sea, and over the fowl of the air, and over the cattle, and over all the earth, and over every creeping thing that creepeth upon the earth. (Genesis 1:26)

When you are given great possessions, you are also given the responsibility to be a steward over those possessions. Therefore, throughout the *Bible,* God has sought out men to bless, men with whom he could enter into a covenant: men of honor, who would abide by their covenants. In this vein God entered into a covenant with Abraham and through his seed with Jesus Christ, who through his death on the cross took our sins and in their place gave us grace and all of the blessing of his covenant with God.

God said to Abraham:
"I'll bless you and I will make you a blessing." (Genesis 12:2)

*If ye be Christ then are ye Abraham's seed,
and heirs according to the promise.* (Galatians 3:29)

Referring to Christ: But now that he obtained a more excellent ministry, by how much also is he the mediator of a better covenant which was established upon better promises. (Hebrews 8:6)

Through the blood of Christ we have an even better covenant than Abraham, so surely God will bless us abundantly. Let's take a look at a few of the promises God made to us.

If ye then being evil, know how to give good gifts unto your children,
how much more shall your Father which is in heaven give things to
them that ask him? (Matthew 7:11)

But God shall supply all your needs according to his riches in glory
by Christ Jesus! (Philippians 4:19)

He that spared not his son, but delivered him up for us all, how shall
he not with him also freely give us all things.
(Romans 8:32)

Ask, and it shall be given you; seek and ye shall find, knock, and it
shall be opened unto you. (Matthew 7:7)

God is able to do exceeding abundantly above all that we ask or
think. (Ephesians 3:20)

Thus saith the Lord, the Redeemer, the Holy One of Israel: I am the
Lord thy God which teaches thee to profit, which leadeth the way
thou shouldest go. (Isaiah 48:17)

This brings us to an interesting question. What is God referring to
in Isaiah 48:17, when he says *"which leadeth the way thou shouldest*
go?" God is telling us that there is no free lunch. With our promise
of prosperity comes the obligation to keep God's commandments. We
must learn to seek prosperity God's way not the world's say. Per *Prov-*
erbs 10:22 he promises to **make us rich and to add no sorrow.**

I know that for those of you who are not religious, all of these *bible*
verses must be getting tedious. I ask you to hang in with me for just a
little longer. I will soon wrap up all the loose ends, and I promise you I
will leave you with a practical **"seven step plan"** for how to gain prosperity God's way, which means that you will be able to have financial
prosperity without it making you unhappy as is the case when you get
financial prosperity man's way.

I am sure we can all agree that though money is important, it benefits us little if in the getting of it we become indentured servants **who**
by virtue of our debt are daily subjected to the torment of fear,
distress and discontentment. What do we do if the car breaks down?

What if we lose our job? What if, what if, what if? Who knows what could go wrong? That is not the point! The point is whether you are in control of your finances so that no matter what goes wrong you are in a position to weather it and be okay, or will it throw you into a crisis that threatens your finances, your health, your marriage and who knows what else! Put another way, do you own your possessions or do they own you? Do you have money in the bank for a rainy day, and equally important have you made deposits in God's bank so that in an emergency you can count on Him being there to supernaturally bring you and your family through any crises you could imagine? Are you depending on uncertain riches or on the living God?

> *Charge them that are rich in this world, that they **be not
> high-minded, nor trust in uncertain riches, but in the
> Living God***, *who giveth us richly all things to enjoy:
> that they do good, that they be rich in good works,
> ready to distribute, willing to communicate.* (Timothy 6:17-18)

At this point I will make a confession. I was not always a Christian, and I learned the hard way what can happen to a man who is high minded and who depends on uncertain riches rather than the living God. That is why I am writing this book. I have learned some hard lessons that in all honesty I wish I could have avoided. It has given me compassion, and I want to do everything in my power to keep others from having to go through the pain that I had to go through. I had to learn humility the hard way and I had to learn, the hard way, how important it is not to hoard your wealth but instead to use it to bless others. Truly, if you are in covenant with God, he will prosper you and bless you so that you may be a blessing to others. Believe me; I learned the hard way that this is not some abstract religious principle. It's a tangible and practical business principle, which underlies the wealth of truly prosperous people who are both rich and happy! I urge you not to be stiff necked like I was! I urge you to listen and pay attention! There are some hard economic times coming and those that are not prepared will surely suffer! Those that do not have their financial houses in order will surely suffer! Those that do not have their relationships on solid ground will surely suffer. And, most important, those that do not heed the warning of God and get in line with His will for them will greatly suffer!!!

Hear now this, O foolish people, and without understanding;
which have eyes, and see not; which have ears and hear not.
(Jeremiah 5:21)

God warned Noah before the flood! God warned Abraham before he destroyed Sodom and Gomorra! And now He is warning those with eyes to see and ears to hear! As surely as the sun will come up tomorrow the time is not far off when this great nation, this mighty nation, this proud nation, The United States of America, will experience economic tribulation such as it has never experienced in history! Woe be unto to those who do not heed this warning, for the time of which I speak shall surely come. I don't mean to scare you. Yes I do. I want to scare some sense into you. Folks, this country is in for some hard times and those who have their finances in order will fare much better than those who don't. Those who are also in covenant with God will fare better yet, but those who are not financially prepared and not in covenant with God will suffer greatly. I hope I have your attention! If so, we can cut to the chase and take a look at:

GOD'S SEVEN-STEP PLAN FOR FINANCIAL AND PERSONAL PROSPERITY!

Step 1: Give that you may receive!

In the physical world you have to make an investment (plant seeds) before you can earn a profit (reap a harvest)! In the spiritual realm you must first give in faith that you may receive according to your faith. At first glance these two statements seem to be opposites, but in reality they are not. You always have to give something to God, so he can multiply it and return it to you more abundantly. For example, John 6 tells of how Christ took five loaves of bread and two small fish and blessed them and multiplied them and fed 5000 people. It's no different in the business world. You have to work to earn a living. You have to invest money and time into a business in order to grow it. That is no different from multiplying the bread and fish. You must first have something to multiply. The only distinction is that in the physical realm we are dealing with tangible goods, with substance, so little faith is required. We can trust in our good judgment. We can trust in the advice of our advisers. We can trust in the stock market, in our 401(k)s in our corporations and our government! Or can we? Or should we? Or dare we? Dare we trust in **"uncertain riches?"** How much better is it to trust in the all Mighty God whose word never returns void and who promises to prosper us abundantly!

So shall my word be that goeth out of my mouth;
it shall not return unto me void, but it shall accomplish that
which I please, and it shall prosper in the thing where to I send it.
(Isaiah 55:1)

God is able to do exceeding abundantly above all
that we ask or think. (Ephesians 3:20)

In the spiritual realm, we are dealing with intangibles so more faith is required, but God has made a covenant with us, and He promises us that if we keep up our end of the deal He will keep up His end as well. *And now, O Lord God, thou art thy God and thy words be true, and thou hast promised this goodness unto thy servant. (2 Samuel 7:28)* As I said, I learned the hard way to put my money on God not man. You can take my word on this or you can learn the same way I did. I recommend the former rather than the latter.

Will a man rob God? Yet ye have robbed me. But ye say, when have
we robbed thee? In tithes (a tithe is 1/10 of your gain) and offerings.
Ye are cursed with a curse; for ye have robbed me, even this whole
nation. Bring ye all the tithes into the storehouse that there may be
meat in mine house, and prove me now herewith, say the Lord of
hosts, If I will not open you the windows of heaven and pour out a
blessing that there shall not be room enough to receive it.
(Malachi 3:10)

And it shall be given unto you; good measure, pressed down, and
shaken together. And running over, shall men give unto your bosom.
For with the same measure that ye met withal it shall be measured to
you again. (Luke 6:30)

*Ye have sown and bring in little, ye eat, but have not filled with
drink; ye clothe you, but there is no warm, and he that earneth
wages earneth wages to put into a bag with holes.*
(Haggai 1:6)

God certainly makes it clear! Tithe and he will prosper us. If
we choose not to tithe, *"our wages shall go into a bag with holes!"*
Again, I will admit to a time in my life when I did not tithe. I made
good money, so it wasn't like I was broke. The difference was that I
had to work extremely hard for my money, and I was always afraid I
was going to lose what I had because I saw a limited supply, my mind-
set was that if something went wrong I could lose what I had. Fear was
my master. This limited outlook came from the fact that I grew up in
poverty and as a result I was afraid of being poor. Job was afraid of
losing what he had, and the devil saw to it that his fear came true. The
moral is be careful what you think and say, because your words and
thoughts have power.

*So shall my word be that goeth out of my mouth; it shall not return
unto me void, but it shall accomplish that which I please, and it shall
prosper in the thing where to I send it.* (Isaiah 55:11)

And also take heed that you don't cheat God, so that when you need
Him you find out that your bank account is overdrawn and He will not
send out his word to prosper you in your time of need. Incidentally the
10 percent tithe that we are to give God is the same amount we need
to set aside for retirement if we want to retire and be able to keep our
present life style, whatever that is. Isn't it interesting how that works?
Now, according to God's promise, if we give God his 10 percent first,
he will multiply it and return it to us so in this instance we can use it to
fill our warehouse just as God's warehouse was filled.

Step 2: Praise God and thank Him even before you receive!

*God promises: Therefore I say unto you,
what things so ever ye desire, when ye pray, believe that
ye shall receive them, and ye shall have them.* (Mark 11:2)

Your prayers are answered according to your faith. So, pray a prayer of gratitude, thanking God for having already answered your prayer. Thank Him for financial abundance or for whatever it is you are praying for. This is a crucial step in prayer. We must have faith that whatever we are praying for has been given to us the moment we ask for it. The *Bible* promises that *"it shall be given unto you according to your faith."* So, if you don't believe, it surely will not be given unto you. If you want to be wealthy, proclaim it! If you want prosperity, proclaim it! Shout it to the roof tops and thank God ahead of time!

Among his many names God is called:

"The Great I Am"

The words "I am" are the two most spiritually powerful words in the *Bible* so when you pray say "I am" wealthy or happy or whatever it is you are praying for.

Everyone prays differently, but I would like to share with you how I pray. It works for me, and I am sure it will work for you also.

MY SEVEN STEPS OF PRAYER

1. I **praise God, thank Him** and get in communion with Him.

2. Before praying, I make sure that what I am praying for is in my best interest, and I **choose my words carefully!** Just to be sure that I am praying according to God's will.

3. When praying, I don't ask God; instead I **proclaim** that He has answered my prayer the instant I pray, and I pray using the most powerful words in the universe: "**I am!**

4. I **see (visualize)** what I have prayed for and **have faith** that God has answered my prayer!

5. I **take actions** that are congruent with my prayer!

6. **I am vigilant,** so that I recognize it when my prayer has been answered!

7. **I am grateful** because it is an affirmation of my faith, and according to my faith shall it be given unto me! And lastly, I tithe on any increase I receive!

If a people want their prayers answered they need to have faith, take action based on that faith and make sure they are praying according to God's will, which means they are praying out of love, forgiveness and selflessness.

I want this book to be more than a philosophy book, or a spiritual book or a finance book. I want it to be a practical book that can truly change people's lives. I want to give the reader the benefit of a lifetime of hard lessons. I have made a lot of mistakes in my life, but I have learned from each and every one of them. I want to share with you the wisdom that I have worked so hard to acquire. The Christian often snubs his nose at anything not spiritual and the non-Christian often snubs his nose at anything spiritual. I am here to tell you there is a place for both. Faith without works is futile and, in the same vein, works without faith are equally futile.

Expect to succeed; believe it in every fiber of your body; have the faith of a small child and you will be successful! But there is one additional equally important component to your success. You have to have a viable plan, and you have to be willing to work your plan until you are successful, no matter how long it takes.

Whether you expect to fail or whether you expect to win, your predominant thoughts will be realized.

"There is nothing either good or bad, but thinking makes it so."
  –William Shakespeare

Most people have no shortage of dreams, but what many of us fail to realize is that dreams are just idle wishes, and no amount of wishing will make your dreams come true. **To be realized, your dreams must be given power by formulating a clearly defined plan, believing that you can achieve your plan and taking specific, incremental steps to achieve that plan.**

For Example: Bruce Jenner was an Olympic gold medalist for the decathlon. In interviews he has explained that he constantly visualized himself winning the decathlon. He knew the current world record for each event, so when he trained he was constantly focused on breaking each and every one of those records. Is it any wonder he realized his dreams? You can realize your dreams too, if you just believe you can and if you focus your mind on achieving them. Remember, whether you expect to fail or whether you expect to win, your predominant thoughts will be realized. Also remember to start thanking God now and don't stop till you get what you want and then especially, when you do get what you wanted, prayed for, and worked so hard for, remember that God was with you every step of the way. Don't forget to thank Him and praise Him and give Him the first fruits of your reward. If you do these things, you will come to know the meaning of "true wealth," which is God's plan for you to be both wealthy and happy. He wants the best for you and God's worst is better than man's best. I don't know about you, but I can't think of anyone who I would rather have as my partner in any venture than God.

Step 3: Practice, patience, persistence and trust in God to provide!

After saying your prayer of affirmation, **(I am)**, you then need to be **patient and vigilant** so that you recognize it when your prayer has been answered. Prayers are answered in God's time, not man's. The *Bible* tells us that a day in heaven is as unto a thousand years on earth. So, things happen considerably slower here on earth than they do in heaven. This is actually a safeguard. This gives us time to make sure that what we think we want is actually what we want and that what we think is good for us actually is. Also, we need to recognize it when God has answered our prayer. Sometimes God will answer a prayer outright in an instant. This is what we call a "miracle," but most of the time God does not answer our prayers in such a direct fashion. Instead He will bring into your life a person or circumstance that is intended to guide you to where you want to go. It will happen out of nowhere. You might say it will be providential. You want to be on the look out for these supposed chance occurrences, because they are God answering your prayer. You see most of the time God does not choose to directly intervene, because if He did we would not learn the lesson that our difficulty was sent to teach us. God gave us free will, and He wants us to use it. All prayers are answered, but most times we are too distracted to see the answer when it arrives, so be watchful.

In my case, I have noticed that out of the clear blue I will meet someone who will have information pertinent to something I have been praying about. I have come to pay particular attention to my dreams. If I wake up, between 5 a.m. and 5:15 a.m., I know that, that is the time when God sends me messages, so I act on the information He sends. As an example, several years ago my wife and I were looking for a new house. The town we lived in had failed to pass three school bonds and we felt we had to move to a town with better schools. In this case my prayer was answered in two parts. The first part came when my children had a sleep over and we were asked to return our neighbor's child to his grandparents who lived in a nearby town called Naperville. We dropped the child off late at night and as we drove into the subdivision my wife said "I think every other house looks like it is missing." I commented that that was not the case, the lots were just big. In addition to finding a good school district we were also looking for a large yard for our children to play in. The next day, we did some investigating and found out that not only were the lots in the subdivision big, but the schools were rated in the top 5 percent of the nation. Our prayer seemed to be answered. The problem was there were not many homes for sale in the subdivision. Finally, we put in an offer on a house, but we didn't really like it. There was a house in the subdivision that we really liked, but there was a problem. It was For Sale by Owner (FSBO) and though we had been by the house several times we could never find the sellers at home. Enter God with the answer to the second part of my prayer. At 5:15 a.m. I woke up, bounded out of bed and told my wife we had to cancel the contract we had in on the other house. I explained that the seller would call that morning and agree to our price, so we needed to withdraw our offer before that happened. I went on to tell her that she had to call a real estate agent immediately, because the house we really wanted was coming on the market that day. No questions asked my wife did as I suggested. She had come to understand that when I have one of these dreams we have to do what we are told. That morning I had to go for jury duty, so I left things in the competent hands of my wife. By 10 a.m. I got a call from my wife. The seller had left a message, he had caved on the price, but in the meantime my wife had already left her message canceling the contract. However, that wasn't the reason for her call. The house we wanted had in fact come on the market just like I told her it would. The problem was I was being interviewed for a murder one jury trial and wasn't free to go see the house. By 11 a.m. my wife called again. She had not even seen the house yet and it had an offer on it. Then came the question, could I get out of jury duty so we could see the house. You are probably thinking fat chance, right? I ask the sheriff who immediately said "no way." Half an hour later my wife called again. This time she was frantic! There was a second offer on the house. I went back to the sheriff and ask him to let me plead my case to the judge. A few minutes late, I was called into the court room where four lawyers, the judge and the defendant sat looking at me like I was crazy. The judge was in his late 60s and didn't appear to have much of a sense of humor. I pleaded my case. The judge looked at me in disgust and told me to get out of his court room. I was about half way down the aisle when he yelled for me to turn around. My heart almost stopped. As I turned the judge smiled and laughed and said, "According to Illinois statutes participation in a court case shall not cause marital disharmony, so go get that house for your wife." Do I even need to tell you the ending? If you have faith, God always answers your prayers! YES, WE GOT THE HOUSE! Thank you, God!

Step 4: Be present minded. Take action in the present in order to reap your reward in the future!

No man can live in the past or the future, for they have no substance. We can only reflect on the past and postulate about the future. So for man to live, he must live in the present, or he doesn't live at all. For only in the present can man make the CHOICES that define his future. Only in the present can man take the ACTIONS that define who he is. The apostle Paul said, **I have but one desire, that I mayest live in the present.**

Though we cannot live in the past, the past is still a part of us. It influences our present CHOICES and ACTIONS. If we lament over past losses or use our past circumstances as an excuse for our current circumstances, our past governs our present. Instead of learning from the past, we use it to excuse our present circumstances and failures. We're frozen in time, and our lives become stagnated because we refuse to learn from the past as we should. The past gives us the opportunity to learn from those who preceded us. It gives us the opportunity to reflect on our successes and failures. It is a wellspring of knowledge that allows us to make better more informed CHOICES in the here and now.

The future has its distinct role to play as well. Our goals, dreams and aspirations are projected into the future. They represent our as-yet unrealized potential. Without DREAMS a man loses his drive, his purpose, his very self and slips into a lament of despair. But caution must be taken, that the future isn't also used to excuse or escape the present. **To realize our DREAMS we must focus them and take continuous action in the present moment.** The future is often used to excuse our lack of action! There's always tomorrow! I will do it tomorrow! Remember:

> *"Tomorrow is promised to no man."*
> – Author unknown

Don't procrastinate! Take action now! For who knows what tomorrow will bring?

Just as the past is the wellspring of knowledge that allows us to make better more informed CHOICES in our here and now, many misuse the future so it becomes a stagnant pool of despair into which they project all of their fears and negative thoughts. Fears paralyze us and rob us of our hope, happiness and success in the here and now. Moreover, fears by and large never materialize, or even worse do materialize because we invited them into our lives creating an unfortunate self-fulfilling prophecy.

> *Whatsoever a man soweth, that shall he reap.*
> (Gal. 6:7)

> *"Do the thing you fear, and the death of fear is certain."*
> –Ralph Waldo Emerson

So, to those of you who would know yourself, realize your potential and find the happiness we all seek. I say to you, live in the here and now, in the present moment! Learn the lessons of the past and use them to make better choices each and every day. Don't procrastinate! Take action now and realize your dreams! Don't lament over the past and don't project your fears into the future! Live now! Make

CHOICES now! Take ACTION now! Be HAPPY now! **For now is
the only moment in time in which you actually exist. All else is
illusion!**

One more thing, don't allow yourself to become discouraged on
your journey. It takes time to get it right. The more you try, the more
you fail and the closer you get to your goal.

*No thing great is created suddenly any more than a bunch of grapes
or a fig. If you tell me that you desire a fig;
I answer you that there must be time. Let it first blossom,
and bear fruit, and then ripen.* (Ecclesiastes 55:135)

Step 5: Be content where you are so God can prosper you!

Wouldn't it be nice if we always got what we wanted? Wouldn't
it be even nicer if we got what we wanted the instant we asked for it?
Who wouldn't like to have immediate gratification? As wonderful as
this sounds if we had this we would become spoiled brats. If you have
ever known a true spoiled brat, you probably did not like him or her.
God doesn't want us to be spoiled brats, so He always gives us what
we need, but He doesn't always give us what we want. That is why we
always want to pray, saying **God's will not mine.** This is especially
true if we want some kind of material reward that we may not be ready
to handle. As they say, "Power corrupts and absolute power corrupts
absolutely." God has to humble us and prove us before He can give us
what we want. Once we have demonstrated that we can handle what
we want without being spoiled or corrupted then and only then will He
give it to us. Then and only then will we pass God's test and be given
what we want. Then and only then is our will in line with that of God.
Because then and only then can God give us what we want without it
harming his children whom he loves and protects.

*And thou shalt remember all the way which the Lord thy God
led thee... to humble thee, and to prove thine heart, whether thou
wouldest keep my commandments or no.*
(Deuteronomy 8:2)

*Let your conversation be without covetousness; and be content
with such things as ye have; for he hath said I will never leave the,
nor forsake thee.* (Hebrews 13:5)

So just what do we have to do to pass the test and be given what it
is we are praying for? Sometimes we are not yet ready to handle what
it is we are asking for, so God lets us teeth on a smaller venture and
learn what it is we truly need to know in order to be successful. That
is why patience is a virtue. By being patient we get the opportunity to
learn what it is we need to know in order to be successful. If we get
ahead of ourselves in a thing, it almost certainly spells catastrophe!
Also if we are discontented with where we are and are envious and or
covetous toward another person, we are almost certainly guaranteeing
that we will stay where we are, because we are not ready to pass the
test. Our heart is not in the right place. Basically what God wants is for
us to prove ourselves. He wants us to put others first.

*... be not high-minded, nor trust in uncertain riches, but in the
Living God, who giveth us richly all things to enjoy:
that they do good, that they be rich in good works,
ready to distribute, willing to communicate.* (Timothy 6:17)

Basically what God wants from us is for us to prosper, and to
prosper we need to not only be financially successful, but also good,
honest people of integrity and character. People He can use, because
he can trust us to put others first in the certain knowledge that having
done so He will add all things to us.

**Step 6: Be humble and acknowledge God as your abundant
source!**

When we attain humility we come to understand our role in the
grand scheme of things. We become naturally unpretentious and
grateful and finally capable of the kind of love that God wants us to
express.

*For who ever exalteth himself shall be abased and he that
humbleth himself shall be exalted.* (Luke 14: 11)

Being humble is an absolute requirement for walking upright with God in his covenant. God insists that we give him the credit, and He further insists that we are not prideful in our relationships with other people. A humble person is not only meek, but also cooperative, supportive, giving, caring, willing to share and, most of all, capable of unselfish love! To be humble is in some small measure to be God-like, and that should be our highest pursuit in life!

Step 7: Remember God and be grateful when you are successful!

God is very specific that He wants us to recognize Him as the source of our prosperity. He says it very clearly:

Charge them that are rich in this world, that they
be not high-minded, nor trust in uncertain riches,
***but in the Living God**, who giveth us richly all things to enjoy:*
that they do good, that they be rich in good works,
ready to distribute, willing to communicate. (Timothy 6:17)

Again in Deuteronomy 8:11, God very clearly warns us to remember Him and to give Him the praise:

Beware that thou forget not the Lord thy God, in not keeping his commandments, and his judgments, and his statutes, which I command thee this day. Lest when thou hast eaten and art full, and hast built goodly houses, and dwelt there in: And when thy herds and thy flocks multiply, and thy silver and thy gold is multiplied, and all that thou hast is multiplied; Then thine heart be lifted up, and thou forget the Lord thy God… And thou say in thine heart, My power and the might of mine hand hath gotten me this wealth.

I don't want to scare you, or maybe I do. Remember there are two ways to get rich: man's way and God's way. Man's way leaves you open to **fear, distress and discontentment!** Man's way leaves you wide open to **covetousness, greed and envy!** Man's way can very likely lead to the accumulation of wealth and power, but it will not likely lead to true happiness.

He that loveth silver shall not be satisfied with silver; nor he that loveth abundance with increase. This is also vanity.
(Ecclesiastes 5:10)

*The blessing of the Lord it maketh rich,
and he addeth no sorrow.* (Proverbs 10:22)

So once again I point out that true wealth is having both wealth and happiness, and that requires you to get your wealth according to God's plan not man's plan.

GOD IS OUR PROTECTOR AND OUR SHIELD AGAINST TROUBLE!

This may be over the top for some of you, but I am going to share it anyway. I was called to do this work many years ago and since then I was in a head-on auto accident that should have killed me, but I came away with only superficial scratches and bruises. While working in construction years ago I was on the outside of a building five stories up. I hooked up my safety harness and leaned back and it broke. I fell and surely should have died, except for the fact that my foot caught and I hung upside down on the outside of that building for 45 minutes while rescuers tried to figure how to get me down. I dared not move, because I didn't know what was holding me. On three other occasions I had accidents that should have killed me, but in each instance I came away unscathed. I don't know about you but given my experiences I believe in angles, divine intervention, miracles and God's promises. I guess I am saying that I will put my money on God every time. I certainly wouldn't want to bet against God. How about you? Where are you going to put your money?

No weapon formed against us shall prosper. (Isaiah 54:17)

If he is for you who can be against you? (Romans 8:31)

That all things work for the good of those who love him.
(Romans 8:28)

*In all these things we are made more than conquerors through him
who loved us.* (Romans 8:37)

I will call on the Lord, who is worthy to be praised;
so shall I be saved from mine enemies.
(2 Samuel 22:4)

SUMMARY

Through prayer man has the power to tap into the spiritual realm and attract to him whatever he wants. This is to say that man can manifest or bring into material form **(just like Jesus did)** anything that he prays for in faith. To accomplish this, he must expect to get what he wants, be patient and persist until his prayer is answered. He must bolster his belief by saying a prayer of gratitude, knowing that his prayer has been answered according to his faith. He must freely give back of that which has been given to him (tithe) or else what he hoards will be taken away from him. He must also live in the present, because the past and the future have no substance. Lastly, he must be humble and give God the credit for his increase and not be prideful and think that his increase came by his hand. We are responsible for whatever is in our life. Nothing is by accident. Life is by invitation, so be careful what you invite into your life.

Make this seven-step prayer a part of your life and your life will be transformed according to your faith! I suggest you write it on a card and carry it in your wallet or purse and refer to it daily, especially if you start to doubt. Remember:

All things work for good for those who love him.
(Romans 8:28)

SEVEN-STEP PRAYER!

1. I **praise God, thank Him** and get in communion with Him.

2. Before praying I make sure that what I am praying for is in my best interest and I **choose my words carefully!**

3. When praying, I don't ask God; instead I **proclaim** that He has answered my prayer the instant I pray, and I pray using the most powerful words in the universe: **I am!**

4. I **see (visualize)** what I have prayed for and **have faith** that God has answered my prayer!

5. **I take actions** that are congruent with my prayer!

6. **I am vigilant** so that I recognize it when my prayer has been answered!

7. **I am Grateful** because it is an affirmation of my faith and according to my faith shall it be given unto me! And lastly I tithe on any increase that I receive!

I want to leave you with one final thought. You can get rich man's way or God's way but God's way has definite advantages.

The Blessing of the Lord it maketh rich, and he addeth no sorrow
(Proverbs 10:22)

So shall my word be that goeth out of my mouth; it shall not return unto me void, but it shall accomplish that which I please, and it shall prosper in the thing where to I send it.
(Isaiah 55:11)

God is real and prayers do work!
You can be both rich and happy if you just believe!

Part III

Developing Your Financial and Personal Life Plan

Chapter 6: Why Most People Retire Poor

The Six Keys to Financial Security:

1st Key – Chapter 7: Automate Your Savings

2nd Key – Chapter 8:
Pay Off Your Credit Cards And Be Debt Free

3rd Key – Chapter 9: Have A Realistic Retirement Plan!

4th Key – Chapter 10: Diversify Your Assets!

5th Key – Chapter 11: Diversify Your Income!

6th Key – Chapter 12:
Own A Home And Pay It Off Before You Retire! (Learn how to pay
off your home in as little an 1/3 the normal time)

Chapter 13: Why Real Estate is a Wealth-Building Vehicle
In Any Market!

Chapter 14: How to Buy A Home If You Have Credit Problems

Chapter 15: Above All Be Happy!

Hopefully by now you are motivated to make some changes in your life and get on with the job of implementing your seven-step, wealth-building plan. But first you need to know why most people retire poor, so you can avoid their mistakes.

Once you know what not to do, all you need is to know exactly what to do. You need a step-by-step plan for building wealth so you can retire well-off. Another thing you need is the will and determination to make your goal of being wealthy an **"absolute must!"** Hopefully, you have decided that being wealthy is a must, and you are ready to take the necessary changes in your finances to ensure that you will retire well off. But remember you also want to be happy so you need to be mindful of doing things Gods way, not mans way!

CHAPTER 6

WHY MOST PEOPLE RETIRE POOR

We all dream of living out our "golden years" with a comfortable retirement program. We dream of traveling and doing all the things we were too busy to do when we were working. But, most of us simply will not retire with enough money to live out our dreams. Most of us will have a declining standard of living in our retirement years.

According to the U.S. Department of Health, Education and Welfare, if you take an average sample of 100 people, by the time they reach the age of 65:

- 36 will be dead
- 54 will be living on government or family support
- 5 will be still working
- 4 will be well-off
- 1 will be wealthy

In other words, only 5 percent will be well-off or wealthy! Are you going to be one of the 5 percent who make it, or one of the 95 percent who only dreamt about making it?

The Poor Are Poor Because: (assuming they make a living wage in the first place). If they are poor it is because they are hooked on Madison Avenue consumerism, demand immediate gratification, and spend their money on non-income-producing consumer goods, which are liabilities that drain their cash and reduce their net worth. In effect, their materialism causes them to **lose control of their finances** which, in turn, puts them in debt and turns them into stressed-out, unhappy, indentured servants. In addition, they derive their income from a <u>single source</u> (their salary), so regardless of how much they make they are dependent on their companies for continued financial security. If the company they work for gets into trouble, as many have, they likewise get into trouble. Also, they live off the money from their paychecks, which are immediately taxed, as opposed to earnings from capital gains and profits from real estate, which are tax deferred (more on this later). Finally, they live to the full extent of their means, so if adversity hits they have inadequate reserves to fall back on.

What Else Did the 95 Percenters Do That Caused Them To Retire Poor?

The 95 percenters didn't have a realistic estimate of how much income they needed in order to retire! Most people mistakenly think that when they retire, their cost of living will greatly diminish. After all, they plan on having their home paid for and the kids off on their own. Also, they won't have the travel and other expenses associated with working. In truth, during retirement your living expenses do go down, but only slightly. At the same time, however, your medical expenses generally go up dramatically. If you don't retire with enough income you could be one of the millions who are faced with the decision of whether to pay for their medicine or buy groceries.

The 95 percenters overestimated their net worth! This is because they typically include their personal residences, automobiles, furniture and other personal property in their **"net worth calculations."** They don't understand the difference between "a**ssets and liabilities."**

Their personal residences, automobiles, furniture and other personal property are assets, but they are actually **"depreciating assets,"** which actually makes them **"liabilities."** For example, the 95 percenters mistakenly think of their personal residences as an asset, because the value of real estate has historically appreciated. They can't live off the appreciation (equity) of their homes unless they borrowing against them or sell them, and then where would they live? In addition, the appreciation (equity) that they can't tap causes their property taxes to go up. So, in truth your personal residence is a LIABILITY not an ASSET.

Most people overestimate just how much of a tax break they get on their personal (non-revenue producing) residence. They focus on the gross interest deduction, rather than the net interest deduction. **Specifically, the U.S. government allows you to deduct approximately 30 percent of the actual interest payment. This means that the net interest deduction is approximately 70 percent lower than most people think.** Say you paid $1,200 per month in interest on your home, which is $14,400 per year. Assuming you are in the 28 percent tax bracket, the tax deduction on your home would be $1,209, not $4,032 as generally believed. ($14,400 x 30% = $4,320 x 28% = $1,209 actual tax deduction). To make matters worse, most people are unaware that after their personal income reaches approximately $125,000 their interest deduction starts to go down. As a result, the people in this income bracket further overestimate the value of the tax deduction on their personal residences.

Similarly, your car, even if it's paid for, is also a liability. You have the expenses of gas, oil, maintenance, license plates, insurance and eventually replacement. Neither your home nor your car creates any income, so by default they are liabilities not assets! This said it would be advisable to recalculate your **"net worth"** and remove any items you listed as assets that do not generate income, because they are in fact liabilities. Also reevaluate how much **monthly income** you realistically need to cover your cost-of-living. Do a financial plan based on your expected retirement expenses. How much do you need for taxes, food, clothing, medical, entertainment, travel and other things? Once you have enough **"income producing assets"** to cover your monthly expenses, you will be able to retire without financial worries.

The 95 percenters miscalculated the contribution of Social Security! Depending on their income levels, most people can plan on getting $1000-$1400 per month from Social Security. The 95 percenters are depending on the monthly income from Social Security during their retirement. The problem is, after they have retired, having miscalculated how much income they actually need to retire and having miscalculated their net worth, they may find that **they don't have enough income to live on.** This problem is compounded by the fact that, if they have to go back to work because they don't have enough money to live on, **the Government will reduce their Social Security payments!**

In other words, there is a real catch-22. Whether they go to work or not they lose. In my mind, there is an even worse problem, which is **counting on Social Security at all!** There are 75 million baby boomers nearing retirement. Based on $1,000-$1,400 per month, the Social Security fund will be paying out between $75 billion and $105 billion per month in payments. I sincerely hope the money is there, but I am not counting on it. If it's there, that's a bonus, but if it's not I will still be fine, because I am not depending on it. I plan on being one of the 95 percenters. How about you?

The 95 percenters invested the majority of their retirement money in portfolio investments! Portfolio investments are paper investments, such as stocks and bonds. Portfolios are generally where the majority of the 95 percenters have the majority of their retirement funds invested. If you have enough dividend income coming in from these investments you can certainly retire off of them, but your income fluctuates in line with fluctuating interest rates and stock market performance. The 95 percenters generally don't have enough dividend income coming in from their portfolio investments to live on. If this is the case, they end up setting up a **"declining annuity program,"** under which an actuarial calculation is made that predicts their life expectancy. Their portfolio is then systematically sold off over their projected life expectancy, and they are given the proceeds as monthly income. If your money is in a 401(k), you don't have any choice as to whether or not you sell the stocks. When you hit 70 ½, you have to start selling your stocks in order to pay the government tax deferments. Systematically selling off your assets leaves you at risk. **If the portfolio declines in value, you risk not having enough money to live on. If you live longer than expected, your portfolio is depleted and you end up with nothing left**. In other words, you run the risk of ending up destitute. In my opinion, the biggest problem with portfolio investments is that they are tied to the ups and downs of the stock market. In 1929 the stock market fell 42 percent and it took 25 years, until 1955, for it to recover to pre-1929 levels. The 1929 crash was blamed in large part on the regulations governing margin calls. The regulations were changed and the market was supposed to be safe.

Despite these changes, in the 1980s the market had another crash. Things were so bad that on Black Friday the markets were closed, and when they opened on Monday the banks were planning to call in all of their loans, effectively causing a catastrophic collapse of the market. This catastrophe was barely averted, because over the weekend the U.S. Federal Reserve, headed by then newly appointed Chairman Alan Greenspan, contacted all the banks and guaranteed their loans.

In the 1990s, the market had an unprecedented bull market. Despite the normal indicators, stocks continued to go up and up and up. They were being driven in part by excitement over dot-com stocks, but the money to fund this bull market was coming from the 75 million baby boomers that were experiencing their peak income earning years, and were putting their considerable discretionary income into the stock market as part of their retirement plan. The economy couldn't sustain the bull market, so stocks crashed and millions of people lost their life savings.

Most recently between March of 2000 and the summer of 2002 the stock market lost a staggering $6.9 trillion. As a result, millions of people have been forced out of retirement and back to work and millions of others who were planning to retire soon were left wondering if they will ever be able to retire. They are left scratching their heads, asking themselves what went wrong.

Fast-forward to 2010-2020 when the baby boomers start to retire in large numbers. Not only will they be pulling $75-$105 billion per month out of Social Security, but also the majority of them will be retiring on declining annuity retirement programs and, thus will see their retirement portfolios systematically sold off to provide them with monthly income. Who knows what this drain on both the Social Security fund and the stock market will do, but for my part I am glad I have a substantial portion of my retirement invested in real estate!

Let's assume that you retire at age 65 with $1,000,000 in stocks, you receive $500 per month in dividends from your portfolio and $1,400 per month from Social Security. That means you have $1,900 a month coming in, but you need $6,000 per month or $72,000 per year to live at your current standard of living. This means you have a monthly short fall of $4,100 per month. If you were projected to live 20 years and you withdrew $4,100 per month for the balance of your life, your $1,000,000 portfolio would be reduced by approximately $984,000, leaving you with a net worth of just $1,600 based on straight line depreciation and not adjusting for ups or downs in the stock market. If you live longer than expected, or if, as in the examples above, the stock market goes down you would likely end up destitute.

The 95 percenters generally don't adequately consider the tax consequences of their investments! Take a 401(k) for example. You are generally able to invest your money in a 401(k) and avoid the 20 percent capital gains tax on your earnings, that is, as long as you don't take the money out. The problem is that a 401(k) does not create any income that can be used to live on. It instead creates equity, which can only be tapped by selling off your asset. When you take money out of your 401(k) retirement, it is taxed as earned income, rather than as capital gains! The importance of this is that capital gains are taxed at 20 percent, but earned income is taxed at a much higher rate. In summary, 401(k)s work best for the 95 percenters who retire on low incomes. For the 5 percenters who retire with higher incomes, taxes go up. Depending on your income level, the taxes on your 401(k) could be as high as 35 percent versus 20 percent for capital gains.

The 95 percenters use their own salary (immediately taxed money with accumulative taxes which average 50 percent) to invest, rather than investing with other people's money! When you use other people's money you are **LEVERAGING YOUR INVESTMENT!**

Let's look at saving. The 95 percenters think saving their money is prudent, and if they can save enough money they will retire rich. It's true you can put your money in the bank and earn compound interest, which over the course of a lifetime can make you a millionaire. However, ask yourself this question. What do you think the banker is doing with the hard-earned money you put into savings at his bank? He's using your money by lending it out in order to leverage it so he can make money off your money. If you want to be one of the 5 percenters, you need to learn to **use other people's money** just the way the banker does. As a matter of fact, you need to learn to use the banker's money! I don't want to give you the idea that saving is bad or that there is no place in your retirement program for portfolio investments. At the same time, I want you to recognize that there are other investment strategies that will allow you to build your wealth at a faster rate. This distinction will be covered in detail in a future chapter.

At this moment the operative question is: how can you use other people's money (i.e. the banker's money) to leverage your retirement? To put things into perspective, imagine what would happen if you ask your banker to loan you money to invest in stocks, bonds, or your 401(k). He would look at you like you were crazy! This said your banker would be more than happy to loan you money to invest in real estate. Why do you think he will loan you money on real estate and not other paper investments? When all is said and done, paper investments have no inherent value, which means their value can go to ZERO! On the other hand, real estate has inherent value in and of itself, so it can be used to secure your loan.

The 95 percenters turned control of their retirement over to others and hoped they would perform well! It's so easy to let the "experts" invest your money for you. After all they know more than you do! That's right, they know how to use other people's money, in this case yours.

As employees, your company makes it easy to buy its stock through payroll deductions. Financial planners and mutual fund managers will be only too happy to invest your money for you. They tell you not to worry about the volatility of the market, because you are investing your money for the long haul, so over the long term all those peaks and valleys will average out. The also assure you they will further reduce your risk by diversifying your investments. So, if you take their advice, you give them your money and go about the business of earning a living, all the while hoping your money is busy multiplying. Your investment might do well, but it might also be wiped out, but in either case you don't have control, because you gave control to the experts!

The 95 percenters failed to pay themselves first! This is perhaps the most important distinction of all. They may have had every intention of saving their money for retirement, but the reality is that each month they barely managed to pay their bills. They allowed their wealth to slip through their fingers and had no idea where it went or why they were never able to get ahead. **One of the key reasons the 95 percenters fail to pay themselves first is because they don't see it as a <u>must</u>.** Deep down inside they don't think they could ever save enough to make a difference. That is because they don't understand the power of COMPOUNDING. At first the money grows painfully slowly and it seems like it will never amount to anything, then all the sudden it takes off and the growth rate is nothing short of astonishing.

Let's look at an analogy to make the point of the power on compounding. What would you say if you were playing golf and your buddy wanted to make a friendly wager, say ten cents a hole? That's a friendly wager that most of us could afford. Now, suppose that when you got to the first hole, your buddy suggested that in order to make it a little more interesting you double the bet with each hole? That's ten cents for the first hole, twenty cents for the second, forty for the third and so on. No big deal you think, what could it amount to $50 or $60 at most? Wrong! You just made a huge bet, and I hope you are one heck of a good golfer. By the sixth hole you are at $3.20, which still doesn't seem too bad, and you are 1/3 of the way through, so again you think no big deal. By the time you get to the 12th hole you are getting nervous, because that little dime has become $204.80. By the

15th hole that dime has grown to $1,638.40 and by the 18th hole it is a whopping $13,107.20. So what is the lesson here? Though compounding isn't sexy, it is powerful, and it can make you rich, but it takes time. You can't afford to wait another day! In the analogy above we went from $1,638.40 on the 15th hole to a whopping $13,107.20 just three holes later!

In the subsequent chapters we are going to explore other even more powerful investment strategies, but for now the lesson is that you can't afford to wait! You need to get started saving today!

CHAPTER 7

AUTOMATE YOUR SAVINGS!

*"In life, it's not how much money you make that determines how
wealthy you become. What's more important is how much
of what you make you save for the future."*

−Larry Ballard

THE PSYCHOLOGY OF WEALTH

Our finances are driven by our emotions and our values. They
define how we earn our money, how we spend it, how much (if any) of
it we save, how we invest and, ultimately, if money will be a source of
security, peace of mind and happiness or if it will be a source of stress,
conflict and unhappiness.

This reality is exemplified by the true story of two of my clients.
One is a retired school teacher in her mid-60s who has always had a
modest income. The other is an executive in his mid-40s who for the
last several years has made a salary of $350,000-$400,000. Which of
the two do you think is wealthier, the teacher or the executive? It's the
teacher by a landslide.

Prior to September 11, 2001, the teacher lived in a modest condo-
minium, and for the past 30 years she had scrimped and scraped every
extra dollar she could to buy condos and town houses as rental investments. By contrast, the wealthy executive lived in a multimillion dollar home, drove a Mercedes and spent his money on extravagances.

In the period following September 11, 2001, neither the teacher's
income nor her lifestyle was impacted, because she had rental income

coming in from a wide variety of people with diverse jobs. Currently, she is living her dream of traveling the world. Even though she never made big money, she paid herself first, lived debt free and retired a bona fide multimillionaire!

In contrast, in the period following September 11, 2001, the executive's company got in financial trouble and he was laid off. He was unemployed for a long time and when he got a new job it was at a much lower salary. He is on the brink of bankruptcy and may never get another job making as much as he once did. In net terms, he has nothing to show for his big salary except even bigger debts. With his savings gone and giving his financial problems, it is likely he will retire in poverty. Even if he is lucky and learns from his mistakes, he has a lot of catching up to do.

I see this story repeated over and over again in the community where I live. I can't tell you how many times I have gone into a million-dollar home, with his and her Porsches or Lexuses in the garage. When I enter the property I am flabbergasted to walk into a cavernous home and hear my footsteps echo, because the family literally has no furniture. They put 10 percent down on a million-dollar home and are living hand-to-mouth. I call these people "penny millionaires," because to the outside world they look like millionaires but in truth, at the end of each month they don't have two cents to rub together. They are stressed and unhappy, because they have given up control of their lives in exchange for Madison Avenue materialism. They are indentured servants with a pair of golden handcuffs, living in a gilded cage, and any way you look at it they are prisoners to their excess consumption.

At same time, I've also been surprised to walk into a modest home and find out that though the person I was talking to didn't look wealthy they actually were. There was one client in particular who surprised me. He was an older man in his late 60s. He didn't have a college education. He wore bib overalls, smoked cigars, liked his beer, drove a 15-year-old pickup and didn't much care what people thought of him. You might say he was a cantankerous old cuss, but from where he sat he had the last laugh, because he was in the catbird seat. It turned out he owned a window and siding business that he was in the process of turning over to his two sons. I found out that, although he lived in a modest home, he owned a several hundred-acre farm in Wisconsin, and his hobby was collecting and restoring classic roadsters.

Not exactly the hobby of a poor man. Looks can be deceiving! Unlike the families in the previous example, he didn't own a lot of investment property; instead, he invested and reinvested his money in his company to the point that when he wanted something he paid cash. No credit cards, just plain old-fashioned cash. Despite appearances, this unlikely looking man turned out to be wealthy. I want to point out that, although he did not invest in real estate, he had leveraged his assets by investing in his company. Like the school teacher, he made money whether he went to work or not.

WHY MOST PEOPLE SPEND THEIR LIVES ON THE PROVERBIAL TREADMILL!

Most people are on the 40/40 program. That is to say they work 40 hours a week, spend what they make, work some more, spend what they make, repeating this cycle over and over for 40 years and end up with nothing to show for all their hard work. The answer to getting off the treadmill is to **pay yourself first so you are always building wealth.** It's easier than you think, because if you save first you never miss what you never had. The simple truth is that if we make saving painful we won't save and by default we will condemn ourselves to retiring in poverty. By contrast when we save first we eventually reach the point where our savings hit a critical mass, which is the point at which we have enough monthly cash flow to pay all our living expenses whether we go to work or not. In other words, your goal is to go to work, save, work some more, save some more, until eventually you can quit work and go play. That is the quintessential definition of FINANCIAL FREEDOM.

You don't have to save a lot of money to become a millionaire. Say, for example, you saved only $5 a day, which is $150 a month. At 10 percent annual return, in 30 years you would have approximately $340,000. In 40 years it would amount to approximately $950,000. If you saved $10 a day, which is $300 a month, you would amass approximately $1.9 million over 30 years. If you wanted to get aggressive and saved $20 a day, which is $600 dollars a month, in 30 years you would amass approximately $3.8 million. **The logical question then is can you afford not to save first? Only if you plan on retiring poor!**

Credo of the Wealthy!

*"If you want to be wealthy: Live within your means, depend on
yourself not others, diversify your holdings, avoid consumer debt and
instead invest in leveraged assets that provide cash flow.
And most importantly, pay yourself first!"*

–Larry Ballard

WHY CREDIT CARD DEBT IS A POVERTY SENTENCE!

The average American has approximately $8,400 in credit card
debt. Assuming a minimum monthly payment at 18 percent interest,
it will take approximately 30 years to pay off the credit card debt at
a total cost of $20,616. That is $20,616 that, if invested at 10 percent annual return, would have resulted in a savings $413,913 over 30
years. Note the most resent numbers have gone up to $10,000.

WHY THE GOVERNMENT PAYS ITSELF FIRST!

Prior to 1943, individual wage earners received their paychecks
and didn't have to pay income taxes to on their earnings until April of
the following year. The problem was many Americans couldn't budget, so when it came time to pay the government they didn't have the
money. The government decided that if people couldn't budget, they
would just take the money up-front through automatic payroll deductions. As a result, before you even see your paycheck the government
takes out on average 30 percent to 40 percent. We pay federal withholding plus state taxes, social security, Medicare and unemployment,
which combined can be 40 percent or more of our gross salary.

If the American public couldn't budget money to pay the government income taxes, what makes us think we will be any more successful at saving money for retirement? Current statistics tell us in
no uncertain terms that we are <u>not</u> successful at saving. Consider the
following:

- Half of all Americans have less than $25,000 in savings.

- One fifth of all Americans have nothing, zero, nada in
  savings.

■   The average baby boomer approaching retirement has approx-
    imately $1,000 in savings.

WHAT HAPPENED TO THE AMERICAN DREAM?

The short answer is we got caught up in the glitter of Madison Avenue consumerism and while we weren't looking, the world changed
and America found itself in a situation where it had a hard time competing with the lower labor cost available in emerging countries. As a
result our standard of living started to decline, slowly at first and now
the rate of decline is increasing. The simple truth is that it is difficult to
save when your salary is stationary or declining and your cost of living
is increasing. Add to this the fact that we are addicted to consumerism,
so we just keep buying things whether we can truly afford them or not.
Anyway you look at it, this is a recipe for financial ruin.

There is another problem that is that most of us are living paycheck
to paycheck. To make matters worse, three out of four American households are two-income households. If one of the parties loses their job,
they can be upside down in financial difficulty in no time flat. The first
thing most people do as soon as they get paid is pay their bills. Then,
they put aside something for spending money and, if there is anything
left, they save it. This habit is why they will never get off the treadmill.
Instead, what we have to learn to do is what the government does: **"pay
yourself first!"**

YOUR FUTURE IS IN YOUR HANDS!

When it's all said and done the question is: **Are you willing to
throw your credit cards away and pay yourself first in order to
change your destiny and retire wealthy?**

I am sure, by now, most of you agree that this is absolutely what
you should do! The problem is that many of you are drowning in debt,
so even though you may agree in principle with the idea of paying
yourself first, from a practical point of view you don't know where you
would get the money. So the operative question is: how are you going to
miraculously save this money? The good news is you don't have to put
yourself on a budget. Budgets don't generally work, because they are
painful and by human nature we try to avoid pain. The answer is really

quite simple. Almost all of us waste $150 - $300 dollars a month, month in and month out. We just don't realize it. All we have to do is find out where we spend the money we waste and then commit that from now on instead of wasting it we will religiously save it. *People Magazine* created an internationally recognized metaphor to explain this phenomenon. It's called the "latte factor."

> *"A latte spared is a fortune earned."*
> –People Magazine

It is $300 or possibly even $600 a month if you really want to. **Unless you want to retire in poverty, you can't afford <u>not</u> to pay yourself first. All you have to do to be a millionaire is do without a few nonessential items that you currently waste your money on.**

EXERCISE #1
FINDING YOUR WASTED DOLLARS!

STEP 1:
Directions: For the next five days record all of your nonessential purchases and their cost in the table below. At the end of the five days, review your purchases and honestly ask yourself which items on your list you could live without. Underline those items **(YES)** indicating that you intend to divert their cost into savings. Carry their cost over to the last column and total the amount to be saved. See example below, obviously in your best interest to save so you can retire wealthy. The exercise below will show you that whether you think so or not, you can pay yourself first. You can save $150.

DAY # I LOG OF DAILY NON-ESSENTIAL PURCHASES

ITEM PURCHASED	UNIT COST	CONVERT TO SAVINGS	
1. Latte	$ 3.77	YES	$ 3.77
2. Cigarettes	$ 7.00	YES	$ 7.00
3. Diet Coke	$ 1.24	YES	$ 0
4. French Fries	$ 0.99	YES	$ 0.99
5. Candy Bar	$ 1.25	YES	$ 1.25
6. Donuts	$ 1.25	YES	$ 1.25
7. Dinner out with family	$ 95.67	YES	$ 0
8. Bottled Water	$ 1.19	YES	$ 0
9. Pack of Gum	$ 0.75	YES	$ 0
10. Ice Cream Cone	$ 3.00	YES	$ 3.00

TOTAL COST OF ITEMS TO BE CONVERTED TO SAVINGS $17.26

NOTE: We are all going to have different lists and different ideas of what we consider essential, but if you are brutally honest, you waste at least $150 a month and probably a lot more. You will note that I considered the $95.67 dinner out with the family to be a necessity, but if you are like many Americans and you eat dinner out three or four times a week, you have just identified a huge opportunity. Say we cut out two dinners a month, that's nearly $200. You just funded your savings program and changed your destiny!

STEP 2:

Directions: Carry forward only those items that you underlined **(YES),** indicating their cost is to be converted into savings. Estimate the number of times per month you purchase the item and multiply the cost by that number. This will give you an estimate of monthly savings.

FIVE DAY TOTAL OF ITEMS
TO BE CONVERTED TO SAVINGS

ITEMS CARRIED FORWARD	# PURCHASED PER MONTH	EXTENDED COST
1. Latte	30 Times @ $ 3.77	$113.10
2. Cigarettes	30 Times @ $ 7.00	$210.00
3. French Fries	5 Times @ $ 0.99	$ 4.95
4. Muffin	2 Times @ $ 1.95	$ 3.90
5. Candy Bar	1 Times @ $ 1.25	$ 1.25
6. Ice Cream Cone	2 Times @ $ 3.00	$ 6.00

TOTAL MONTHLY SAVINGS OPPORTUNITY $339.20

$339 at 10 percent for 30 years = $776,277. Now you know the cost of not paying yourself first and it is truly enough to make you a millionaire. If, as suggested above, you cut out two dinners per month at $95 each, that's an extra $190 a month and that makes our adjusted total $529.00, and we really haven't given up anything essential. $529 at 10 percent for 30 years equals $ 1,211,358. Also remember, we want to make this achievable and relatively painless so say for example that you really love your latte and can't bear to give it up. Instead of cutting it out completely, cut down from a latte a day to a latte twice a week. That still makes a savings of approximately $83 a month and you get your latte to boot. That's a win-win outcome.

STEP 3:
Directions: Complete the five daily logs below, following the directions in steps 1 and 2 above, in order to get a snapshot of your spending habits.

DAY # 1 LOG OF DAILY NON-ESSENTIAL PURCHASES

ITEM PURCHASED	UNIT COST	CONVERT TO SAVINGS	
1.	$	YES	$
2.	$	YES	$
3.	$	YES	$
4.	$	YES	$
5.	$	YES	$
6.	$	YES	$
7.	$	YES	$
8.	$	YES	$
9.	$	YES	$
10.	$	YES	$
11.	$	YES	$
12.	$	YES	$
13.	$	YES	$
14.	$	YES	$
15.	$	YES	$

TOTAL COST OF ITEMS TO BE CONVERTED TO SAVINGS $

DAY # 2 LOG OF DAILY NON-ESSENTIAL PURCHASES

ITEM PURCHASED	UNIT COST	CONVERT TO SAVINGS	
1.	$	YES	$
2.	$	YES	$
3.	$	YES	$
4.	$	YES	$
5.	$	YES	$
6.	$	YES	$
7.	$	YES	$
8.	$	YES	$
9.	$	YES	$
10.	$	YES	$
11.	$	YES	$
12.	$	YES	$

13.	$	YES	$
14.	$	YES	$
15.	$	YES	$

TOTAL COST OF ITEMS TO BE CONVERTED TO SAVINGS $

DAY # 3 LOG OF DAILY NON-ESSENTIAL PURCHASES

ITEM PURCHASED   UNIT COST   CONVERT TO SAVINGS

1.	$	YES	$
2.	$	YES	$
3.	$	YES	$
4.	$	YES	$
5.	$	YES	$
6.	$	YES	$
7.	$	YES	$
8.	$	YES	$
9.	$	YES	$
10.	$	YES	$
11.	$	YES	$
12.	$	YES	$
13.	$	YES	$
14.	$	YES	$
15.	$	YES	$

TOTAL COST OF ITEMS TO BE CONVERTED TO SAVINGS $

DAY # 4 LOG OF DAILY NON-ESSENTIAL PURCHASES

ITEM PURCHASED   UNIT COST   CONVERT TO SAVINGS

1.	$	YES	$
2.	$	YES	$
3.	$	YES	$

4.	$	YES	$
5.	$	YES	$
6.	$	YES	$
7.	$	YES	$
8.	$	YES	$
9.	$	YES	$
10.	$	YES	$
11.	$	YES	$
12.	$	YES	$
13.	$	YES	$
14.	$	YES	$
15.	$	YES	$

TOTAL COST OF ITEMS TO BE CONVERTED TO SAVINGS $

DAY # 5 LOG OF DAILY NON-ESSENTIAL PURCHASES

ITEM PURCHASED	UNIT COST	CONVERT TO SAVINGS	
1.	$	YES	$
2.	$	YES	$
3.	$	YES	$
4.	$	YES	$
5.	$	YES	$
6.	$	YES	$
7.	$	YES	$
8.	$	YES	$
9.	$	YES	$
10.	$	YES	$
11.	$	YES	$
12.	$	YES	$
13.	$	YES	$
14.	$	YES	$
15.	$	YES	$

TOTAL COST OF ITEMS TO BE CONVERTED TO SAVINGS $

STEP 4:

Directions: Carry forward only those items that you underlined **(YES)** indicating their cost is to be converted into savings. Estimate the number of times per month you purchase the item and multiply the cost by that number. This will give you an estimate of how much you are committing to save monthly.

FIVE DAY TOTAL OF ITEMS
TO BE CONVERTED TO SAVINGS

ITEMS CARRIED FORWARD	# PURCHASED PER MONTH	EXTENDED COST
1.	__ Times @ $ ____	$
2.	__ Times @ $ ____	$
3.	__ Times @ $ ____	$
4.	__ Times @ $ ____	$
5.	__ Times @ $ ____	$
6.	__ Times @ $ ____	$
7.	__ Times @ $ ____	$
8.	__ Times @ $ ____	$
9.	__ Times @ $ ____	$
10	__ Times @ $ ____	$
11.	__ Times @ $ ____	$
12.	__ Times @ $ ____	$
13.	__ Times @ $ ____	$
14.	__ Times @ $ ____	$
15.	__ Times @ $ ____	$
TOTAL MONTHLY SAVINGS OPPORTUNITY $		

Use the calculator @ www.moneychimp.com to calculate how much your incidental purchases are costing you in retirement dollars. $_____ @ 10 percent for ___ years = $_____. Now you know the cost of not paying yourself first. It is truly enough to make you a millionaire.

Hopefully you have calculated approximately how much money you let slip through your fingers each and every month and have made the commitment to convert at least some of that money into savings. If so, read and sign the pledge below committing yourself to this course of action.

I PLEDGE THAT based on a review of my current spending habits, I will save $_____ per month. I further pledge that I will immediately stop using my credit card(s) and as I pay off my credit card(s) I will retire it/them and no longer go into debt for consumer purchases. The only instance in which I will buy anything on credit is when I am making a "leveraged purchase" of either a personal residence or the purchase of income producing investment property.

SIGNED:_____ **DATE** _____

NOTE: If you have no credit card debt or very little then you want to put the entire amount you pledged to save into savings. On the other hand, if it's going to take you a year or more to pay off your credit card debt you don't want to wait that long to start saving. In this instance take the amount you pledged to save and save half of it. Put the other half toward retiring your credit card debt faster.

AUTOMATE YOUR SAVINGS PLAN!

Paying yourself first assures you that you will regularly put aside money toward your retirement. Otherwise the money just gets wasted and you end up poor when you could have ended up wealthy. The key to paying yourself first is to have the money automatically deposited in your investment vehicle of choice. More on this later.

CHAPTER 8

PAY OFF YOUR CREDIT CARDS!

Achieve A Debt-Free Lifestyle!

Having identified where we are going to get the money to fund our savings program, the next step is to figure out how we are going to pay off our credit cards so we can honor our pledge to live a debt-free lifestyle.

The goal is to figure out exactly what our monthly credit card debt is and then develop a plan that will either allow us to lower our monthly payments and accelerate our payment schedule so we can stop throwing away our hard-earned money on non-tax-deductible credit card interest payments and instead convert it into savings so we can retire wealthy.

EXERCISE # 2

CONSOLIDATING YOUR CREDIT CARD DEBT
AND NEGOTIATING A LOWER INTEREST RATE!

STEP 1:

Directions: List all of the credit cards for which you are responsible. This includes yours, your spouse's and your children's cards if you make the payments. Enter the balance from each card and then total all the cards to derive your TOTAL DEBT. Next, enter your minimum monthly payment for each card and then total them in order to determine your TOTAL MINIMUM MONTHLY PAYMENT. Next, calculate the # OF PAYMENTS REQUIRED TO PAY OFF EACH OF YOUR CARDS. You do this by dividing the current balance by the minimum monthly payment i.e. (See Visa below. $2,250 divided by $65 = 35 payments.) Last, call each credit card company and ask them what the **"EFFECTIVE RATE"** is for your card. When you get the rate, put it in the last column of your worksheet on page 134. **NOTE:** You do not want the percent above prime. They must by law give you the effective rate if you ask.

Credit Cards	Current Balance	Minimum Payment	Number Payments to Pay Off	Effective Interest Rate
1. Visa	$2,250	$65	35	18 percent

STEP 2:

Directions: Call each of your credit card companies and ask them the questions listed below.

1. Tell who ever answers that you want to talk to a supervisor about **consolidating all of your credit card debt with their company.** You want to speak to a supervisor, because they have the authority to lower your rate on the spot if they so choose.

2. Ask the supervisor if you transfer your **entire debt balance of $_____** (insert your actual balance from your worksheet on page 134) to their company, what interest rate will they give you? Your goal here is to get your interest rate reduced, hopefully, to as much as half the national average. With this in mind, you need to get educated so go online to either www.lowermybills.com or www.bankrate.com or check your local newspaper. Also ask, if in order to keep your business, would they be willing to waive your annual fee? If they say no to waiving your annual fee, it's no big deal. On the other hand, if they say no to lowering your rate then you have to be prepared to tell them that "if they are not willing to lower your rate you intend to close your account." Tell them that "you intend to transfer your account to the **company that gives**

you the lowest rate. From your research above, have the name of a competitor and their rate ready to throw out in conversation.

3. Once you have successfully negotiated a CONSOLIDATED RATE with one of the companies, enter your new rate on your worksheet on page 134. At this point you will also have **ONE MONTHLY CONSOLIDATED PAYMENT** to make to a single credit card company. Enter that number on your worksheet as well.

All that is left is to determine how much your monthly payment has been reduced. You do this by taking the total minimum monthly payments for all your individual credit cards from column # 3 of your worksheet from page 134 and subtract your consolidated minimum monthly payment the worksheet. Enter your SAVINGS on the last line of the worksheet.

STEP 3:

Directions: Following the directions in steps 1 & 2 above, complete the table on the next page with your specific data and determine how much you can reduce your monthly payment by consolidating your debt to a single card.

WORKSHEET

Credit Cards	Current Balance	Minimum Payment	Number Payments to Pay Off	Effective Interest Rate
1.	$	$		percent
2.	$	$		percent
3.	$	$		percent
4.	$	$		percent
5.	$	$		percent
6.	$	$		percent
7.	$	$		percent
8.	$	$		percent
9.	$	$		percent
10.	$	$		percent
11.	$	$		percent
12.	$	$		percent
13.	$	$		percent
14.	$	$		percent
15.	$	$		percent
TOTALS	$	$	********	Avg. percent

CONSOLIDATED RATE percent	CONSOLIDATED MINIMUM PAYMENT $

MONTHLY REDUCTION IN PAYMENT
(Original monthly – consolidated payment) $

STEP 4:

Directions: Tell your credit card company you want to arrange **to have your bill paid automatically.** Ask them if they can debit your checking account monthly. If they can't do it, call your bank and see if they offer on-line bill paying services to transfer money to your credit card company on a specified day each month. **REMEMBER YOU DON'T MISS WHAT YOU NEVER SEE!**

EXERCISE # 3
WHAT TO DO IF YOU HAVE SO MUCH DEBT THAT NO CARD COMPANY WILL CONSOLIDATE YOUR DEBT!

If you cannot consolidate all of your cards into one single payment because your total debt is too high, the next best thing is to target one card at a time and pay it off.

NOTE: At some point you will have paid off enough debt that you can go back to the card companies and approach them again about consolidating all of your debt into one payment on one card.

STEP 1:

Directions: Look at column #4 of your worksheet on page 134 and identify the cards with the shortest pay-offs and pay them off one at a time. Once you have completed your list, all that remains is to start paying off the first card. To do this you pay the minimum payment on all of the cards except the one you are targeting to pay off. You make accelerated payments (½ of what you pledged to save) on that card so that you can pay it off faster.

WORKSHEET

CREDIT CARDS: (Listed from lowest # payments to highest # payments to pay off date)	# PAYMENTS TO PAY OFF
1.	
2.	
3.	
4.	
5.	
6.	
7.	
8.	
9.	
10.	
11.	
12.	
13.	
14.	
15.	

NOTE:

This strategy will not work if you keep racking up credit card debt, so remember your pledge to stop using your cards immediately and to cancel each card as you pay it off. **Remember, the strategy requires that going forward you pay cash for all consumer purchases.** The only debt you take on is for leveraged investment purchases, specifically your home and investment property.

GET CREDIT COUNSELING IF YOU NEED IT!

If you have so much debt that you cannot get a credit card company to agree to consolidate your debt service, it is a good idea for you to seek credit counseling. There are many companies that offer credit counseling. Before you go with any of them, check with your local Better Business Bureau. Also, before you sign up, ask if using their service will damage your credit rating. One highly regarded credit counseling service is Consumer Credit Counseling Service (CCCS). They are a spin off of The National Foundation for Credit Counseling, the nation's oldest national nonprofit organization for consumer counseling and education. With approximately 1300 offices nationwide, there is a good chance they will have an office in your area. You can call them toll free at 1-800-388-2777 or visit their site online at www.nfcc.org.

Remember:
> *"In life it's not how much money you make that determines how wealthy you become. What's more important is how much of what you make you save for the future."*
>
> –Larry Ballard

CHAPTER 9

HAVE A REALISTIC RETIREMENT PLAN!

General Guidelines of Your Millionaire Retirement Plan!

In the previous two chapters, we learned what the 95 percenters did wrong that caused them to fail to realize their dreams of retiring wealthy. If you learn from their mistakes, you will be well on your way to retiring as a 5 percenter who realizes his dreams of retiring wealthy. Therefore, take into account that you must:

- *Realistically estimate how much income you need to retire on!*

- *Properly estimate your net worth!*

- *Understand that, if you have to work while you are collecting Social Security the government will reduce your Social Security payments so budget accordingly!*

- *Understand that if your retirement is heavily dependent on portfolio money there are two possibilities.* 1.) Even if you have adequate dividend income to live on, your income will still fluctuate, because of fluctuating interest rates and stock market performance! 2.) If you don't have enough dividend income to live on, your portfolio will be systematically sold off in order to provide monthly income for the duration of your projected life expectancy. This is called a declining annuity retirement program, and the problem with it is that if your portfolio goes down in value or you live longer than expected you will be destitute!

■ *Understand the tax consequences on your investments* so you don't end up with less after-tax income than you expected! Profits from real estate can be deferred as long as the investor wishes. By contrast "earned income" is immediately taxed!

■ *Learn to leverage your investments* by using other people's money in order to increase the yield on your investments.

■ *Take control of your investments*, so you can optimize the return on your investments and minimize your risk, and so when you make a mistake you can learn from it!

■ *Pay yourself first through an automatic forced savings program!* If you always spend everything you make and never put anything away for retirement, how can you possibly expect to retire wealthy? Why work for the government and the credit card companies and fail to work for yourself? So pay yourself first and you will retire rich.

Knowing what the 95 percenters did wrong and doing the opposite isn't enough. If you want to retire as a 5 percenter who realizes his/her dream of retiring wealthy, you need to know exactly what the 5 percenters did and you need to do the same thing. It's that simple! If it worked for them, there is no earthly reason it will not work for you. Therefore, in addition to the above you need to:

■ *Pay cash for all your consumer purchases. Carry no consumer credit card debt.* Instead, spend your money on "leveraged debt" that generates income and builds wealth.

■ *Own your own home and have it paid off by the time you retire* (more on this later). A home is a forced savings program that will substantially increase your wealth.

■ *Live within your means* so you have the financial resiliency to withstand vacillating changes in your financial situation. To this end, keep an emergency fund that has at least thee to six months' living expenses, preferably a year.

■ *Don't be dependent on a job for __all__ of your income.* Instead derive your income from several sources, so if you lose your job you have alternate income. Ultimately, your goal is to create enough recurring revenue that it covers all of your monthly expenses. At that point you have reached the critical mass that determines you are financially independent, because you can pay your bills whether you work or not.

- **Cut your wasteful spending.** This is your latte factor from Chapter 6. Keep your pledge to save the money you used to waste or, if you have credit card debt, apply half of the money you save each month toward paying off your credit card debt and put the other half into savings. If you don't pay yourself first, you will never retire wealthy. It's that simple.

- **Develop a specific savings and investment plan and set it up so it is automatically funded.** Later in this chapter, we will cover exactly how to accomplish this.

- **You _MUST BELIEVE_ that you can be a wealthy 5 percenter** or you are defeated from the get go. Even if you try, you will not be committed. Your prominent thoughts will be realized, so think like a wealthy "can do" person and it will be so.

- **Don't make your definition of wealth a moving target.** By this, I mean learn to live within your means. Don't get caught in the trap where you make more money, but you spend it all instead of saving it. To this end, set up your savings program so it is based on a percent of your income. That way, whenever your income goes up your savings will likewise increase as well.

- **Make being wealthy a _MUST!_** If you don't, you will never be wealthy. You will simply be a 95 percenter who gave it his best shot, but didn't quite make it. It has to be an absolute must!

- **You have to be flexible and you have to be in control of your investments.** You can take advice from the experts, but you need to be ultimately in control. Otherwise, you will not be in a position to learn from your mistakes. Every investor makes mistakes. The point is to learn from them.

- **Follow your plan unwaveringly.** Once you have established your investment plan and allocated your funds, you need to stick to your plan. Don't allow yourself to be tempted by some great deal and risk your retirement on some get-rich-quick scheme. If you stick to the game plan it will work. Remember "pigs get fat, but hogs get slaughtered."

Believing Makes It So!

In life the quality of the questions we ask often determines the quality of our life. This is one of those instances. How you answer the questions below will determine your financial future.

1. Are you committed to becoming a millionaire? By this, I mean is it an absolute must for you?

2. Are you committed to taking a predetermined percentage of your income (per your pledge in Chapter 6) and setting up an automated savings program that pays you first?

If you honestly answered "yes" to both of these questions, you will become a millionaire! You see, the hard part is in your mind. If you can see it and if you truly believe it, then it will come to pass! It's that simple. It's just the way things work in God's kingdom. At that point, the only thing remaining is to define your specific action plan and for you to unwaveringly execute your plan and constantly visualize yourself having achieved your goal. See yourself wealthy! See yourself enjoying the good life! See it in detail and see it often! Never lose sight of your dream! Claim it as your reality and refuse to see it as anything but your God-given right. See yourself as deserving, and **live with an attitude of gratitude.** The only way you get past scarcity is by starting with gratitude. If you see yourself as having reached your goal of being a millionaire, there is no place in your thinking for thoughts of scarcity and poverty. All you have to do is execute your plan and stay the course. The rest is history. God will keep his promise and prosper you if you keep your promise and keep up your end of the deal.

So shall my word be that goeth out of my mouth; it shall not return
unto me void, but it shall accomplish that which I please,
and it shall prosper in the thing where to I send it.
(Isaiah 55:11)

God is able to do exceeding abundantly above
all that we ask or think.
(Ephesians 3:20)

CHAPTER 10

DIVERSIFY YOUR ASSETS!

Developing Your Unique Millionaire Retirement Plan!

You already know most of what you need to know. That is to say, you have a basic understanding of how to build wealth. All that is missing is your step by step action plan. Believe it or not, that is the easy part. It's easy because it's a process, and the great thing about a process is that it doesn't discriminate. It doesn't care if you are male or female, brilliant or average. It doesn't even care how much money you make. All that is important is that you follow the plan. It's like the paint-by-number oil-painting kits that make everyone look like an artist. Just follow the process, and the process will make you look like a shrewd millionaire investor.

The key to your wealth-building process is to **safely grow your money, yet accelerate your rate of return without jeopardizing what you have already saved."** Impossible you say. No! It's not only possible, but also there is an easy three-step process!

STEP 1:
Set your savings goal and adhere to it! What percentage of your income are you pledging to save (5 percent, 10 percent, 15 percent 20 percent) _____ percent. At a minimum you should be pledging to save the wasted money you identified when you calculated your latte factor in Chapter 6. If you are really serious about becoming a millionaire, you should commit to save 10 percent or more of your gross income. How much are you pledging to save per month based on a percentage of your current income?

Regardless what anyone says, it does take money to make money, so the question is how aggressive do you want to be. Obviously, the more you save, the faster you will become a millionaire. When I started out, I had very little money left over from my paycheck. In order to save seed money, I sold antiques at local flea markets and saved my money to buy my first investment property. Is there anything you could do to make supplemental income in order to jump start your retirement fund? Your sacrifice pays double dividends because it will not only allow you to save more aggressively, but also provide you with an alternate source of income to insulate you in the event you lose your job or have some sort of financial setback. Who knows, you might even find a new career.

He who gathers money little by little makes it grow.
(Proverbs 13:11)

STEP 2:
   Decide how you are going to allocate your investments for optimal growth and security! We will get into specific investment vehicles in a second, but for now we need to define the process. The key to this process is **controlled growth coupled with risk management,** and the key to achieving this objective is a process called "**asset allocation**." Before anyone heard of Warren Buffet, there was a famous British investor by the name of Sir John Templeton. To the best of my knowledge, Sir John was the originator of the concept of asset allocation. It is a simple, yet brilliant concept. It is based on the assumption that none of us is perfect. No matter how astute we are, we can and will make bad decisions. We can and will make bad investments. The beauty of asset allocation is that it expects us to make mistakes, so it allows for our mistakes. In essence it protects us from ourselves. Here is how it works. You divide your investments into four buckets as follows:

Asset Allocation Investment Strategy

1) **Emergency Bucket:** Minimum of three to six months' living expenses in low risk, liquid investments. One year of living expenses is ideal.

Used to cover living expenses in case of a true emergency, such as job loss, health issues, and so forth. This money is only to be used in the direst of situations. It is to keep you from going upside down in an emergency and for no other reason, absolutely none! These funds need to be liquid, so you can get to them quickly in an emergency. Typically your emergency bucket will have some cash and a money market account and/or U.S. savings bonds. You never want to put large amounts of money in a savings or checking account, because they pay little to no interest.

2) **Security Bucket:** Low risk, low-yield investments that you allow to grow by means of **"compound interest."**

   Once you put money in your security bucket you never— and I do mean never—touch that money until you retire. It may seem at first like it grows at a snail's pace, but over time it accumulates into a sizeable sum. Say, you saved $10 dollars a day or $300 dollars a month from the age of 20. By age 60, assuming a 10 percent annual rate of return, you would have amassed approximately $1.9 million. This money is your security net to retire on. It is there for no other reason. It's your protection against the possibility that you make some bad investments in your growth bucket and lose a substantial portion of those funds. Examples of typical investments are fixed-income investments such as T-bills, money market accounts, U.S. savings bonds, corporate bonds, whole life policy and your personal residence. (You need a place to live)

3) **Growth Bucket:** (Higher-risk, higher-yield investments that increase the "velocity" at which your money grows and that takes advantage of leverage in order to allow you to use other people's money to substantially increase your rate of return).

   Once you put money in your growth bucket, you don't touch it until you make a profit. When you make a substantial profit, you divide your profit up. Put one third into your security bucket to grow for retirement; reinvest one third back into your growth bucket; and put one third in your reward bucket to be used to pay cash for whatever luxury item you want. Your growth bucket can generally grow at two to five times faster than your security bucket. Examples of typical investments are mutual funds, collectibles, real estate, securities and stocks.

4) **Reward Bucket:** (Profits from growth bucket are used to pay cash for items on your wish list. It's your reward and your motivation).

In terms of how you actually ALLOCATE your funds, think of your emergency bucket and security bucket as being essentially one bucket. This is because they are both low-risk, low-yield investments that pay a fixed rate of return over a specified period and that grow based on accumulation of compound interest. The only difference in your emergency bucket and your security bucket is that your emergency bucket is invested in more liquid assets, so that in an emergency you can access your funds quickly. Jointly, both buckets exist to provide you both short- and long-term security, which is why we view them as essentially one bucket. In terms of asset allocation your second bucket is your growth bucket. It is comprised of higher-risk assets that have the potential of allowing you to grow your assets at a faster rate due to either higher yields and or leverage.

With higher return comes higher risk, therefore, more caution is required. This is why you segregate the funds into two buckets. Every person is unique in terms of his/her tolerance for risk, so I can't give you an iron-clad formula for how to allocate your funds. Nevertheless, generally the younger you are, the more risk you can afford to take, and the older you are, the less risk you can afford to take. This is because the younger you are the more time you have to recover from a loss, while the older you are the less time you have to recover. This said, a high risk taker in his 20s or 30s might choose to split his investments 30 percent to 40 percent in security and 60 percent to 70 percent in growth. By contrast, a person in their 40s or 50s might choose to be more conservative and divide his funds so that 60 percent are for security and 40 percent are for growth. At the same time, a person in his 50s or 60s might choose to be even more conservative and divide his funds so that 70 percent or 80 percent are for security and 20 percent to 30 percent are for growth. It is your individual decision. The point is that you do not want to risk the money in your security bucket, because that is your retirement. Your growth bucket just feeds your security bucket in order to accelerate its growth, but you retire off of your security bucket. Decide now what percentage you are going to put into security and what percentage you are going to put into growth. Then, do not under any circumstances change your ratio just because a supposed good deal comes along. Stay the course. The only reason you change your allocation is to adjust your risk as you get older.

STEP 3:

Decide on the specific investments you intend to make and then automate the process so you always pay yourself first! This process involves you deciding on the specific investments you want to put in your 1) emergency bucket, 2) security bucket and 3) growth bucket. The decision as to what specific investments you choose to make will in large part be based on your age and how much risk you are prepared to take for the potential of higher profits. You are looking to achieve a balance between risk and reward so you grow your wealth rapidly while not taking excessively high risk.

Note: It's important to note that over time your mix of investments can and should change. This is because when you are young you can afford to take more risk than you can as you get older. When it comes to exactly how to automate your savings plan the definitive book on the subject is THE AUTOMATIC MILLIONAIRE and accompanying work book by author David Bach. I highly recommend the book.

—— YOUR EMERGENCY BUCKET ——

Most Americans live from paycheck to paycheck. To make matters even worse, nearly 75 percent of all American households are two-income households. What happens if one of those paychecks is lost? Without adequate reserves, that family can be in serious financial trouble in six months or less. People can and do file bankruptcy and/or lose their homes to foreclosures simply because they were living too close to the edge and something unforeseen happened. With the corporate instability we are experiencing, you simply can't afford to have less than three to six months' living expenses on hand at all times. A year is ideal.

Whatever you do, don't put your emergency money in with your regular bill paying account! It's too easy to borrow from Peter to pay Paul and never pay Peter back.

Emergency bucket investment vehicles:

- **Cash:** Every retirement program needs some cash for those times when you have to have money immediately. Generally 5 percent to 10 percent cash is ample. If you are over 60 you may want to have as much as 15 percent.

- **"Liquidity and low risk,"** money market accounts have been the investment vehicle of choice. They have been considered to be some of the safest investments, on par with bank certificates of deposit. When you invest in a money market account, you are actually buying shares in a money market fund (mutual fund) that invests in short-term government bonds and sometimes in highly rated corporate bonds.

  Recently, however; *"low interest rates"* have made money market accounts less attractive. As I write this book interest rates are low and if they stay low, banks and brokerage firms will have difficulty making money on them. Rates could go back up again so don't rule out money market accounts.

  NOTE: <u>Not all money market accounts are federally insured.</u> Given the current low rates, I would recommend that if you decide to open a money market account that you go with one that is **federally insured,** which means you will be trading a higher rate for lower risk.

QUESTIONS TO ASK WHEN OPENING A MONEY MARKET ACCOUNT:

✓ What is the minimum required to open an account? Typically, the minimum to open an account is between $1,000 and $2,000, but it can be as low as $1, so shop around.

NOTE: If you decide to open a money market account you need to decide how much you are going to put in it each month. The more you put in, the faster your money compounds. If possible, put in 5 percent of your net take home pay per month.

✓ Do they offer systematic investment programs? This is an account where you agree to have money taken out of your checking account and transferred to the money market account on a regularly scheduled basis. If they offer a systematic investment program what you want to know is whether it has a lower minimum required to open an account and if so what it is?

NOTE: Generally, if you sign an agreement to make systematic deposits they will allow you to open an account, often with as little as $1. You should know that if you open an account this way, you generally do not get check writing privileges.

✓ Do they offer federally insured accounts and if so what is the rate on an insured account vs. a noninsured account?

NOTE: You can visit www.bankrate.com and 1) compare interest rates; 2) determine the minimum amount required to open an account; and 3) sort banks by state, which is important because some states offer tax-free checking on money market accounts. You can also check rates in financial publications, like the Wall Street Journal and Barron's. Call local banks and brokerage houses and check their rates. Brokerage houses generally pay higher rates than banks.

✓ Does the account come with check writing privileges; and if so what is the smallest check you can write? Also, ask if the account comes with an ATM card.

✓ Is there a low balance charge; and if so what is the balance and associated fee?

NOTE: It's important to have check writing and/or ATM privileges so you can get access to your money in an emergency.

How to <u>automate</u> the funding of your money market account!

✓ Ask your employer if it can direct deposit funds from your paycheck into your money market account. If your employer can't do this, arrange to either have funds automatically transferred from your checking account into your money market account or arrange for a systematic withdrawal from checking into the money market account.

■ *U.S. savings bonds* are easy, convenient and low risk. They:

   • Can be purchased on line at TREASURYDIRECT.GOV

   • *Are guaranteed by the federal government.*

   • Allow you to invest as little as $50 a month automatically into either *"I Bonds," also known as "inflation bonds" or "EE bonds," which are also known as "patriot bonds."*

NOTE: You can get the current rates for both types of bonds by going to WWW.TREASURYDIRECT.GOV and clicking on "For EE/E Bond Investors" and "For I-Bond Investors."

■ *I Bonds/Inflation Bonds* get their name from the fact that their earning's rate is tied to the inflation rate. Specifically, their earning's rate is a combination of a fixed rate and a semiannual rate that is based on the consumer price index. The benefit to investors is that in the event of inflation the rate of return on the bonds is increased so you are not stuck with an unattractively low rate. Features of I bonds include:

   • Minimum purchase is $50.

   • Maximum amount you can purchase in one year is $30,000.

   • They are sold at "face value," which means a $50 bond costs $50. They earn interest for up to 30 years.

   • They can be sold after one year with a three-month interest penalty. This seems like a steep penalty, but given their high rate of return and protection against inflation, they are still a good deal.

   • For current rates on I Bonds go to savingsbonds.gov.

■ **_EE Bonds/Patriot Bonds:_** The name Patriot bonds comes from the fact that these bonds were issued following the terrorists attacks of September 11, 2001. Features of EE/Patriot bonds include

- The rate of return is 90 percent of that paid on five-year Treasury notes.

- They are sold at 50 percent of their face value, which means that a $100 Patriot Bond costs $50. When they come due in 30 years, you get $100 plus interest.

- They can be sold after one year, but if they are sold before five years you are penalized three months' interest.

How to <u>automate</u> the purchase of U.S. savings bonds!

✓ Just go to www.savingsbonds.gov and click on "easy saver plan," which will take you to a page that explains how to purchase bonds via an automatic debit from your checking or savings account or through payroll deduction.

YOUR EMERGENCY BUCKET IN REVIEW

✓ You always need some cash on hand for emergencies.

✓ The advantage of money market accounts over bonds is that they are more liquid, so you can get your money out quicker without having to pay a penalty.

✓ Government bonds generally pay a higher rate of return than money market accounts because they are considered a longer-term investment.

✓ It's up to you to decide if, given your situation, one of these investments makes more sense for you than the other, but for many people having both isn't a bad idea.

✓ You want to keep a minimum of three to six months' living expenses in your emergency bucket at all times. A year is a safer number.

—— YOUR SECURITY BUCKET! ——

Per Chapters 2 & 3, I foresee a time in the not too distant future when the American economy will suffer a virtual collapse, resulting in a severe stock market collapse and possibly even currency devaluation. Despite this, the stock market is an intricate part of our economy and system of commerce. As such, it is a principal component of most people's retirement programs. Nevertheless, it is prudent to consider the possibility of a stock market crash and adjust our investments, so they will be as insulated as possible from the ups and downs of the market.

NOTE: If the dollar collapses completely, which could happen in the other nations of the world were to decide to abandon the dollar as the world's currency. The more debt the U.S. amasses the more likely this scenario becomes. In such an event we would most likely go into hyperinflation leading to a total collapse of the dollar and a state of anarchy. Note normally in times of economic instability gold and silver are a safe haven, but I fear that by the time this book gets out the cost of gold and silver will be too high to be a practical haven for the average person.

We don't have to look back too far to find an example of how the ups and downs of the market can affect people's lives. Over the spring and early summer of 2002, the U.S. stock market lost a staggering $6.9 trillion. This was far more than a hiccup. This was a catastrophe of major proportions. Millions of Americans lost their life savings and were forced out of retirement. Still others who were looking to retire in the next five to ten years were left with the possibility of having to work for the rest of their lives.

The question is what can we learn from what happened, so we can insulate ourselves from similar events in the future? The lesson here is that this is your security bucket. Its function is to provide you long-term security. As such, you need to be conservative with respect to how you invest these funds. There is a time and place for high risk, high reward, but it has no place in your security bucket. Given this, you want to make sure your investments in your security bucket are diversified in a combination of stocks, bonds and Treasury bills. The easiest way to accomplish this is through a balanced fund or asset allocation fund that automatically diversifies your investments for you.

Security bucket investment vehicles:

■ *Company Stock:* Remember, this is your security bucket, so no matter how great you feel your company is you want to resist the temptation to put too many eggs in one basket. The key to security is diversification, so don't put more than 5-15 percent in your company stock. Also, remember what happened to the employees of Enron, Lucent Technologies and World Com. They thought their companies were wonderful, but the employees took a bath on the company stock. Don't let that happen to you. When you invest in a single stock, you have no diversification and it's not backed by the government, so no matter how solid you feel your company is, you should consider your company's stock to be a high-risk growth investment.

■ *Your Home:* Buy a home and get it paid off before you retire.

You sure can't get rich renting. If you rented for 30 years and paid $1,200 a month you would have spent a whopping $432,000 and would have absolutely nothing to show for it.

According to a survey published by the Federal Reserve in 2000, the net worth of renters was $4,200 versus $132,000 for home owners. In other words, home owners were 31 times wealthier than renters.

There are lots of reasons why real estate is the "Consummate Wealth Building Vehicle." For Example:

• It is a **forced savings program.**

• It has **inherent value in and of itself** where stocks do not.

• Your purchase can be **leveraged** while portfolio investments generally cannot. Say you purchased a $300,000 home with 20 percent down, which comes to $60,000. This means you have 80 percent leverage. Put another way, you have 5-to-1 leverage. Now, let's assume your home experienced 10 percent appreciation over a three-year period. Because of the 5-to-1 leverage, you have made $30,000 on a $60,000 investment, which is a 50 percent return. I know housing prices are flat right now and we don't know what the future holds, but none the less you need to understand the concept of leverage which has allowed real estate to historically be such a good investment.

- Unlike stock, real estate allows investors to get **immediate equity** by buying below market value.

- Unlike stocks, real estate can be **refinanced** to pull out equity without having to liquidate the asset.

- When you buy a home using a mortgage, you are **using other people's money** to make a leveraged purchase. This means your money can be working for you elsewhere making compound interest.

- Provides **superior tax benefits.** You can deduct interest payments up to a maximum of $1,000,000. The higher your tax bracket the more you benefit.

- Provides **hands-on control,** which means its value can be substantially increased. For example, you can fix your home up and substantially increase its value. You have no such control over stocks.

- **Real estate has inherent value:** So unlike stocks even in a down market real estate retains value where stocks can go to zero.

Pay your mortgage off early:

Most Americans have no idea of how much money their home mortgage is actually costing them. If they did they would be highly motivated to pay it off as soon as possible. A 6 percent interest rate may not sound too bad, especially when compared to a credit card, which could be as much as 18 to 30 percent. *But, in actuality a 30-year mortgage is a "30-year sentence of indentured servitude designed to keep you poor and make the bankers rich."* You may be surprised to find out just how much that 6 percent loan actually cost you. For example, if you had a $200,000 mortgage at 6 percent amortized over 30 years with a monthly mortgage payment of $1199.10 you would pay $231,677 in interest over the term of the loan. Your total pay out would be $431,677. The true interest rate is more like 115 percent than the 6 percent you were told. If that doesn't make you mad you are a lot more tolerant than I am. Fortunately, there is a better way. In Chapter 12, I will show you how you can pay off your 30-year mortgage in as little as 8 to 11 years and spend the next 19 to 22 years investing in your retirement program so you can retire in comfort. I don't know about you, but that sounds like a good deal to me.

Right about now, I am sure you are thinking that is too good to be true, but I assure you it isn't. As a matter of fact it is easy and you can do it on your current income without making any major changes to your life-style.

■ Your Self-Directed Retirement Plan through Work: Most companies offer 401(k) retirement plans or if you work for a nonprofit organization, such as a school or hospital, it would be a 403(b). Regardless of which plan your employer offers, they are essentially the same. Despite the availability of these programs the unfortunate truth is that 25 percent of all Americans who are eligible for such plans have not even signed up and the majority of those who do participate do not contribute the maximum. What follows will show you why these plans are important to your financial future.

NOTE: For those of you who are self-employed we will be discussing your options shortly.

What a 401(k) or 403(b) can mean to your financial future!

- These are pre-tax retirement programs, which means that the government allows you to pay yourself first.

- Your earnings are also tax exempt until you take the money out.

- As of 2005, you can contribute up to $14,000 if you are less than 50 years old and $18,000 if you are over 50.

- Most employers do not charge an administration fee.

- Many employers offer matching funds. Generally, it's 25 percent of what the employee puts in.

- Your investment accrues compound interest.

- ***Contributions can be made <u>automatically</u> through payroll deductions.***

What tax deferred investing means to your bottom line!

When you make a regular investment, you are investing with post-tax dollars. For example, let's assume the government takes 30 percent out of your paycheck up front. In effect, this means that for every dollar you invest, the government takes 30 percent off the top, leaving you with only $0.70 to actually invest. If you made a return of 10 percent on your $0.70 you would have a total of $0.77 after one year. In contrast, if you put the same dollar in a pre-tax retirement plan you would get the entire dollar to invest, so if you earned 10 percent on your investment, in a year you would have $1.10 as opposed to $0.77, or $0.33 more per dollar. In addition, gains on the $1.10 are not taxable, while they are taxable on the $0.77.

THE POWER OF EMPLOYER MATCHING!

Many employers offer to match a portion of the employee's contribution. Hopefully, your company is one that does. The typical employer contribution is $0.25 for every dollar the employee invests. Using the example above, this means that for every pre-tax dollar you invest, the company puts in $0.25, so you are actually investing $1.25 at 10 percent, which yields a total of $1.38 after one year versus $0.77 with a regular post-tax investment. That is a huge difference.

What do you do if your company doesn't offer a retirement program? You open an Individual Retirement Account (IRA)! You have two options.

Option 1: Traditional IRA: This is an individual (**<u>tax-deferred</u>**) retirement program. You can make tax deferred contributions up to a maximum of $3,000 a year if you are under 50 years old and $3,500 if you are 50 or older. To give you an idea of how this breaks down, there are 260 working days in a year, so a $3,000 contribution is $11.54 a day or $250 a month and a $3,500 contribution is $13.46 a day or $292 per month. Other things to consider include:

- Your contribution is taken out before taxes, but when you

withdraw the money you pay income tax on the money you put into the account.

• In order to satisfy your tax obligations, you must start systematically withdrawing money by age 70 ½.

NOTE: A Traditional IRA may not be tax deductible if you are covered by a plan at work, so to be sure of your eligibility check IRS Publication #590.

Option 2: Roth IRA: This is an individual retirement program that is not tax deductible. This means that you pay taxes up front when you contribute. Other things to consider include:

• Depending on your income level, you may or may not be eligible for participation. You can contribute up to $3,000 per year if you are single and earn less than $95,000 a year and for a married couple you must earn less than $150,000 per year. If you earn more than the above amounts, you can still participate but the amount of contribution is reduced based on your income. If you are single and earn more than $110,000 per year or are married and have a combined income over $160,000 you are not eligible to participate at all.

• Unlike a Traditional IRA, you are not required to start withdrawing money at 70 ½ years of age.

• The good news is that if your money has been in a Roth IRA for five years or longer and you are 59 ½ years old, you can withdraw your money with no tax obligation!

Which is better a Traditional IRA or a Roth IRA? Obviously, the answer to this question depends on your particular situation. Consider the following:

• If you can't get a tax deduction on a Traditional IRA because you have a tax-deferred retirement plan at work, a Traditional IRA isn't even a consideration. You want a Roth IRA.

• There are two key decision making factors:

1) Do you feel that in your situation you would benefit from taking the up-front tax deductions of a Traditional IRA,

or would you be better off with the tax-free pay out of a Roth IRA? To me, the answer to this question somewhat depends on whether or not you can fully fund the programs.

2) With a Traditional IRA, it is easier to fund the maximum because you are contributing with pre-tax dollars. For Example:

- With a Roth IRA, in order to contribute $3,000 you actually need approximately $4,000, because you have to pay taxes on your income before you can contribute.

- If you are confident you can contribute the maximum and if you are 15 years or more away from retirement, a Roth IRA is a good choice, because when you retire all the money you take out will be tax free. For more information visit www.rothira.com.

How do you set up an IRA and automate your contributions?

You can set up an IRA at a bank, a brokerage or online. Look for a large company with online service and phone support. You have three options as to how you automate your contributions. They are as follows:

Option 1: Ask your employer if it can make a **"payroll deduction,"** which takes money directly from your paycheck and transfers it directly to your IRA. If your employer is set up to do this, you will need to complete a form providing your employer with the account number and routing information for your IRA.

Option 2: If your employer doesn't offer payroll deductions, ask if they can make **automatic direct deposit of your paycheck into your checking account.** Most employers can accommodate this request. Once the money has been deposited in your checking account, you can have your bank or brokerage firm transfer the money into your retirement account. Have funds transferred every pay period, the day after your check clears.

Option 3: Find out if your bank offers **online bill payment** capability. If so, this is an incredibly **simple way to pay all your bills on line.** All you do is open an online bill payment account and from that point all of your bills go to your service provider, which scans them and provides them to you online. All you have to do is click a button and the funds to pay each bill are transferred out of your checking account and your bills are paid. The cost of opening an automatic bill paying service usually run $13 a month for 30 bills or $5 a month plus fifty cents per bill. The following are websites for three bill-payment companies: www. paytrust.com, www.statusfactory.com and www.quickbillpay.com.

What do you do if you are self-employed?

The government knows that small business is the backbone of this country, so it gives business owners the best tax breaks of all. There are a variety of programs available to business owners, such as 401(k) profit-sharing plans, money purchase plans, profit sharing plans and defined benefit plans, but to keep things simple, I am only going to discuss two of the more exciting and simpler plans.

Option 1: The Simplified Employee Pension (SEP IRA, also known as the self-employed retirement program

- If you are self-employed and do not have any employees, you can contribute up to 25 percent of your gross income, up to a maximum of $40,000. The exact figure is adjusted annually based on inflation.

- If you are like many self-employed people, you may not take a regular salary, in which case it is difficult to fund the plan automatically, so you will have to rely on yourself to make sure you fund it.

Option 2: The one-person 401(k) profit-sharing plan

- You can open up a 401(k) for a one-person business for as little as $150. In the first year the maximum salary deferral contri-bution is $15,000 for people under 50 years old, and $20,000 for those 50 and older. Profit-sharing contributions can also be made each year up to 25 percent of compensation. Combined salary deferral and profit-sharing contributions cannot exceed the lesser of 100 percent of compensation or $44,000 per per-son per year. Note: These figures may change over time so make sure you get current information when investing. My intent here is only to explain how the plans work.

——— YOUR GROWTH BUCKET ———

This is where you go beyond the power of compounding. Instead of investing in things that provide you a fixed rate of return, you are investing in things that have the potential of providing considerably higher returns, but with higher associated risk.

Growth bucket investment vehicles:
- ***Individual Stocks:*** Obviously, any time you buy an individual stock as opposed to participating in a mutual fund you have a higher risk, because you have no diversification. But by the same token, your profits have the potential of being higher as well. For example, if you had had the foresight to buy McDonald's, Block Buster, Wal-Mart, Subaru or Microsoft stocks early on, before these companies took off you wouldn't be reading this book. Instead you would be lounging on a beach in some island paradise. For example, a $6,000 dollar investment in Subaru made in 1967 and sold at its peak would have put approximately a million dollars in your pocket. Similarly, a $100 dollar investment in Wal-Mart made in 1989 and sold at its peak would have yielded you over $40,000. By the same token, you could have lost your shirt on the dot-coms, so it's important to remember that the sword can cut both ways. The thing to remember about stocks is that a savvy investor can make money whether the market goes up, down or sideways, but the average investor only knows how to make money when the market goes up. That means the odds are two to one against the novice. With this in mind, invest according to your knowledge level and let the novice be weary. Having said this, I don't want to discourage you from picking the next Microsoft, just resist the temptation to put all your eggs in one bucket.

I have often said that most times the difference between success and failure is the quality of the questions you ask. Why did Wal-Mart take off like a rocket and pass its larger competitors, K-Mart and Sears? In 1978, Wal-Mart had 78 stores while K-Mart had 1326 and Sears had 851. The combined market value of K-Mart and Sears was 65 times that of Wal-Mart, but today Wal-Mart is worth considerably more than K-Mart and Sears. How and why did this reversal of fortunes take place? Sam Walton did two things that catapulted his company to the stars. He spent two days a week going out to his competitors and modeling absolutely everything they did right and avoiding what they did wrong. He also motivated his employees to provide a higher quality of customer satisfaction than had ever been achieved in that market segment. He made shopping at his stores a pleasurable experience. In other words, he did his homework and kept his fingers on the pulse of the market. That is exactly what you want to do. Become an informed investor. You don't have to be a Sam Walton. All you have to do is be well informed enough to see an opportunity when it presents itself.

Let me provide a couple more examples. Why do you think McDonalds has done so well? The answer is laser targeted marketing. They targeted children, because they understood kids are vulnerable to advertising and they knew that if they could hook them as children they would have them for life. They made our children what McDonald's calls users. It is arguable whether Microsoft has the best operating system in the world, but it is not arguable who has a lock on the world computer market. What distinguished Microsoft from its competitors? Bill Gates had a single-minded vision of being the operating system for the world. He wasn't building a computer company. He was building a vision. In my area there is a restaurant chain called "Lettuce Entertain You." Its founder, Rich Melman, had a vision also. He saw dining out as a total experience. He saw his mission as more than providing a good meal. It was about the experience. It was about being entertained. He created a chain of theme restaurants that excited the customer's senses. He also understood customer service, so he brought in the best chefs he could find and motivated them to excellence by giving them a piece of the action.

That is enough examples. What is the point? The point is you should be on the look out for the next visionary who has a better vision, better product, or a better process. You should be looking to the future and asking yourself how changes in society are affecting the way we live and the products and services we want and need? How is the aging of the world's population changing the demand for products and services? How is globalization changing

our economy and how will it positively or negatively affect corporate America and the stock market? How is technology changing
our lives, and how can you capitalize on those changes?   What
are the new frontiers in science? For example will nanotechnol-
ogy and bioengineering be the next breakthrough technologies?
Are concerns about global warming going to create investment
opportunities and if so which technologies have the best chance of
emerging victorious? Will the government impose Cap and Trade
Legislation (see my book Modern Slavery for details on Cap and
Trade) and if so what will it do to the price of oil, natural gas and
coal? What does the future hold that presents an opportunity for
those that have the vision to see it and the wherewithal to invest in
it?

In essence, I challenge you to become an informed investor. Along
with your questioning, you need some concrete knowledge, so
subscribe to a financial publication and begin to educate yourself.
Hire a financial adviser and take what he tells you under advise-
ment. Notice I didn't say let him invest for you. I said listen to his
counsel and then make an informed decision and, if you make a
mistake, learn from it and go on.

■ *Real Estate Investing:*
To begin, it is important to note that your personal residence is not
considered an investment. It is a forced savings program. Though
it may increase in value, because it has expenses such as principal,
interest, taxes and upkeep and does not generate income it is not in
this context an investment.

The quintessential difference between real estate and stocks is that
real estate has inherent value in and of itself, because it serves
the essential function of providing us shelter. The same is true
of factories, warehouses, schools, libraries, parks and other real
estate. It touches nearly every aspect of our life. In **The Wealth of
Nations, Adam Smith observed that real estate along with raw
materials for the manufacture of finished goods is the basis of
all wealth.** Stocks by comparison are merely a convenient means
of conveyance. They represent things of value, but they themselves have no value except the value which consumers place on

them. Given this, one of the essential differences between real estate and stocks is that real estate has inherent value. It can go up and down with interest rates or economic upheavals but, because of its utility, it continues to have value, while stocks can go to zero and the companies that issue them can go out of business, leaving investors with nothing but worthless paper.

The primary advantage of stocks is their liquidity as opposed to the lack of liquidity associated with real estate. This distinction is one of the primary reasons it is advisable to have both stocks and real estate in your retirement plan. In Chapter 12, I will show you how to tap into the equity in your home in order to have it at your disposal in the event of a financial setback. This knowledge is absolutely vital to your financial security. Given the effects of globalization, corporate America is not as safe a place to work as it once was. I don't know about you, but I could sleep a lot better at night if I knew that if I lost my job that I would not automatically lose my home.

—— DISASTER PROTECTION ——

What steps can you take to protect your wealth?

What if this so called recession (2008 sub-prime collapse) becomes the Second Great Depression and what if it results in another stock market crash and eventually a currency devaluation/collapse? In such an event, does history give us any indication of how to protect our assets? Actually it does. Some investments are more vulnerable than others. The day after a devastating stock market crash you get up and you still need food and medicine and other basic necessities, so the companies that make those types of items will do well, because there will still be demand for their products. Ironically, history has actually shown that in times of hardship people will give up almost anything except their vices. They need their crutches even more in bad times, so history has shown us that tobacco and alcohol sales will remain strong.

If we look back at the spring and early summer of 2002, the U.S. stock market lost a staggering **$6.9 trillion.** Generally speaking those who were conservative and diversified their investments between stocks, bonds, and Treasury bills lost very little, while those who invested solely in stocks lost a substantial portion of their holdings.

This essentially means that in the event of a stock market crash the low-risk investments in your emergency and security buckets would be expected to do much better than those in your growth bucket, so you would want to weight your investments accordingly. This said nothing will protect us if our currency fails.

History also shows that there are definitely places not to have your money. In hard times, people can and will do without luxury items, so companies that make non-essential items, like TVs, MP3 Players, and Play Station 3 will see demand for their products fall off sharply and with the reduction in demand will come a proportional reduction in the value of their stock. History has also shown us that demand for big-ticket items, even those that we might view as necessary, like cars, washers, dryers, and refrigerators will fall sharply because, as long as they are working, people will not replace them.

It goes back to Adam Smith's definition of financial wealth as those things with **inherent value in and of themselves!** It's really quiet simple. Stocks, and bonds and, for that matter, currency are essentially just paper promissory notes. If investors lose confidence in the promise of the issuer to pay, the paper itself has no value. By contrast, no matter how bad things get, you still need a house to live in, food to eat, clothes to keep you warm, gas for your car and medicine in case you get sick. All the goods that you need because they are essential have to be manufactured, so the raw materials used to manufacture them are also essential. Finally, you still need essential services, such as medical attention, electrical and gas service, and so forth. These things are literally essential for our survival; therefore stocks or bonds offered by these companies will retain value. The currency may change and the economy may be in upheaval, but you still need essential goods and services, so they will retain value. Therefore, if you can find a way to invest in these essential goods and/or services, then you have taken an important step toward protecting your assets in the event of a stock market crash and/or currency devaluation.

ALTERNATIVE INVESTMENT STRATEGY TO HEDGE AGAINST LOSS OF YOUR WEALTH IN TIMES OF ECONOMIC CRISIS!

To put things into perspective, let's look at seven different assets and see how each might perform in the event of a stock market crash and or currency devaluation.

1. ***Currency:*** For the purpose of this example, let's assume a currency devaluation of $10 to $1. At a $10 to $1 exchange rate, $100,000 would be worth $10,000.

   The above cartoon depicts exactly what happened in post World War I Germany. Their money was essentially worthless. In this scenario, the people who had too much of their assets in cash were devastated, while the people who had less cash on hand actually fared better. This is because once the devaluation occurred, and a new currency was issued everything was more or less relative, because the cost of everything had gone down in response to the currency devaluation. If, as previously recommended, you keep no more than 5 to 10 percent of your wealth in cash you will limit your exposure.

2. ***Precious Metals:*** Gold and silver are actually commodities, because they can be used as raw material in the manufacture of finished goods. Given this, they do have intrinsic value in and

of themselves. They are also generally considered to be a hedge against economic downturn. For this reason, their value can fluctuate drastically as people rush to them for security. This creates both a problem and an opportunity. Any time the market senses a problem, the value of gold and silver go up, so on the surface it would appear that in the event of an economic upheaval they serve to protect your wealth, and they do, at least in the short run. The problem is that as soon as the public feels the crisis is over the flight to precious metals ends as abruptly as it started and prices fall accordingly. Therefore, if you get caught holding too much of these commodities you can take a financial bath. There can be another problem as well. For example, in the aftermath of the crash of 1929, America had a currency devaluation. The government called in the currency and reissued new currency. The problem was it had to get the public's buy-in as to the value of the new currency, so the government backed it with gold and silver. The only catch was that the government didn't have enough gold and silver to back the new currency, so the government made it illegal for private citizens to own gold or silver. Safety deposit boxes were seized and people's gold and silver were confiscated and they were given currency in exchange.

NOTE: None of us know what the government is going to do, but for my part I do not trust them. There is no way of knowing if the government will call in the gold and silver. There is one other possibility which we have not discussed. There is the possibility that they might capitalize on a currency collapse to force us into a paperless system, but in any event you still want to hedge your bets with some gold and silver if you can. Over the last several years gold has gone from around $300 to $1,000 an ounce so unfortunately if you haven't already bought it is too late for the average American.

3. *Coins:* Historically, a devaluation of the currency only affects paper currency, not coins. This is because most people don't generally keep much change on hand. Also, relative to the amount of currency in circulation, it's too costly to mint new coins. This said, let's say you had $1,000 in change and the currency was devalued $10 to $1 as in the previous example. If the government

doesn't call in the coins, they would have a relative increase of $10 to $1 so $1,000 in coins would, relatively speaking, be worth $10,000 in buying power. By comparison if you had the same $1,000, but it was in currency that was called in and reissued at $10 to $1, you would get back $100. In simple terms, an ounce of prevention is worth a pound of cure. I keep a five-gallon jar of quarters and dimes in a safe place just in case. I know I don't get any interest on this money, but it makes me sleep better at night and that is more important to me. I hasten to add; I see currency devaluation as inevitable. As to when it will occur that depends on a lot of variables. The more debt the U.S. incurred the more likely devaluation will occur. As I have said before there is a limit as to how much U.S. debt the rest of the world will underwrite.

We also have to consider the possibility that the U.S. dollar will at some point in time be replaced with the Amero which is a combined U.S., Canadian and Mexican currency. See my book <u>Modern Slavery</u> for more on this subject. If we go to the Amero it is more likely that they will call in the coins than if we stay with a U.S. currency. This said there are no certainties in uncertain times, but none the less I don't think you have much to loose by keeping some coins on hand as a hedge against a devaluation of the dollar.

4. *Raw Material Commodities:* A commodity has intrinsic value in and of itself because it is a raw material used in the manufacture of finished goods. In addition, the government can't easily call in commodities and exchange them the way it can currency. Because of this, holding commodities is a means of transitioning wealth during an economic upheaval. Say you had 10,000 barrels of oil. The government can't very easily call in your oil, so when the devaluation is over and a new currency has been reissued, you still have your 10,000 barrels of oil you, which you can sell. The cost per barrel may have dropped, but the relative value of the oil will have remained constant because it was not turned in and exchanged for some lesser quantity. So your assets have bridged the economic restructuring, and your relative wealth has been retained. The unfortunate thing here is that most of us don't own any oil wells, natural gas wells or other large quantities of commodities so it begs the question:

How can the public practically invest in raw material/commodities as a hedge against economic crisis? The answer is really quiet simple. We can buy stocks in those companies that do own lumber, coal, iron, gas, oil, iron, aluminum, and so forth.

However, it is important to note that history shows that not all commodities will perform equally. For example natural gas and oil are more or less necessities and would be expected to do well. By contrast, coal is used primarily in industry so if heavy manufacturing declined as would be expected the demand for coal would likewise fall. Lumber, iron and aluminum would likewise be expected to fall, because manufacturing and new construction would be expected to fall. Nothing can be manufactured without raw materials, so though the value of companies that own commodities would likely go down in the event of a stock market crash, they are much less likely to go off the boards than companies who manufacture products that are non-essentials. The key to economic survival is to stay in the game. It's like high stakes poker. As long as you are in the game you have a shot at taking it all. The point is that everything is cyclical. What goes down eventually goes back up, that is unless it goes off the board, in which event all bets are off and you lose, pure and simple.

5. ***Stocks and Other Portfolio Investments:*** It's impossible to predict with any accuracy how much a given stock would go down in the event of a stock market crash, but the key is to be invested in stocks that stay on the board so that eventually you can recoup your losses. An astute professional investor can make money in a down market as well as an up market, so he could quite possibly get rich in the face of currency devaluation and its impact on the stock market. On the other hand, the average American who has his/her money invested in a defined contribution retirement program isn't an expert investor. He/She has likely been advised to "invest in mutual funds, diversify and hold for the long run." As we saw earlier, this type of diversification does provide some protection, but you are not likely to make money in a stock market crash with this strategy. However, you will hopefully stay on the board, so you can recoup your losses when the market comes back up.

You can hedge your risk by investing some of your GROWTH money in stocks of companies that supply products that are essential. For example, we need to eat, so a company like Proctor and Gamble is probably a safe bet. Similarly, we need medicine, so stocks like Walgreen's, CVS Rx, and Baxter and Abbott Labs might also be safe bets. More so than the individual company, what is important is what it manufactures. So, in essence, I recommend investing in toilet paper, soap, medical supplies, and companies that make products that are considered "necessities." This is because historically no matter what happens to the economy, there will still be a demand for these types of products where there may not be a demand for luxury items. **Demand drives value.** Therefore, it follows that the stocks of those companies that manufacture necessities will fare better than the stocks of those companies that manufacture luxury items. (Again I am not making recommendations. These are only examples.)

Also, having U.S. savings bonds and T-bills in your portfolio (per the recommendations for your emergency and security buckets) substantially reduces your risk. This is because if you have U.S. savings bonds and T-bills they are backed by the government. So, in anything short of a collapse of the government, your money is protected.

6. *Your Home:* In the event of a currency devaluation, the value of your home would decline based on the law of supply and demand. The devaluation may or may not be proportional to the exchange rate for the currency, but in any event the value of your home would decline substantially. Having said this, I would reiterate that your home is not an investment. It is not an asset. It is simply the place you reside. Given this, investing a lot of money in a residence is contrary to the rules of wealth building. Nevertheless, if at all possible, you want to have your home paid for.

7. *Real Estate Investment Property:* More millionaires have been made in real estate than any other field and more people put their money in real estate for safe keeping than any other place! This said, I believe it is a wise decision to put a portion of your assets

in real estate as a means to transition it through times of economic crisis. Prices have fallen drastically and depending on future events they might fall even more but unlike stocks real estate serves a function and will therefore retain value. Additionally real estate has tax benefits and **cash flow benefits** which are valuable even in a down turn economy. Just like your personal residence, the value of your real estate investment portfolio would decline, probably markedly. However, like any commodity, real estate has intrinsic value so it can allow you to bridge times of economic crisis with your wealth intact. Say, for example, if you had 10 rental properties pre-devaluation, you would still have 10 rental properties post-devaluation, so your "relative wealth" has been retained. The fair market value of your holdings will be appreciably less, but so what? What is important is that in "relative post-devaluation dollars" your rental income remains unchanged, which means your standard of living is unchanged. **Note:** In the event of a major economic downturn such as we are in **you do not want to be over leveraged,** because it could get you in trouble.

In the above examples, the hedge investments discussed allow you to not only survive an economic crash, but also to retain your relative level of wealth. They could even allow you to actually emerge from the economic crisis wealthier than you entered.

If for argument's sake I am wrong and the dollar does not collapse, the investment strategies that I have outlined are still sound. If, on the other hand, I am correct, my strategies will protect your wealth and allow you to bridge any economic crisis with your wealth intact.

CHAPTER 11

DIVERSIFY YOUR INCOME!

What would you do if you went into work tomorrow and found out you were being laid off? Even worse, what would you do if you got into an automobile accident and couldn't work for six months to a year? The real question is, if an unexpected emergency of any kind hit, would you be okay financially, or would you quickly be in financial trouble? Would the bill collectors be knocking at the door? Would you lose your home? In other words, would it be an inconvenience or would it be a catastrophe of monumental proportion?

If you don't have at least six months of living expenses (preferably one year) in the bank, you are at high risk in the event of an unforeseen financial setback. Unfortunately, most people don't have adequate savings to protect them from life's ups and downs and peaks and valleys. Things never stay up forever, so we need to have a contingency plan for what to do when one of life's valleys hits.

That is exactly why you need a financial plan, and as part of that plan you should have a security nest egg of 6 to 12 months of income. Equally important, you should have more than one revenue stream, so if one revenue stream, say your job, is lost, you have others to fall back on, so the loss of your job though not a good thing is not a catastrophe.

Going forward we need to consider reducing our dependency on the government and the corporations and learn to be responsible for our own financial security. Until recently most of us considered working as an employee to be safer and more secure than being in business for ourselves. Globalization has changed all that. Our jobs are not nearly as secure as they once were. Every time you turn on the TV or open a newspaper you hear about another merger, or acquisition, or a company that is downsizing or outsourcing, or being negatively impacted in some way. America is losing jobs to China and India, and due to our trade deficits there is a flight of capital from America to foreign markets. All of this is destabilizing our job market. As a result we are well advised to have an alternate source of income, so if we loose our job we still have income.

Some of you may see this as an opportunity to start your own business, but others of you may have absolutely no interest in owning a business. You may not want to be in business for yourself, but like it or not you need to explore alternate sources of income, so you are not totally dependent on your job. In this day and age there are all types of opportunities for part-time, at-home businesses. As an example I recently had a garage sale, and an older lady came by and made several purchases. I noticed that she was very specific about what she wanted. As it turned out, she was looking for collector items, which she purchased and turned around and sold on EBay. I didn't think much about it, but as we got to talking I realized she had a real business. She was averaging $6000 a month as a retired grandmother. Another guy I know buys used CDs and sells them on the Internet. He makes pretty good money too.

The question is whether there is something you like to do that you could turn into a side business in order to make some extra money. I know several tradesmen who make some serious money buying distressed properties and fixing them up and either selling them or renting them out. They generally got their seed money by doing side jobs and putting all the money away in order to get the money to buy their first property. There is a family in my neighborhood that purchased a used air compressor for a few hundred dollars and put out flyers, offering to blow out people's sprinkler systems in the fall. They got a ton of business and as fate would have it their little side business saved them from financial ruin. He lost his job that winter and the money from the side business carried them through till he got another job. I know another man who was a tool and die maker, and he could see that business was slowing down as more and more work was going overseas to China. With very little capital investment, he started a pest-control company on the side. He eventually lost his job, but by the time he did it was okay, because he was actually making more at his side business than he was from his regular job. I could go on, and on and on, but you get the idea.

THE FIVE WAYS TO MAKE MONEY AND BUILD WEALTH

1. *Portfolio Investments: (Paper Assets)* Regardless of my concerns about the collapse of the stock market, there is a place in every-one's retirement program for selected portfolio investments. See Chapter 9.

2. *Business: (manufacturing, marketing, delivery of products and services)*

   This does not mean you have to be an employee. You could choose to start your own business. If you do you will need expertise, con-tacts, some money and a well-thought-out plan.

3. *Intellectual Property:* This includes patents and copyrights. It's the domain of inventors, writers and musicians. The beauty of intellectual property is that it creates on-going annuity revenue streams. If we truly think about it, every product ever made, every book ever written, and every song ever sung originated as an "idea," so this is the domain of creativity where our ideas are made manifest. Chances are at some point in your life you have had an idea that could have made you rich and you didn't act on it. Do you have any ideas now that could make you rich? You probably do!

4. *Real Estate Investing:* More millionaires have been made in real estate than in any other field, and more millionaires put their money in real estate for safe keeping than in any other invest-ment.

5. *The Internet:* This delivery system levels the playing field between big corporations and individual entrepreneurs. You don't need a brick-and-mortar building. You don't need manufacturing capability; all you need is a product or service and the ability to effectively reach your target market with a compelling reason to buy from you. The potential is almost unlimited.

If you want to protect your financial future, you are well advised to look at these five vehicles for "wealth building" and ask yourself if one or more of these wealth-building vehicles attracts you. Is there anything that sparks your imagination, anything that you think you would love doing? If you find something you truly love, it's not work; it's joy. For me it's writing. It's a joy to do something I love, something that helps others and something I would do for the sheer pleasure of it. Is there something that strikes a similar chord with you? If so, you will find the meaning of true freedom.

CHAPTER 12

WHY REAL ESTATE IS A WEALTH-BUILDING VEHICLE IN ANY MARKET!

"Every person who invests in well selected real estate in growing sections of a prosperous community adopts the surest method of becoming independent for real estate is the basis of wealth."
                                                    –Theodore Roosevelt

If you want to be among the 5 percent of Americans who retire well off, you not only want to own a home, but also have it paid off by the time you retire. You will still of course have taxes and upkeep, but you will be out from under the interest payments, which are generally the largest expense. In the next chapter I will tell you how you can:

■   Pay off your home and be mortgage free in as little as 8 to 11 years.

■   Take the money you save in interest payments and put it to work to make you wealthy.

You can retire wealthy on your current income if you know how, which I will show you, but first you need to understand the basics of why real estate is a wealth-building vehicle.
    In order to understand the power of real estate as a wealth-building and protection vehicle, it is necessary to understand the basic principles that underpin the U.S. tax structure. Robert Kiyosaki, in his best

selling book, *Rich Dad Poor Dad*, coined the term first, second, and third class money. According to Mr. Kiyosaki:

- **First-class money** is tax-deferred money on real estate taxed at 0 percent!

- **Second-class money** is tax-deferred capital gains money taxed at 15 percent!

- **Third-class money** is immediately taxed money from your salary taxed at 50 percent!

NOTE: Third-class money is the earned income from your job. It's taxed when you get your paycheck and taxed again each time you spend the money until on average you are taxed at 50 percent.

First-class money (0 percent tax-deferred money from real estate)

First-class money is actually tax-deferred capital gains money that is normally taxed at 15 percent, but in this instance the 15 percent capital gains tax is deferred for as long as the taxpayer chooses. He can choose to defer the tax indefinitely. He can even choose to set up a family trust and pass his property on to his children without ever having incurred tax consequences. The taxpayer is able to take the 15 percent profit from his investment and, instead of giving it to the government, reinvest it with zero tax consequences. This is the money you're taxed least on, at 0 percent. This capital gains tax deferment is granted to real estate, royalties and intellectual properties. In the instance of real estate, the tax deferment is done through what is called a "1031 like kind exchange." (More on this subject later.)

Why do you suppose the government allows this 0 percent money? The answer is because the government feels it is in the best interest of the economy to do so. The government is mandated, by its constituents, we the American citizens, to provide among other things, jobs and a robust economy so the citizenry can maintain a high standard of living.

So, how does the government create jobs? Royalties and intellectual property are the fruits of creative endeavors. They essentially start with an idea and the next thing you know Bill Gates has revolutionized the computer, changed our lives, and created untold wealth and lots and lots and lots of jobs. That's obviously good for the economy.

Likewise, Baxter or other pharmaceutical companies create a wonder drug that saves millions of lives and generates lots of money and lots of jobs. These endeavors have to be underwritten, in the form of tax incentives, or these modern creative marvels would never come about and we would all be intellectually and economically poorer.

Where does real estate come in? Why is the government willing to underwrite investment in real estate? Real estate stokes the engine of the economy like nothing else can. It creates a domino effect that triggers spending, growth, expansion and prosperity! For example, following the events of September 11, 2001, the American economy went into recession. It was still recovering from the collapse of the dot-coms and the corporate scandals of Enron and other companies, whose accounting practices were being questioned. In order to pull the economy out of recession, the government lowered interest rates to 1.1 basis points. The last time interest rates were that low was during World War II. The real-estate market responded with one of the strongest, most sustained real-estate booms in history. People bought homes like wildfire. They bought appliances, furniture, drapes, paint, and so forth. All of that buying created jobs and fueled the recovery of the American economy.

The recession aside, the government always wants real estate investors to be willing to buy property. And that's why it allows them to defer their capital gains and reinvest the profits with absolutely no tax consequences. They also want investors to improve and maintain their properties, so they allow them to depreciate the property. Imagine this, you have a property that is appreciating in value and in addition it has a positive cash flow, or in other words you are making a profit. Since the government wants to encourage you to keep the property up, it allows you to depreciate the improvements. Or, in other words, they give you a tax break on your gain, rather than having you pay taxes on it. Put another way, the government is letting you make a profit and counting it as a loss. Sweet! It doesn't get much better than that!

Second-class money: (15 percent tax-deferred money from capital gain)

Second-class money is comprised of paper assets, such as stocks, bonds, and T-bills, which are taxed at the 15 percent capital gains rate.

So again, why would the government be so generous as to allow this tax break? Though the government established Social Security to provide a safety net, it was not intended to provide 100 percent of the recipients' incomes during retirement. The government wants to encourage people to invest in stocks, bonds and other paper assets as a vehicle for retirement and in order to fund corporate growth. It knows that if it takes too much out of our profits, we won't be motivated to invest, so the government restrains itself.

The government also wants to encourage us to invest in stocks, bonds, T-bills and other paper assets, because it wants to fund such things as municipal utility projects, its debt service and, most important, it wants to keep a steady supply of money going into the corporations in order to create jobs and fuel the economy.

Third-class money: (50 percent immediately taxed money from your paycheck)

Third-class money comes from your paycheck, where it is **immediately taxed** when you receive your salary and again each time you spend money. Because there is no tax deferment on this class of money, it is the most heavily taxed of the three classes of money. The cumulative tax on this third-class money is generally in the range of 50 percent. This is because you are taxed when you get your paycheck, when you spend it on the things you need, when you save it, when you invest it, and when you die your estate is taxed as well. As they say the only two things you can't avoid are death and taxes.

So why does so much of the tax burden fall on the average American? Why do we wage earners have to pay the highest taxes of any of the three classes of money? First of all, we are all wage earners, whether we are a CEO, an entrepreneur like Bill Gates, a doctor, a lawyer, or a factory worker. We are all wage earners. **The tax rate we pay is driven by where we are in the wealth-building process.** Zero percent and 15 percent money create jobs and fuel the economy. You could argue that when we spend our 50 percent money on consumer goods we create jobs. To an extent that is a valid argument. But our salaries do not in and of themselves create wealth. They are the result of the wealth-building process that has funded our salary. In reality, our salaries are a debit, because every dollar paid as salary by a corporation is a dollar that won't drop to the bottom line as profit! As I said a moment ago, we are all wage earners so we all get paid the 50 percent money that comes from earning a salary. However, we don't all earn 15 percent and 0 percent money because not all of us have portfolio assets, nor do we have investment property or intellectual property.

So what's wrong with third-class (50 percent) money? Those of us who only receive 50 percent money from a salary are at a real disadvantage. We are forced to make our consumer purchases with after-tax dollars. In other words, we are taxed on our salary and then taxed again when we spend what is left. There is no leverage in this scenario. We don't have any employees to earn money for us. If we save or invest, we are using 50 percent after-tax dollars, which are the highest taxed of the three classes of money. We do not create any annuity revenue stream to generate future wealth. **We simply get a day's pay for a day's work!** That's a sure fire way to be one of 95 percent of Americans who never realize their retirement dreams!

So, what's wrong with 15 percent capital gains money? It's the second-highest taxed class of money. It's based on your portfolio assets, which float with the stock market so the income it generates can fluctuate with the changes in interest rates and stock performance. In addition, if you don't have enough 15 percent money to live on, you will have to retire on a **declining annuity retirement program,** which may see you live longer than expected, or see your portfolio decline in value, leaving you destitute. Remember, this is where most of the population's retirement funds are held. They are parked out of their control, being controlled by others. Sounds risky to me! Though 15 percent money is better than 50 percent money, it's nowhere as good as 0 percent money!

Why the first-class (0 percent) money of real estate is a wealth-building vehicle!

1) ***Real estate allows optimal leverage.*** Say you wanted to buy $250,000 in stock. How much money would you need? The answer is $250,000, because you can't generally leverage a stock purchase. (The exception being the commodities market where speculative items like gold, silver, grain futures, and pork bellies are bought on margin) With just $50,000 of your own money, you could reasonably purchase a $250,000 investment/rental property.

You put 20 percent down ($50,000) and leverage $200,000, using the bank's money. Now, let's say the stocks went up $25,000. Congratulations, you just made a 10 percent return on your $250,000 investment. Now lets say you made the same $25,000 on the property you purchased using $200,000 of the bank's money. Your return on your investment would be 50 percent, because you only used $50,000 of your own money. Put another way, your leveraged real estate purchase provided a return that was 5 times higher than the stock purchase. Put yet another way, for the stock purchase to have yielded the same return as your real-estate purchase, it would have had to yield $125,000 in profit. When you sell the stocks at a profit of $25,000 how much do you owe the government? The answer is 15 percent or $3,750, so in reality you did not make $25,000. You actually made only $21,250. Now, let's say you made the same $25,000 on the property you purchased. How much do you owe the government? The answer is $0. You can do a 1031 **like kind exchange** and defer your tax consequences. Put another way, your $50,000 leveraged real-estate purchase has returned its original investment plus $25,000, so you now have $75,000 to invest with 20 percent down, allowing you to purchase a $375,000 property. Now you see why real estate is a wealth-building vehicle?

Also, unlike the 50 percent money from your paycheck, the 0 percent money of real estate often requires little of your time or effort, because it is simply the leverage from an investment that has generated a profit. It is profits you were able to keep and reinvest without paying the government its 15 percent capital gains, because you have chosen to defer the tax. You simply do a 1031 like kind exchange that allows you to defer your tax consequences as long as you purchase other investment property of equal or greater value than the real estate you just sold.

NOTE: The Government has very specific requirements for how a 1031 is transacted. You need to hire an "intermediary" to hold and disburse the funds from the transaction. The intermediary may be an attorney or an employee of an exchange company. From the time you close on the property you are selling, you have a maximum of 180 days to identify and close on a new property or else your tax deferment is not allowed. I strongly recommend that if you are considering a 1031 exchange contacting a professional intermediary for legal assistance. Many banks have 1031 Exchange Departments, or can refer you to a reputable exchange company.

2) *Real estate provides asset management:* A 1031 exchange can also help real-estate investors to be able to optimally manage their assets. Say, for example, if I have a property in an area that I believe is topping out in terms of appreciation. Say that this was a property I had a substantial amount of equity in. Let's assume I was in a position to sell the property for a $500,000 profit. The potential tax consequences on this transaction, based on 15 percent capital gains, would be $75,000. This is enough to make me think twice about selling the property. But, by using a 1031 exchange, I can move my money from this property to a new property in an area that is experiencing faster appreciation and/or to a property that would yield higher cash flow and incur no capital gains. This is an example of managing my assets so that they yield the highest possible return. I have a "leveraged asset" that I am able to sell and "reinvest the profits" without any tax consequences. This is the quintessential definition of asset management, which in turn, is what wealth building is all about!

3) *Real estate provides hands-on control.* Real estate gives an investor much more hands-on control than other investments. Say you have $100,000 in the stock market. Is there anything you can personally do to increase the value of your asset? No! You can choose to sell the stocks, but that's about the only control you have. And if you did sell it, you would have to pay capital gains.

By contrast, there are many ways you can substantially increase the value of your real estate. For example, you could:

- Buy a property in need of light or extensive "rehabbing," and you could fix it up and increase its value.

- Fix up a four flat and then raise the rents which would, in turn, raise the value of the property. To give you an idea of how this would work, let's say you raise the rent $100 in each unit. That's $400 a month or $4,800 a year extra income. Because of the additional $4,800 annual income, the property would probably go up about $48,000, (based on a 10 percent capitalizing rate).

■ Increase the value of the property by changing the use of the property. Say, for example, you purchased a piece of vacant land in Florida, where the weather is nice year-round. Now say there are a lot of low-income retirees in the area. You could get the property re-zoned and put in a trailer park, which could potentially have a much greater value than the vacant land. I could go on and on, but suffice it to say.

4) **With real estate you have control over your asset, and you have many ways to increase the value of your asset**! This is not the case with most non-real estate assets!

5) **Real estate often allows you to buy below market value.** For example; any time the seller is driven by an event outside his control he is likely motivated to sell the property as quickly as possible, which generally means at below market value. The following are some examples:

■ **FORECLOSURE:** Given current market conditions there are tons of foreclosures.

■ **TAX LEAN**: Likewise you can pick up properties cheap at tax sales. This is a little complicated and is not recommended for a novice investor.

■ **SHORT SALE:** Willing to sell below fair market value in order to avoid foreclosure.

■ **DIVORCE:** Need to liquidate.

■ **ESTATE SALE:** Out-of-state siblings anxious to liquidate property.

■ **ELDERLY:** Quick sale due to going into nursing home.

- **RUNDOWN PROPERTY:** Can be purchased below market value, fixed up, and sold for a profit.

- **TRANSFEREE:** Has two mortgages and needs to get out from under one of them.

As property owners are painfully aware, real-estate values have been under pressure since approximately 2006 and in 2008 the bubble burst resulting in a nation-wide drop in housing values. In some areas prices have dropped 30-50%. Even though this has made investing in real estate look on the surface to be less attractive, this may not actually be the case. For example, say you have a property to sell, and it sells for less than the expected amount. The low sales price could be offset by you being able to pick up another property at an equally low or lower price. In this instance, the price issue is a wash. Likewise, say you are picking up an investment property that you intend to rent. If you were able to pick up the property at a depressed price that would make the property easier to cash flow, so again what looks bad isn't necessarily the case. There are even instances where selling or renting a property at a loss can even be an advantage. Wealthy people use real estate to offset their federal tax obligations, so there are instances where losing money in a real-estate transaction can be a good thing.

Regardless of whether real-estate prices are appreciating, stagnant or actually declining there are reasons to invest in real estate. One primary reason that the truly wealthy park their money in real estate for safe keeping is that real estate is historically much less volatile than stocks, which can loose 100 percent of their value. This is especially true for stocks in luxury items that people can do without in hard times. Conversely, everyone needs a place to live. The real problem with real estate is that it is not typically a liquid asset. In the next chapter I will show you how to get around that problem.

6) *Real estate allows you to refinance the property and keep the asset.* With most investments, the only way you can get your money out is to liquidate the asset. For example, the only way

you can get your money out of stocks is to sell them and pay capital gains taxes. With real estate, you can refinance the property and keep the asset. This has several advantages. For example, you get money for which you have expended little time or labor. All you did was refinance to tap into your equity. Say you refinance a property and get $60,000 out of it. How much would you have to pay the government in taxes? "NOTHING!" You get $60,000 and you pay no taxes. By contrast, if you earned $60,000 or sold 60,000 worth of stocks you would most definitely have tax consequences. This means that the money from your refinance is yours to spend with no tax consequences. They are tax-free dollars you can invest or spend any way you choose. Finally, your interest payments, closing costs and property taxes are tax deductions, so you win all the way around.

7) ***Real estate generates both income and appreciation.*** Other than stocks, most financial investments generate income or appreciation. Real estate generates both income and appreciation, which is one of the reasons it outperforms most investments and is an excellent retirement vehicle.

8) **Real estate provides substantial tax advantages.** For example, you are able to:

   ■ Deduct closing costs the year they are incurred.

   ■ Deduct mortgage interest payments.

   ■ Depreciate the property.

   ■ Defer capital gains on the sale of a property through a 1031 like kind exchange.

   ■ Get tax credits on historic buildings. Tax credits are even better than tax deductions, because they come right off the top.

9) **Real estate provides lower risk than most investments.** For a variety of reasons, real estate is generally a lower risk than most other investments.

   ■ Stock prices vacillate up and down and can quickly lose most or all of their value.

■ Real estate by contrast historically goes up and down much more slowly and holds its value much better. In addition, it always retains some value because at a minimum the land has value.

■ Rental property enjoys monthly income and substantial tax benefits, which make it a lucrative investment even if it does not appreciate as expected.

In summary real estate is the consummate wealth-building vehicle because:

■ It yields the investor 0 percent tax-deferred money.

■ It's taxed the least of any of the three classes of money. (0 percent, 15 percent and 50 percent)

■ It provides optimal leverage. You are able to use other people's, particularly the banks' money.

■ It facilitates asset management, because the investor can control his asset; he can manage it so it achieves the highest possible return in the shortest possible time.

■ It allows hands-on control of the asset, so the investor has the ability to substantially increase the value of his asset.

■ It can be purchased below market value, thus providing immediate equity.

■ The investor can refinance the property to pull out equity and still keep the asset.

■ It generates both monthly income and appreciation.

■ It offers substantial tax advantages.

■ It's a lower risk than most investments.

For all these reasons, real estate is the ideal investments to build wealth! It is the ideal place to put your wealth to protect it! And it should clearly be an investment option for the 5 percent of Americans who intend to RETIRE WELL OFF!

CHAPTER 13

OWN A HOME AND PAY IT OFF BEFORE YOU RETIRE!

How to pay off your house in as little as 8 to 11 years and why this is the key to financial security

Imagine the freedom you would have if your home was paid off!
What would you do? Where would you go? Who could you help? What dreams could come true? Just let your mind run free. Are you on vacation on a Caribbean Island with the soft trade winds blowing in your hair? Are you taking a romantic walk along the beach with the stars as your canopy? Are you on a cruise ship headed to some exotic port? Perhaps you are just relaxing on your patio about to have your kids and grandkids over for a family barbecue, and all the sudden it hits you. You just made your last mortgage payment. Your home is paid off. For perhaps the first time in your life you are in control. Perhaps for the first time in your life you don't have to worry. You can just sit back, relax and, enjoy those that you love. Wouldn't that be just a little like experiencing heaven on earth? Don't just dream about it. Let me show you how your dreams can come true. As unbelievable as it may sound, I will show you how you can pay off your home **"FREE AND CLEAR"** in as little as 8 to 11 years and in the process save tens of thousands if not hundreds of thousands of dollars in interest payments. Even more unbelievable, I will show you how it can be done on your current income without negatively impacting your current life style. Finally, I will show you how you can take all that money you

saved in interest payments and invest it in order to retire in comfort. Before you finish this chapter you will know how to accomplish all these things. However, before I can do that I have to correct some important misconceptions about home ownership.

Who owns your home—you or the bank?

Flash back to when you first bought your home. Do you remember how excited you were? You could hardly contain yourself. You had realized the American Dream. You were a home owner!

Or were you? Or are you? If your home isn't paid off **"free and clear,"** you don't own anything. The bank owns your home and you don't realize it, but you are the bank's "indentured servant". You have a mortgage, and the bank owns the house. *You just got a 30-year sentence of indentured servitude. Would you like to get an early parole? Say 19 or 20 years early.* Wouldn't that be wonderful! Just imagine the wealth you could build if your home was paid for in 10 years and you could *"divert your mortgage payments into savings."* Just imagine how it would feel to not have any financial worries. Wouldn't life be a lot sweeter?

The key to wealth is to own a home and pay it off before you retire!

It's an unfortunate fact but, for a variety of reasons that we will explore, most people will never pay off their homes, even fewer will be debt free and still fewer will ever have financial security. What a shame. If you want to be among the 5 percent of Americans who retire comfortably with no financial worries, you need to not only own a home, but also you need to have it paid off by the time you retire. You will still of course have taxes and upkeep, but you will be out from under the interest payments, which are generally the largest portion of most people's mortgage payments.

Most Americans have no idea how much money their 30-year mortgage is actually costing them. If they did they would be highly motivated to pay it off as soon as possible. A 6 percent interest rate may not sound too bad, especially when compared to a credit card that could be as much as 18 to 30 percent. *But, in actuality, a 30-year mortgage is a 30-year sentence of indentured servitude designed to keep you poor and make the bankers rich.*

WHY YOUR 30-YEAR MORTGAGE IS A 30-YEAR POVERTY SENTENCE!

A Conventional Loan (first mortgage) is what is known as a "close-end loan." A closed end loan:

- *Is amortized,* which means it is for a specified period, such as a 3- or 5-year adjustable arm or a 15- or 30-year fixed rate mortgage.

- *It is front-end loaded,* which means that initially and for the first several years the vast majority of your mortgage payment goes to interest with only a small amount going to principal. In addition, the principal contribution increases minimally from month to month.

- *Allows only one payment per month* to be applied to principal, which restricts your ability to make extra payments in order to pay down your interest on an accelerated schedule.

- *Is based on the average monthly balance*, which means you cannot affect the amount of interest due each month. Interest is derived solely from where you are on the amortization table.

- *Allows only a one-way flow of money,* which means that you can make payments, but as principal accumulates you cannot tap into your equity.

In the context of what you have just learned about a conventional loan, consider the following situation. There are three home owners who all work at the same company; they all get laid off on the same day. The first person has 10 percent equity in his home, the second has 50 percent equity and the third has 75 percent. Who will be more likely to borrow money against the equity in his home in order to pay his monthly bills until he gets a new job, person 1, person 2 or person 3? Sorry, this is a trick question. The answer is that none of them will likely be able to borrow any money. This brings us to the first misnomer.

- *The 1st Misnomer: is that "you borrow against collateral" in this instance "the equity in your home."* If this were the case the person with 75 percent equity would be in an excellent position to borrow all the money he needed, but it is not the case. The reality of the situation is that "you borrow against your income," so if you have no income you most likely won't get a loan.

Now let's look down the road nine months later at these same three people and assume that none of them have been able to get a job. They have gone through their savings and are all three months behind on their mortgage payments. The bank is after all of them for back payments. Which one of the people is most likely to be foreclosed on; the one with 10 percent equity, the one with 50 percent equity or the one with 75 percent equity? Who said the one with 10 percent equity? Wrong! The bank doesn't care how much equity you have. All the bank cares about is protecting their investment. So from this prospective they are actually more motivated to work with the person with either 10% or 50% equity than the one with 75%. Lets take a look at the situation from the vantage point of the bank and their profit motives. By the time you factor in late payments, real estate commissions and closing costs, if the bank sells the home with 10% equity they stand to loose a lot of money. Even the loan with 50% equity could be upside down in a situation like we are experiencing where homes in many areas have lost 30% or more of their value. If you have no income they are going to foreclose, pure and simple, but say you were a two income family so you have income, but you are coming up short each month. In such an instance the bank might be willing to work with you. They might say something like this:

"We at People First Bank have your best interest at heart. We don't want to see you lose your home, so we will do what ever we can to work with you. Perhaps we can lower your interest rate or take reduced payments until you get on your feet and we will just add what you owe us to the back end of your loan and extend the term of your loan. Aren't we compassionate?"

Compassionate my XXX!
Greed comes in many disguises!

Who said the one with 75 percent equity? Unfortunately, this is true! The one with the most equity would be most likely to be fore-closed on. Again, the motivation is that the bank is in business to make money and when push comes to shove, they have little if any compassion. Simply put **the bank can sell the home of the person with 75 percent equity substantially below fair market Value** and satisfy its board of directors. If the unlucky home owner doesn't get any money out of his house, that's just too bad. There is a saying:

> *"Owe a person a little and they own you.*
> *Owe them a lot and you own them."*

In this instance, the home owner owed the bank a little, so the bank owned him. In the first example, the home owner owed the bank a lot, so he a modicum of leverage, which points out one of the problems with a closed-end loan. The further down the amortization table you go, the more equity you build up; but, at the same time, the more the bank can hold you hostage. Imagine how it would feel to have a home with $400,000 in equity and one day you are in an auto accident and can't work for several months. Your monthly expenses are $5,000 per month so, if you could access even 80 percent of your equity you could pay all your bills for 64 months or 5.33 years, but instead you can't get your money, and you loose your home and everything you worked a lifetime to amass. Are you just a little mad? I certainly hope so!

Obama's Foreclosure Rescue Plan: Here are the general guide-lines. If you are unemployed and have no monthly income you don't qualify, not even if you have a large amount of money in savings because the plan does not take savings into consideration. It looks solely at income. Say you were a two income family and one of you lost your job so you have income, just less than previously. You may qualify. You will be asked to submit a financial statement/monthly budget, bank statements and two years income tax statements. If you qualify you could be eligible to get your interest rate reduced to as low as 2%. The key decision factor is what percent of your total income is represented by your mortgage. Originally your mort-gage could not exceed 38% of adjusted income, but that number was recently changed to 31%. Here is what I advise. Go to a local branch and get a personal banker to assist you. You will get much better rep-resentation than if you just call up the settlement department. They are swamped and generally won't take the kind of time you need to get comfortable with the program. There are companies who will represent you for a fee, but you can accomplish pretty much the same results if you go to a local branch and find someone who is willing to help you.

- ■ ***The 2nd Misnomer: is that the more equity you have in your home the more security you have.*** Actually, the converse is true. The more equity you have, the less security you have, because the more equity you have the more leverage the bank has over you. There is a very simple solution to this problem but before you can do anything to solve a problem, you first have to be aware of the problem. That is why they say:

"Knowledge is Power"

In this case the knowledge you need is to know how to turn your ***(closed-end)*** conventional first mortgage, which is an "***illiquid asset***" that does not allow you access to your equity into an ***(open-end)*** loan, which is a "***liquid asset***" that allows you access to your equity.

You do this by opening a home equity line of credit (HELOC) You want to set up the line of credit for the maximum amount the bank will allow. It doesn't cost you anything unless you use it, so it is a no-brainer. You don't even have to think about it, just do it and sit back and know that if any of life's unforeseen twist of fate come upon you, you have prepared in advance to take them in stride. This strategy goes a long way toward protecting you from unforeseen economic events beyond your control and should let you sleep better at night. For example, this addresses the problem, from our earlier example, of the man with $400,000 equity in his home who was in a car accident and unable to work. If he had done this, his home equity would have been immediately available to him. All he needed to do was write himself a check. There is no loan application and no explanation to the bank. The loan is pre-approved, so all you do is write a check and tap into the equity in your home to get you safely through your crisis. Thank you, GOD!

Back to our discussion of why your **30-year mortgage is a poverty sentence:**

With this in mind, let's take a look at the amortization table on the next page for an average American family John & Sue Smity. The table is for your reference, but the charts that follow will summarize key points that highlight why most Americans will never pay off their mortgages.

WHY MOST AMERICANS WILL NEVER PAY OFF THEIR MORTGAGES

NOTE: I have highlighted years 5, 21 and 30, because they have special significance that I will explain as we go through the charts that follow.

Mortgage Details
John & Sue Smith

Mortgage Amount	$ 200,000
Interest Rate	6 percent
Remaining Term	360
Interest Payment	$ 1,000.00
Principal Payment	$ 199.10
Escrow Amount	$ 415.00
Total Payments	$ 1,614.10

Current Debt Amortization

Year	1st Mortgage Balance	Total Debt Paid	Total Interest
1	$197,541.99	$ 2,458.01	$ 11,933.19
2	$194,936.50	$ 5,063.50	$ 23,714.90
3	$192,168.20	$ 7,831.80	$ 35,335.80
4	$189,229.13	$10,770.87	$ 46,785.93
5	$186,108.80	$13,891.20	$ 58,054.80
6	$182,796.00	$17,204.00	$ 69,131.20
7	$179,278.87	$20,721.13	$ 80,003.27
8	$175,544.81	$24,455.19	$ 90,658.41
9	$171,580.46	$28,419.54	$101,083.26
10	$167,371.60	$32,628.40	$111,263.60
11	$162,903.15	$37,096.85	$121,181.35
12	$158,159.09	$41,840.91	$130.829.49

13	$153,122.42	$ 48,877.58	$140,182.02
14	$147,775.11	$ 52,224.89	$149,223.91
15	$142,097.98	$ 57,902.02	$157,935.98
16	$136,070.69	$ 63,929.31	$166,297.89
17	$129,671.65	$ 70,328.35	$174,288.05
18	$122,877.94	$ 77,122.06	$181,883.54
19	$115,665.24	$ 84,334.76	$189,060.04
20	$108,007.66	$ 91,992.34	$195,791.66
21	$ 99,877.76	$100.122.24	$202,050.96
22	$ 91,246.43	$106.753.57	$207,808.83
23	$ 82,082,73	$117,917.27	$213,034.33
24	$ 72,353.84	$127,646.16	$217,694.64
25	$ 62,024.90	$137,975.10	$221,754,90
26	$ 51,058.88	$148,941.12	$225,178.08
27	$ 39,416.50	$160.583.50	$227,924.90
28	$ 27,056.04	$172,943.96	$229,953.64
29	$ 13,933.23	$186,066.77	$234,228.03
30	$ 0.00	$200,000.00	$231,677.04

WAIT IT GETS WORSE! FIVE-YEAR SNAPSHOT

This chart highlights the fact that after five years John and Sue have paid $71,946.08 in mortgage payments, ($13,891.20 plus $58.054.80), but only $13,891.20 has been applied to principal. You will recall that their original mortgage balance was $200,000, and five years later it is still $186,108.80.

Current Debt Amortization

Year	1st mortgage Balance	Total Debt Paid	Total Interest
1	$197,543.99	$ 2,458.01	$11,933.19
2	$194,936.50	$ 5,063.50	$23,714.90
3	$192,168.20	$ 7,831.80	$35,335.80
4	$189,229.13	$10,770.87	$46,785.93
5	$186,108.80	$13,891.20	$58,054.80

**Paid one third of original loan amount and have only
$13,891.20 in equity!**

**Over five years 80 percent of mortgage payments
go to interest!**

This punctuates exactly how little of your payment goes to principal in the early years of your loan and therefore why a 30-year mortgage is a poverty sentence.

This brings us to:

■ *The 3rd Misnomer: Moving or refinancing is no big deal!* Make no mistake it is a huge deal, and failure to understand the problem is a financial poverty sentence!

● *Why moving will keep you from ever paying off your mortgage?* With the advent of mega-corporations we have become a mobile society.

"The average American moves every five to seven years."

Unfortunately, most of us move without ever realizing the havoc it plays on our finances. Here is a familiar scene. Your boss calls you in and offers you a promotion, but the catch is you have to move. You get a raise. The company will pay your moving expenses and in some instances they will even give you a cost-of-living differential. Sounds great, doesn't it? Opportunity knocks! Pack the bags, tell the kids, and head out on a great adventure. Each year millions of American executives are faced with this very scenario. Most of them jump at the opportunity with great expectation, but some carefully weigh the cost and say no. Which one are you?

The problem is that most people don't stop to reflect on the impact of the move on their mortgage. Looking back at John and Due's scenario, after five years they had paid $71,946.00 in mortgage payments, but only $13,891.20 had been applied to the principal. In *the first five years 80 percent of their mortgage payments had gone to interest.* At that rate how will they ever pay off their home? This punctuates exactly how little of your payment goes to principal in the early years of your loan and, thus, why a 30-year mortgage is a poverty sentence. It is far more costly to move or refinance than most people ever imagine. This is all the more reason to pay your mortgage off early.

- *Why refinancing will keep you from paying off your mortgage.* Have you ever been approached to refinance? If you are like me it is a monthly event. It goes something like this. Want to get out from under those high credit card bills and gain control of your finances? There is a way! Consolidate all of your credit card debt into your mortgage and reduce your monthly bills. Sounds good to me! Get rid of my high-interest credit card debt at perhaps as much as 18 to 30 percent interest) and trade it in, in this instance for a (6 or 7 percent interest rate) and in the process reduce my monthly payments and get control of my finances! What a deal! I can get out of the pressure cooker and sleep at night. The fact of the matter is that most people who find themselves in this spot *(up to their necks in credit card debt)* are there for a reason. They got snookered by the *Madison Avenue advertising brain-washing campaign* that has turned most Americans into *consumer junkies who have been convinced that their happiness depends on having material possessions.* Their credo is:

> *"I want that; no, I have to have that, because my identity is tied to what I have and how I look."*

What a shame. Given this mentality it is no wonder that most people who refinance in order to lower their monthly bills eventually find themselves in the same fix again; up to their necks in credit card debt and having to refinance again. If you ever find yourself faced with the decision to refinance, remember:

- In first five years of your loan you pay one-third of the original loan amount but 80 percent of your mortgage payments go to interest and only 20 percent to principal.

Now you understand why the banks are all too happy to be nice and help you out from under that credit card debt by refinancing your loan. Let's not forget that they also charge you some pretty hefty refinance fees, which add insult to injury. God wants you to be free and to be able to enjoy your life. That is why he is against debt. Debt is the ultimate boat anchor!

What a shame we have been brainwashed into believing that who we are is defined by what we have and how we look! Our identity should be tied to who we are in God, who we love and how we can serve others, not material possessions.

And it shall be given unto you; good measure,
pressed down, and shaken together.
And running over, shall men give unto your bosom.
For with the same measure that ye met withal
it shall be measured to you again.
(Luke 6:30)

God wants us to have all our needs met. As a matter of fact, he promises to meet all our needs, not our wants, but our needs, not our greed. If we look at the scripture above, we see that as with every promise God gives us there is a condition. In this instance the condition is that: For with the same measure that ye met withal it shall be measured to you again (Luke 6:30), which is to say that we must give. We must serve. We must not become slaves to material possessions. We must not make money our God, because if we do we will surely be unhappy. We will always want more. We will think that if we get that, we will be happy, but we won't be, at least not but for a second. Then we will want the next thing, and the next and the next.

God does not want us to be in debt. He does not want us to be stressed out. He wants us to be able to stop and smell the roses, and He wants us to stop and reflect on what a beautiful world He has created for us. How can we do that if we are constantly stressed out over finances? God has a better plan for your life. He owns all the cattle on a thousand hills; He owns all that there ever was and ever will be; and He wants to give it to you and me.

***But God shall supply all your needs
according to his riches in glory by Christ Jesus!***
(Philippians 4:19)

Yes, He wants to give you riches, but He can't if you are in debt. Debt is a cancer that robs you of your peace, joy and happiness, and that is why God is against it.

***The rich ruleth over the poor and the borrower is
servant to the lender.***
(Matthew 6:1-12)

This book is about helping people break the bonds of financial oppression. Please heed these words and do everything you can to get your home paid for and invest for the future. With this in mind, how many years do you think it takes to pay off half of your loan on a 30-year mortgage?

21-YEAR SNAPSHOT
Current Debt Amortization

Year	1st Mortgage Balance	Total Debt Paid	Total Interest
1	$197,543.99	$ 2,458.01	$ 11,933.19
5	$186,108.80	$ 13,891.20	$ 58,054.80
21	$ 99,877.76	$100,122.24	$202,050.96

It takes 21 years to pay off half your mortgage!

As this table shows, after 21 years of making mortgage payments, John and Sue will have paid off less than half of their $200,000 original loan balance. As I will show you shortly, if they were on the accelerated payment program they would have paid off their home in 10.4 years and would own their home free and clear.

30-YEAR SNAPSHOT

Current Debt Amortization

Year	1st mortgage Balance	Total Debt Paid	Total Interest
1	$197,543.99	$ 2,458.01	$ 11,933.19
5	$186,108.80	$ 13,891.20	$ 58,054.80
21	$ 99,877.76	$100.122.24	$202,050.96
30	$0.00	$200,000.00	$231,677.04

**To pay off $200,000 loan, you pay a total of $431,677.
A 6 percent loan equates to paying 115 percent
of loan amount in interest!**

Finally, after 30 years your home is paid off, that is provided you never moved and never refinanced; otherwise you are still on the treadmill. Your 6 percent loan cost you more like 115 percent than the 6 percent you were told. In order to pay off a $200,000 loan, you ended up paying $431,677, of which $231,677 was interest. What a scam. It's no wonder the banks are rich and only 5 percent of Americans will retire comfortably. They gave their financial future to the banks and didn't even realize they were doing it. Fortunately, there is a way you can pay off your home in a fraction of the normal time. Read on.

■ *The 4th Misnomer: is that your home is guaranteed to appreciate.* Since roughly 1980 the U.S. job market has been under ever-increasing pressure from globalization, specifically from cheap labor costs in India and China. The result has been that relative to the cost of living, salaries have been flat or falling since the 1980s. Despite the falling salaries, driven by demand from the 75 million baby boomers housing prices continued to increase but it was becoming increasingly harder and harder for the average family to be able to afford home ownership. Then the events 9/11/2001 caused the bottom to fall out of both the stock market and the real estate market. The government responded by lowering interest rates to levels not seen since the early 1940s. This resulted in an overheated real-estate market, which drove prices up even higher. As if that wasn't bad enough, mortgage companies driven by greed made millions of questionable zero to 10 percent down loans, and Wall Street bundled them together into (CDO's) Collateralized Debt obligations and sold these toxic investments to unsuspecting investors all around the world. The result was the now infamous sub-prime mortgage collapse of 2008 which saw housing values in many areas fall by as much as 30-50%.

LONG-TERM REAL ESTATE PROSPECTIVE!

In my opinion the housing market will not have a significant recovery for years or decades to come.

This is because of the following considerations.

- The continued degradation of the labor market, owing to globalization will continue to create a negative delta between salaries and the affordability of houses.

- Unless unemployment is reduced we can expect significant numbers of retailers to go out of business triggering a collapse in the commercial market which will negatively impact the residential market.

- The imminent retirement of 75,000,000 baby boomers will create a glut of large expensive homes, because the generation coming up is much smaller and has less discretionary income. Thus, they cannot afford the upper-end homes of the retiring baby boomers. In addition, as the baby boomers retire they will have less discretionary income to spend to stimulate the economy.

- Finally, the American population has just about exhausted the supply of available credit and, given the long-term decline in salaries, credit spending has been a major factor in economic stimulation.

SO WHAT CAN THE AVERAGE AMERICAN DO?

In a soft market with falling prices, people who have minimal equity in their homes are put in an untenable situation where they find themselves upside down on their mortgages, which is to say they owe more on their houses than the properties are worth, especially after you factor in real-estate commissions and closing costs, which can run 6 to 10 percent of the sales prices. Couple this with a recession/depression and it is no wonder that foreclosures are at record rates. This is a serious problem and one for which there was no answer until recently.

The Mortgage Acceleration Program (MAP), which I will discuss later in this chapter, could help many people out of this catch-22 by affording them an alternative method to build equity in their homes. Let me give you an example. Say you had a home valued at $200,000 and at the peak of the real estate boom it appreciated 8 percent in a single year that would mean the home went from $200,000 to $216,000, and the owner's equity increased by $16,000.

Now, let's assume that in 2009 the same house has zero appreciation. In this instance, you might assume that your equity would remain constant, but that is incorrect. Whatever portion of your mortgage payment goes to principal represents your gain in equity for the year. Let's look at the amortization table below for John and Sue Smith and let's assume that they were in the first year on the table. In this instance, we see that they pay $11,933.19 in interest and accrue only $2,458.01 in principal (equity).

Mortgage Details for John & Sue Smith

Mortgage Amount	$ 200,000
Interest Rate	6 percent
Remaining Term	360
Interest Payment	$ 1,000.00
Principal Payment	$ 199.10
Escrow Amount	$ 415.00
Total Payments	$ 1,614.10

Current Debt Amortization

Year	1st Mortgage Balance	Total Debt Paid	Total Interest
1	$197,541.99	$ 2,458.01	$11,933.19
2	$194,936.50	$ 5,063.50	$23,714.90
3	$192,168.20	$ 7,831.80	$35,335.80
4	$189,229.13	$10,770.87	$46,785.93
5	$186,108.80	$13,891.20	$58,054.80

The question is: given a zero appreciation is there another way to gain more than the $2,458.01 in principal? The good news is that there is. Let's go to the next chart, and I will show you how. This is a hint of what is to come. Later in the chapter, I will show you three methods for how to accelerate principal faster than with a conventional mortgage.

Mortgage Details for Mark and Lynn Johnson

	(MAP) Mortgage Acceleration Program	Conventional Mortgage
Starting Balance	$200,000	$200,000
	Balance in 1 year $184,811 $15,189 Principal Increase	Balance in 1 year $187,534 $2,458 Principal Increase
Repayment Time	10.4 years	30 years
Total Interest Paid	$70,422	$231,677

What we see here is that, even in a zero appreciation market, with MAP, the equity in the home increased nearly as much as it had from the earlier example when there was an 8 percent market appreciation. In a flat or falling real-estate market, having a program such as MAP would keep you from going into negative appreciation, or going "upside down," and getting yourself in a position where you are unable to sell your home, because to do so would mean that you would have to take a loss. It doesn't matter whether you gain principal from market appreciation or from accelerated principal build up. At the end of the day when all is said and done, principal is principal. At last what you have been waiting for.

HOW TO PAY OFF YOUR HOME IN AS LITTLE AS ONE THIRD OF THE NORMAL TIME AND INVEST FOR THE NEXT 19.6 YEARS

Assuming that using the **Mortgage Acceleration Program (MAP)** that I will explain shortly, John and Sue were able to *pay off* *their home in just 10.4 years* and if they were to take their $2,199.10 monthly mortgage amount and invest it for the next 19.6 years they would be able to amass $994,540 @ 6%, $1,253,893 @ 8% and a whopping $1,589,535 @10%.

Which would you rather do, pay off your mortgage over 30 years or pay it off in 10.4 years and spend the next 19.6 years investing for retirement? I guess the question is rhetorical, because I can't imagine anyone wanting to go the long route if they didn't have to. You don't have to. You can do the same thing John and Sue did. Based on your unique scenario, you will have a different pay-off date than John and Sue, but it is most probable that you will be able to pay off your mortgage in one third to one half the normal time. I don't know about you, but that sounds like a good deal to me. Right about now, I am sure you are saying that this sounds too good to be true, but I assure you it isn't. As a matter of fact, it is easy and, as I promised earlier, you can do it on your current income without making any major changes to your current life style.

FINALLY, WHAT YOU HAVE BEEN WAITING FOR!

How to pay off you mortgage years early and invest for retirement!
There are three ways to accomplish this and I will cover them all.

Option 1: Automated bi-monthly payment program

This is the least effective of the three methods, but until recently it was the best option available. I present it here, because many will not be able to qualify for the other two programs initially, because they have bad credit or little to no equity in their homes. I would encourage them to go on this program now and then when they qualify go on to one of the other two programs.

The bi-monthly program is really quite simple. All you do is pay your mortgage payment every two weeks as opposed to once a month. The result is that you make 13 payments per year instead of 12. Depending on your interest rate, you will end up paying off your mortgage 5 to 10 years early. The average is 7 years. If your monthly mortgage payment was $1,500 per month and you paid it off seven years early, you would avoid $126,000 in mortgage payments, not to mention you might be able to retire sooner than planned. To calculate exactly how much earlier you could pay off your home by making bi-monthly payments, go to www.bankrate.com for free mortgage calculator.

How to automate your bi-monthly mortgage payments!

Start by asking your bank or mortgage company if they offer bi-monthly payments? If they say yes, then you have two choices as to how you automate your payments.

1st Choice: Go to www.bankrate.com and add 10 percent to your mortgage payment, i.e. current payment $1,500 then add $150 for a total monthly payment of $1,650. This is the same as making a bimonthly payment and will pay off a 30-year mortgage in 22 years. There are no set-up fees or bimonthly charges. All you do is have the 10 percent payment automatically transferred from your checking account to your mortgage account. Check with your bank to find out how they want the payment, i.e. one check for your regular mortgage payment and a second check for the extra 10 percent to be applied to principal.

2nd Choice: In this instance, you are going to use a service to automate the process for you. I suggest you ask your bank or mortgage company who they recommend. There is a one-time fee that can range from approximately $200 to $400 and a transfer fee of between $2.50 and $6.95 every two weeks. You want to be able to calculate your saving which means you need to know how much the service will cost you over the 22-year period. At $2.50 every two weeks, your cost would come to $65 per year, or $1,430 over 22-years, plus the one-time set-up fee. At $6.95 every two weeks your cost would come to $181 per year, or $3,975 over 22-years, plus the one time set-up fee. This may sound like a lot, but it isn't when compared with a savings of $126,000 per the example above.

Questions to ask the service before you decide to go with them:
1. What do you do with my money when you get it? Some companies keep the money until the end of the year and make one lump sum payment. You want a company that sends the money in immediately, so your mortgage is paid off sooner.

2. What are your set-up and transfer fees, and are there any other fees?

3. Do you provide value-added auditing services to see if the bank made any posting mistakes? Many banks will not let you make bi-monthly payments unless you use a service.

Option 2: The Australian method
They say: **"Necessity is the mother of invention,"** and that was exactly the case here. Houses in Australia are generally considerably more expensive than comparable houses in the United States. Going back about 15 years, the high cost of housing in Australia was causing a hardship on families all across the country. As an outgrowth of this problem people were looking for relief from their oppressive mortgage payments. **(Sounds like the United States today!)** The answer to the dilemma came in the form of a best-selling book, **Own Your Home Years Sooner,** which put forth the unorthodox notion that you could use a **HELOC,** with a higher interest rate than your conventional mortgage, to accelerate the pay off of your conventional mortgage and save thousands in interest. I don't know about you, but the idea of paying off a low-interest loan with a high-interest loan sounds like a pretty far-fetched idea. Some healthy skepticism might seem to be in order. But as they say, **"The proof is in the pudding."** Some 15 years after the idea's inception nearly 50 percent of the households in Australia used the approach, and on average they have been able to reduce their 30-year mortgages by 14 to 18 years.

How the Australian method works.

There are three requirements to making the program work.

1) You need to be able to qualify for a HELOC.

2) You need to spend less than you make. In other words, you need some discretionary money to periodically apply to principal-only payments.

3) You need to put all your income into the HELOC and pay all your bills out of the HELOC.

Earlier in this chapter we enumerated the fact that a conventional first mortgage is a closed-end loan. Based on the attributes of a closed–end loan it is a 30-year poverty sentence. As fate would have it, the bankers wanting to **encourage spending** created the **HELOC,** which is an **"open-end loan"**. An open-ended loan:

■ Is bi-directional, which means money can flow in and out.

■ Is based on average daily balance, which means it's simple interest and you can affect the amount of interest due each month.

■ Is not amortized, which means it is open ended and can be paid off at any time.

■ Allows multiple payments and withdrawals per-month, which means it can be used like a checking account.

When the bankers created the HELOC, I am sure they had no idea that they were creating an *"interest cancellation vehicle,"* but luckily for us they were. In and of itself an HELOC is not a debt-cancellation vehicle. What turns it into a debt-cancellation vehicle is the way you use it. Basically what you do is use your HELOC as a consolidated checking account. When you get paid, you deposit your check and from that point you use your HELOC as your checking account, *paying all your living expenses out of it.* I stress that you pay all your bills out of the HELOC, this means your mortgage payment, utility bills and all incidental bills. The longer you keep your money in the account before you pay your bills, the more efficient it is at reducing the average daily balance on the HELOC, which in turn reduces the amount of interest charged in any given month. Your contractual interest rate remains unchanged, but since you are paying interest on a smaller amount, by virtue of using the bank's money, your effective interest rate is substantially reduced. In net terms, you have created an interest-cancellation account. At this point, the effective interest rate on your HELOC, if managed correctly, should be considerably lower than the rate on your conventional closed-end loan. The next step is to use the HELOC to periodically make *principle-only payments* on your first mortgage, which will move you down the amortization table and concurrently cancel all the associated interest. In order to do this the *inflow into the HELOC has to be greater than the outflow.* This is to say that at the end of each month after you have paid your bills, you have to have some money left over. We call this left over amount your *discretionary income,* which is money that is not obligated for specific bills and can therefore accrue in the HELOC until such time that it accumulates to a point where it can be used to make a principal-only payments on your first mortgage.

I know this is confusing, so let's go through some numbers. Let's say Bill and Sharon Johnson earn $5,000 per month and their living expenses are $4,350 per month. This would mean they had a discretionary income of $650 per month, which they leave in the HELOC to accumulate to the point where they are advised, by the program, to make a principle-only payment on their first mortgage. Follow along with me on the amortization table below. Let's say on month two, Bill and Sharon made their normal mortgage payment and in addition they made a principal-only payment in the amount of $1,015.59. That is the precise amount of principal due for months three through seven. By making that principal-only payment, they would move down the amortization table to month seven and, in the process, they would cancel $4,979.91 of interest. Hopefully, you can see how if you did this three or four times a year you could substantially shorten the length of your 30-year mortgage. In the process, you save tens if not hundreds of thousands in interest.

Example of Interest Cancellation on Conventional Mortgage

Payment #	Payment Date	Interest Rate	Monthly Schedule	Principle Paid	Interest Paid	Balance
1	06/01/07	6.000	$1,199.10	$199.10	$1,000.00	$199,800.90
2	07/01/07	6.000	1,199.10	200.10	999.00	199,600.80
3	08/01/07	6.000	1,199.10	201.10	998.00	199,399.70
4	09/01/07	6.000	1,199.10	202.10	997.00	199,197.60
5	10/01/07	6.000	1,199.10	203.11	995.99	198,994.49
6	11/01/07	6.000	1,199.10	204.13	994.97	198,790.36
7	12/01/07	6.000	1,199.10	205.15	993.95	198.585.51
				$,1015.59	$4,979.91	

Making a one-time principal payment of $1,015.59 moves you down the amortization table by five months and cancels $4997.91 in interest.

Summary of Australian program:
Though the Australian program works, it was the proto model. It is a time-consuming manual procedure that requires serious discipline on the part of the user. The typical pay off with the Australian program is 14 to 18 years, which is better than the by-monthly plan, which is 23 years. Option 3, which we will discuss next, has the best pay off of all.

Option 3: The mortgage acceleration program (MAP)
The MAP is based on the same concept as the Australian program in as much as they both use a HELOC to cancel interest and achieve an accelerated pay off of your mortgage. The big difference is that MAP is computerized, which means it is easier to use and achieves a faster pay off of your home—as little as 8 to 11 years.

Let's go through a detailed example so all this starts to make more sense. Let's take a look at the financial profile for Connie Stevens, a single mom and see what using MAP means for her financial situation.

Constants for Connie Stevens:
- **1st Mortgage:** $136,000 at 5.25 percent amortized over 30 years with a monthly payment of $927.

- **HELOC:** 9.5 percent on average daily balance
  - **Monthly Budget:**
    $2,272.98 monthly income
    -$1,927.08 total expenses
    $ 345.90 discretionary income

As you recall, discretionary income is the amount of money left over each month after we pay all our bills. It is what is used to accumulate money to use to make principal-only payments. Now that you know what is at stake if you want to have extra discretionary money to apply to the principal balance on your home refer back to chapter 7 and take a look at your spending habits. Remember:
"A latte spared is a fortune earned."   –*People Magazine*

One-year snapshot with MAP
Follow along on the chart below as I walk you through Connie Steven's one-year snapshot with MAP. Column 2 below reflects the fact that from month three to four the principal contribution increased by only $0.69 per month and following the normal amortization table with no extra principal contributions it only increases a few cents

per month thereafter. However if we look at the last payment for the period (2/12/08) we see that the monthly principal contribution had increased from $156.92 to $199.92, which is an increase of $43.00. How did that happen? In column 5 we see that during the year MAP instructed Connie to make three extra principal-only payments totaling $7,796.69. (Remember Connie only had $345.90 a month discretionary income which comes to $4,159.80 per year.) So the additional $3,636.89 was borrowed from the HELOC at the direction of the MAP software. That action did three things:

1) In column 2 we see that it increased the principal contribution by a whopping $43.00 a month.

2) In column 5 we see that it also reduced the principal balance from our starting balance of $136,058 to a new balance of $126,032 for a **total principal reduction of $10,026 in just one year.** Though not reflected on the table below by following a normal amortization schedule it would take 4.7 years to reduce the principal balance by the $10,026 that the MAP software did in 1 year.

Connie Steven's One-Year Results on Map

Date	Principal	Interest	Extra Principal	Amount	Balance
2/12/08	$199.92	$552.26	$0.00	$927.08	$126,032.06
1/09/08	$199.04	$553.14	$0.00	$927.08	$126,231.98
12/10/07	$198.18	$554.00	$0.00	$927.08	$126,431.02
11/07/07	$197.31	$554.87	$0.00	$911.32	$126,629.20
10/13/07	$196.45	$555.73	$0.00	$911.32	$126,826.51
9/01/07	$195.60	$556.58	$0.00	$911.32	$127,022.96
8/07-07	$194.75	$557.43	$0.00	$911.32	$127,218.56
7/03/07	$193.90	$558.28	$0.00	$911.32	$127,413.31
7/03/07	$0.00	$0.00	$5,169.57	$5169.13	$127,607.21
6/07/07	$170.54	$581.64	$0.00	$911.32	$132,776.78
5/01/07	$169.79	$582.39	$0.00	$911.32	$132,947.32
4/30/07	$0.00	$0.00	$1.534.13	$1,534.13	$133,117.11
4/15/07	$0.00	$0.00	$1,092.99	$1,092.99	$134,651.24
4/07/07	$157.61	$594.57	$0.00	$911.32	$135,744.23
3/0307	$156.92	$956.26	$0.00	$911.32	$135,901.84
Totals	**$0.69**		**$7,796.69**		

One Year Principal Reduction of $10,126

3) Finally 4.7 years of interest was wiped out. But, rather than look
    at that amount let's jump ahead and see the results in 11.33 years.
    (See Chart Below.) Connie's mortgage is paid off and she has paid
    a total of $45,159 in combined interest between the HELOC line of
    credit and the primary mortgage. Comparing this with a conven-
    tional program, it would have taken Connie 30 years to pay off her
    home with a total interest cost of $134,726. The bottom line is that,
    with the MAP, Connie paid off her home 18.67 years early and
    saved $89,566 in interest, which she can invest toward retirement.

Connie Steven's Home Pay off Comparison \
MAP vs. Conventional Mortgage

	MAP	Conventional Mortgage
Starting Balance	$136,058	$136,058
	Balance in 1 year:	Balance in 4.7 Years:
	$126,032	$126,193
Repayment Time	11.33 years	30 years
Total Interest Paid	$45,159	$134,726

Total Interest Savings with MAP: $89,566

SUMMARY OF MAP BENEFITS

I am excited to be able to bring this kind of information to the
American People. As a nation and as individual families, we need des-
perately to get a handle on our debt before we drown in a sea of red
ink. I have presented many financial tips in this book, but I think that
the MAP system is the most powerful debt-reduction tool I have ever
come across. For perhaps the first time in our lives, we have a tool that
will allow people to have a financial speedometer and gas gauge that
will allow them to accurately understand the impact of their spending
habits and take control of their financial futures. If you can pay off your
home early and then invest what you would have spent on mortgage
payments, you have a real shot a retiring in comfort. There are several
companies which offer mortgage Acceleration software but the one I
am most familiar with is UFIRST. Visit http://www.u1stfinancial.com/
for more information on their product. Note I do not sell their software
nor do I receive any financial consideration from them.

CHAPTER SUMMARY

A conventional loan (first mortgage) is a 30-year sentence of indentured servitude, because it is a closed-end loan which means it:

- **Is amortized:** interest is charged solely based on where you are on the amortization table.

- **Is front-end loaded:** for the first several years the vast majority of your mortgage payment goes to interest, and principal contribution increases minimally month to month.

- **Allows only one payment per-month:** this restricts your ability to make extra payments.

- **Is based on the average monthly balance:** which means you cannot affect the amount of interest due each month.

- **Allows only a one-way flow of money:** which means that you can make payments, but as principal accumulates you cannot tap into your equity.

There are four misnomers about home ownership. They are:

1) **That you can borrow against collateral, in this instance, the equity in your home.** Unless you have secured liquid assets you borrow against your **income, not your assets,** which simply put means no job, no loan.

2) **That the more equity you have in your home the more security you have.** Actually the opposite is true. The more equity you have, the less security you have, because the more equity you have the more leverage the bank has over you. Simply put **the bank can sell the home of the person with say 75 percent equity substantially below fair market value,** and satisfy its board of directors. If the unlucky home owner doesn't get any money out of his house, that's just too bad. There is a saying:

> *"Owe a person a little and they own you.*
> *Owe him a lot and you own him."*

With this in mind there is a simple solution to this problem. Take out a **HELOC,** so if you ever have an unforeseen financial emergency, you can tap into the money in your home, be able to pay your bills, and buy yourself breathing room until you get back on your feet. In an extreme case, it could keep the bank from foreclosing on your home. Remember, if your home isn't paid off free and clear, the bank owns it and you are at the bank's mercy.

3) **Moving or refinancing is no big deal!**
Make no mistake it is a huge deal, and failure to understand the problem is a financial poverty sentence!

✓ Why will moving keep you from ever paying off your mortgage?

"The average American moves every five to seven years"

Remember Mark and Lynn's scenario. After five years they had paid $71,946.00 in mortgage payments, but only $13,891.20 had been applied to principal. In the first five years 80 percent of their mortgage payments had gone to interest. At that rate how will they ever pay off their home? It is far more costly to move or refinance than most people ever imagine; which is all the more reason to pay your mortgage off early.

✓ Why refinancing will keep you from paying off your mortgage.

The short answer is because every time you refinance you start all over on the amortization table, with the vast majority of your mortgage payments going to interest and very little of going to principal. All you are doing is making the bankers rich.

4) **Your home is guaranteed to appreciate:**
The fact is it isn't. More important, if it doesn't, what do you do? The answer is to find another way to build principal. Our earlier example showed us that even in a zero-appreciation market, with the MAP the equity in the home increased nearly

as much as it had from the earlier example when their was an 8 percent market appreciation. In a flat or falling real-estate market, having a program, such as MAP, would keep you from going into negative appreciation, or "going upside down," and getting yourself in a position where you could be unable to sell your home because doing so would mean that you would have to take a loss. It doesn't matter whether you gain principal from market appreciation or from accelerated principal build up. At the end of the day when all is said and done, principal is principal.

How to pay off your mortgage years early and invest for retirement! There are three options:

1) **Bi-monthly payment program.** The bi-monthly program is really quite simple. All you do is pay your mortgage payment every two weeks as opposed to once a month. The result is that you make 13 payments per year instead of 12 and depending on your interest rate you will end up paying off your mortgage 5 to 10 years early. The average is 7 years.

2) **The Australian method:** Based on the best selling book, Own Your Home Years Sooner, Australians have on average been able to reduce their 30-year mortgages by 14 to 18 years.

3) **The Mortgage Acceleration Program (MAP):** MAP is based on the same concept as the Australian program in as much as they both use a HELOC to cancel interest and achieve an accelerated pay off of your mortgage. The big difference is that MAP is computerized, which means it is easier to use and achieves a faster pay off of your home: as little as 8 to 11 years.

Home Pay off Comparison with MAP vs. Conventional Mortgage

Figures Based on Connie Stevens Example

	MAP	Conventional Mortgage
Starting Balance	$136,058	$136,058
	Balance in 1 year:	Balance in 4.7 Years:
	$126,032	$126,193
Repayment Time	11.33 years	30 years
Total Interest Paid	$45,159	$134,726

Total Interest Savings with MAP: $89,566

Mortgage Details for Mark and Lynn Johnson

	(MAP) Mortgage Acceleration Program	*Conventional Mortgage*
Starting Balance	$200,000	$200,000
	Balance in 1 year $184,811 $15,189 Principal Increase	Balance in 1 year $187,534 $2458 Principal Increase
Repayment Time	10.4 years	30 years
Total Interest Paid	$70,422	$231,677

For perhaps the first time in our lives we have a tool that gives people a financial speedometer and gas gauge to help them accurately understand the impact of their spending habits and take control of their financial futures. If you can pay off your home early and then invest what you would have spent on mortgage payments you have a real shot a retiring in comfort.

CHAPTER 14

HOW DO YOU BUY A HOME IF YOU HAVE CREDIT PROBLEMS?

For most of us, it's the American dream to own our own home. It gives us pride and a sense of belonging. What we may not know is it also substantially contributes to our wealth.

I know too well from personal experience that, as renters we pay the taxes and mortgage for our landlord and he gets the appreciation and tax write off on the property we pay for, for him. In exchange, he is kind enough to regularly increase our rent. It's been this way since the earliest of times. In medieval times the serfs worked the land and paid the noblemen (landlords) for the right to live on their property. The noblemen got rich and the surfs remained perpetually poor.

I was at a seminar recently where the speaker quoted a statistic that I thought was pretty powerful. He didn't quote the source, but I thought I would share it with you anyway.

"The net worth of a homeowner is about eight times higher than that of a renter."

There's no doubt that there are a variety of factors that account for this statistic. Nevertheless, it highlights the importance of home ownership to wealth building.

I would like to share a personal story with you. The entire time I was growing up my parents rented, because every time they saved enough for a down payment on a house my father would decide it was time for his lucky streak. With lady luck on his side, my father would get into a not-so-friendly poker game. The next thing we knew, our dream of owning our own home would end up as a pile of poker chips on the table of a dark, dank, smoke-filled tavern. When I started college, my father picked up and left. My mother hadn't worked for 20 years and even then she had only done menial jobs for minimum wage. That same month the motor on my junker car blew, and I had no car. Then to top things off, our landlord of 15 years came to the door and told us he was selling the rat trap that we called home. He said he thought he had a buyer, so we should find another place to live.

As fate would have it, the seemingly bleak turn of events turned out to be a turning point in my life. I dropped out of college and got a job as a salesman, which incidentally provided me with the first new car I had ever owned. I sold the only possession I had, a motorcycle, and used the money as a down payment on the house we were renting. It was a duplex, so I immediately became a landlord. Over time, I fixed up the dump to a point where it was the nicest home on the block.

Eventually, I went back to school and got my degree. When I was finally able to move out, I gave my mother the house. With the rent from the other side, she was able to pay the mortgage and live there rent free for the rest of her life. There is a proverb from the Bible that says:

> *"Give a man a fish and you feed him for a day.*
> *Teach him to fish and you feed him for life."*

What that duplex did for my mother was give her the ability to be self-sufficient, and that gave her a sense of dignity and self-respect that she had never had. As for me, I learned the importance of home ownership in wealth building. I could go so far as to say that this book is the result of buying that duplex.

So why did I tell this story? I told this story partly to point out how owning a home can change a person's life and partly to give readers a sense of perspective. I sincerely want to see all of you realize the dream of home ownership!

FREQUENTLY ASKED QUESTIONS (CREDIT COUNSELING)

Is there anything we can do if we don't have the money for a down payment?

First of all, refer to Chapter 9, "Pay off Your Credit Cards and Be Debt Free." This chapter should help those of you who need help getting your finances in order so you can save for a down payment.

Here is a true story that might help motivate you and put things in perspective. When I used to rehabilitate properties, I worked with a crew of Polish men. I learned to have the utmost respect for these men. Most of them were over here so they could make a better living for their families back in Poland. They generally lived with five or six other men in a small apartment. They worked 10 hours a day, 6 days a week, and they never complained. They would generally have a single junker car between them. Their lives were generally made up of hard work and sacrifice. Most of what they made went back home to relatives, but they still managed to be happy and thankful for what they had. Most of the men were here on temporary work permits, but once in a while one would be allowed official immigrant status and would be allowed to bring his family to America to live. Whenever this would happen the man, who generally spoke no English or at most very broken English, would immediately set out to realize the American dream. Sure enough, in a few years I would meet up with him, but now he had his own contracting business and his wife had her own house-cleaning business. They owned rental property, and to say the least they had come a long way.

Here is the difference between a fourth generation American and that first generation immigrant. The American becomes lazy, and he wants something for nothing. He has an attitude that he is owed a good living. The immigrant on the other hand, knows he has no one in the world he can depend on but himself and his family. They will work their hands to the bones to get ahead. No job is too demeaning, because they don't see themselves as a maid or a janitor or whatever. They see themselves as getting ahead. They see themselves as making a better life for their families and when the day is done nothing else is important to them but that they are making progress toward realizing their dream.

I recently sold my lake property, and it gave me great pleasure to sell it to a first-generation polish immigrant family that ran a maid service. They were so excited to have a piece of the American dream. If these immigrants can come over here speaking almost no English and in a few years carve out a life for themselves and their families, what does that say about us Americans who complain that we can't get ahead? To me it says we don't want it bad enough!

What I want to leave you with here, is that you can realize your dream if you want it bad enough. **What you have to do is turn your dream into a plan and work the plan.** Don't take no for an answer and don't depend on anyone but yourself and your family. Take responsibility for your actions and go out and realize your dreams. The only question left is do you want it bad enough? If you do, nothing can hold you back?

Ask yourself what sacrifices you are willing to make. For example, I have a client, who is currently looking to buy his first investment property. He is a painter by trade. He makes a decent living, but he works hard. How he got the money for the down payment is by doing side jobs and saving 100 percent of the money toward his dream. What are you willing to do to make your dream come true? Consider this:

"Nothing in the world can take the place of persistence. Talent will not; nothing is more common than unsuccessful men with talent. Genius will not; unrewarded genius is almost a proverb. Education alone will not; the world is full of educated derelicts. Persistence and determination alone are omnipresent."
– Calvin Coolidge

"People always blame their circumstances for being what they are. I don't believe in circumstances. The people who get along in this world are the people who get up and look for the circumstances they want, and if they can't find them make them."
– George Bernard Shaw

I truly hope you will go out and make the circumstances you want and that you won't stop until you realize your dream. If you want it bad enough, nothing will stop you.

How do you buy a home if you have low income?

There are government assistance programs that can provide down payment assistance for low-income families. These programs provide low-interest rate loans combined with zero interest loans that can increase your buying power by as much as 35 percent. Check with your local county housing authority to find out what programs are available in your area. Also "Section eight voucher recipients" can use their rent voucher toward a mortgage payment, provided they have a down payment for the home and it can be purchased within government price guidelines. Call your local authority for details.

What if you make too much to qualify for government assistance, but are having trouble getting together the down payment?

Given the current tight credit situation, grant programs are less prevalent than they used to be, but they are still worth looking into. Such programs typically provide approximately 3 percent toward down payment and or closing costs. Check with your local mortgage agent to see if there are any programs for which you might qualify. Also, there are FHA and VA loans that you can qualify for with credit scores that are lower than those required for a conventional loan. If there is a family member or someone who is willing to assist you with the down payment you can get what is called a gift letter, in which event the mortgage company will allow you to use the funds toward the purchase of the house. Lastly, you may be able to get the seller to give you assistance with the down payment. Here is how it works. You negotiate the purchase price for the home (say $100,000) and then you add 3 percent ($3,000) to the purchase price. This makes the new selling price $103,000, of which $100,000 goes to the seller and the buyer gets $3,000 to use toward the purchase. The only catch is that the house has to appraise at the higher value and that is tricky right now with housing prices declining. In most areas the comparables are not so tight as to make it impossible. That assumes, of course, that the house was priced at fair market value to start with. Check specific requirements in your area, so you don't violate any laws.

NOTE: You must add a clause to the contract that reads: "Seller to pay $_____ toward buyer's closing cost and/or out of pocket cost."

What do I do if I have had a bankruptcy or if my credit is bad?
If you have filed bankruptcy, you generally have to wait a couple of years before you qualify to buy a home, but you can reestablish your credit. Contact a mortgage company or talk to whoever handled your bankruptcy. While you are waiting, this is what you do:

1) **Check your credit report:** There are three major credit reporting companies. You want to get a consolidated report from at least two or preferably all three of them. The consolidated report is important so that you are sure that all of your credit history is reflected in the report.

   Trans Union Corporation
   P.O. Box 390
   Springfield, PA 19064-0390
   1-800-916-8800   www.tuc.com

   Experian National Consumer Association Ctr.
   P.O. Box 2002
   Allen, TX 75013
   1-800-experian   www.experian.com

   Equifax Information Center
   P.O. Box 740241
   Atlanta, GA   30374-0241
   1-800-685-1111 www.equifax.com

2) **Have any errors on your credit report removed and have letters of explanation inserted in your file to explain any remaining issues:** In addition, the FAIR CREDIT REPORTING ACT requires that the bureaus check out any entry you take exception to and remove any item that can't be validated. The process for having incorrect information removed from your credit report is as follows.

✓ Write a letter to the creditor in question and request they correct your records.

✓ Provide appropriate documents to creditor and/or credit bureau. Provide canceled checks, payment receipts, letters of agreement, and so forth.

✓ Note names and dates of parties you spoke to and any pertinent comments.

✓ In 30 days request a corrected report to verify that your file has been updated to reflect any necessary corrections. Make sure all negative information is explained and or removed.

3) **Find out what your credit score is:**
    You can go to www.myfico.com and pay a fee to get your credit scores. There are a lot of variables when looking at credit worthiness, but generally speaking a score of 730 and up is excellent. A score of 680-729 means you will have no problem getting a loan from most lenders. A score of 660 – 678 means your score is questionable, but you should probably be able to get a loan, though you may have to pay a slightly higher rate. A score of 560 - 600 is highly questionable.

NOTE: For an additional fee you can use the FICO SIMULATOR in order to determine how best to get your score up. For example, they rate recent activity (last six months) highest, so you could run a simulation to see what would happen if you put your credit balance on a card with a lower rate and then paid down your balance at an accelerated rate. Finally you should note that, if you have a lot of credit reports pulled in a short period of time, say by a car dealership, the system will assume you are going to buy a new car on time payments, so your debt service will be going up. Based on this, the system will automatically lower your credit score. If you have not purchased a new car in six weeks your scores will automatically go back up. I mention this because, if you plan on buying a house, you don't want to be making any large purchases or be doing anything that will make the system mistakenly believe you are going to be taking on additional debt.

4) **Reestablish your credit:**
Open a savings account with a local bank. When you open the account, find out what the smallest loan is that the bank will make. That is the amount you want to open your account with. After a month or so go to the bank and ask the loan officer for a loan equal to the amount in your passbook. That way you can use your passbook as collateral. Make sure the loan is for at least six months. The first three or four weeks make weekly payments. Then take your next payment in person, and be sure to talk to the loan officer so he can get to know you. From this point on, make regular monthly payments. After three months go back to the bank and ask to borrow money "unsecured." If they ask you, and they probably will, what you want the money for just tell them you want to establish credit with their bank. When you get the loan make sure you make all your payments on time. If you do this at two, or even three banks you will have a credit history that will allow you to borrow money from them when you need it.

In addition, get a department store credit card. Make a few purchases and pay the bill promptly. Next apply for a Visa or MasterCard. With your new credit history and job verification you should be able to get the credit card. Finally, apply for an American Express or Visa Gold card. As long as you continue to pay on time your credit should be okay.

I should note that when you have gotten your credit cards and reestablished your credit history, you want to use your credit very sparingly, because consumer debt doesn't make you wealthy. It makes you poor. It makes you a 95 percenter. You want the credit so you can use it to borrow money to buy real estate to create cash flow, get tax deductions and build equity all of which contributes to wealth building.

What benefits do I get from owning versus renting?

■   Tax incentives: When you own your home, you get tax incentives equal to approximately 30 percent of your principal and interest payments. This means you have more leverage buying than renting. It also means you can afford to pay more as a mortgage payment than you can as a renter.

■ Control over your property: If you own, you have control over your own property. You don't have to ask a landlord if you can paint or do whatever.

■ If you own property you get equity: You may notice I didn't say appreciation. That is because I don't personally believe the housing market is going to improve for several years, but regardless you will get the equity build up in the home and if you use the MAP program discussed earlier you can accelerate the equity build and potentially pay off your mortgage in as little as 1/3 the normal time. One thing is for certain and that is that if you rent for 30 years, you'll have absolutely nothing to show for it. Let's be conservative and assume the housing market has a reasonable come back and you get a modest 3 percent appreciation, what would that mean to your financial situation? Say you purchased a modest home at $100,000, and it appreciated at an annual rate of 3 percent over the term of a 30-year mortgage. At 3 percent appreciation, your $100,000 home would have appreciated by $142,726 to $242,726. Now what if you owned 10 properties and they each appreciated $100,000. You are a millionaire! Even if they don't appreciate you can retire and live off the rental income.

Real estate has the potential to get you off the 40/40 program

This is where we are taught to:

■ Go to school.

■ Get a 40-hour per week job.

■ Work for 40 years, and if you are lucky get a gold watch and a farewell party. And if you're not lucky, you just get the boot. Either way, it's not much to show for a life's work. You deserve more and real estate can give it to you. For that matter, any leveraged investment that creates an annuity income stream can give you what you deserve, which is the right to retire in dignity with your head held high!

I used this quote earlier, but I think its A GOOD THOUGHT TO CLOSE THIS CHAPTER WITH.

"Every person who invests in well-selected real estate in growing sections of a prosperous community adopts the surest method of becoming independent, for real estate is the basis of wealth"

–Theodore Roosevelt

Owning your own home is after all "The American Dream." It's a dream two thirds of all Americans have realized, and it's about time you realize the dream too. **It's a dream you can realize!**

CHAPTER 15

ABOVE ALL BE HAPPY!

Do you not know that in a race all the runners run,
but only one gets the prize?
Run in such a way to get the prize.
(1 Corinthians 9:24)

Sometimes I think we don't even know what the prize is, much less how to get it! Americans have been brainwashed by Madison Avenue advertisers into thinking that the prize is material possessions. Slowly, but surely we are coming to understand that there is a price to pay for materialism. The pursuit of things exacts a price from us. The more we want, the more of our precious time we have to give up in order to earn the money to buy the things we want. The more we go into debt in order to buy the things we want, the more we become indentured by the things we buy, and they end up owning us instead of us owning them. The more we go into debt, the more we make the money changers rich and ourselves poor. We are working tomorrow and the next day and the next in order to pay for things we have already consumed. We are in effect giving up our future financial security, because we are like little children who say "I want that and I want it now." Without realizing it we are trading peace of mind, financial security, and happiness for material possessions that fill a temporary void in our lives but ultimately leave us unfulfilled so we have to fill the emptiness with more material possessions, like a drug addict satisfying our craving for a time, but each time it takes more to satiate our hunger.

Let no debt remain outstanding, except the continuing
debt to love one another, for he who loves his fellowman
has fulfilled the law.
(Romans 19:8)

What then is the proper role of money and the things it buys? Money is a means to an end and nothing more. Having a certain amount of money can provide us safety and security and allow us reasonable control over the events of our lives. To this extent it will contribute to our happiness. Its primary purpose is to give us control over our time so that by virtue of having money we are able to spend our time in pursuit of things that make us happy as opposed to spending an inordinate amount of our time having to work to earn a living. Having a certain amount of money also provides a safety net that drives the demon of fear away from our door and allows us to enjoy the moments of our lives as opposed to constantly looking to the future wondering what tomorrow will bring. What if we don't get that raise? What if the car breaks down? What if we get sick? Heaven forbid, what if we lose our job? Even worse, what if we retire and find out we were so busy consuming day by day that we neglected to provide for our old age? The golden years can quickly become a nightmare of despair for those who daily have to choose between paying the rent, buying food or paying for prescription drugs.

He who gathers money little by little makes it grow.
(Proverbs 13:11)

If we fixate on money it becomes our God, and it is a cruel God of guile and deception that promises us happiness. Beneath its thin vale of deception it lays a snare that robs us of our happiness. It robs us of control of the day-to-day living of our lives because the making of money dictates what we do and how we spend out time. When our lives are at an end and we are asked what we regret not doing, I doubt if many of us will say we wish we could have spent more time at work! However, I suspect a good number of us might look back and wish we had spent more time with our wives, our children and our friends. We may wish we had taken time to stop and smell the roses. We may wish we had taken more time to travel or enjoy our favorite pastime. We may wish we had taken time to take better care of our health. We may finally understand that no man stands alone! We are a part of the community of man. The pursuit of money isolates us and, thus, makes us unhappy. Given this realization, we may well wish we had spent more time cultivating our relationships with our fellow man as well as with God.

The God of money is particularly cruel to those who are foolish enough to go into debt in order to satiate their material appetites. It creeps up on them at night when they lay their heads on their pillows, and it steals their peace of mind replacing it with fear, anxiety, stress, uncertainty, and a feeling of being powerless and vulnerable. Like a thief in the night it steals their peace of mind without which there can be no joy. And without joy there can be no happiness, there can only be loneness and despair, which make poor bed fellows.

> *I will lie down and sleep in peace, for you alone,*
> *O LORD, make me dwell in safety.*
> (Psalms 4:8)

The lesson to be learned is that being in debt causes us to almost single mindedly fixate on how we are going to pay for the goods we have already consumed, and it causes us to stress about what we will do if we do not have any money when the bills are due. We are in a prison of our own making. We are in a gilded cage, and we have voluntarily put on a pair of golden handcuffs thinking by mistake they were decorative bracelets.

> *The rich ruleth over the poor and the borrower is*
> *servant to the lender.*
> (Matthew 6:11-12)

When we are fixated on the pursuit of money we lose all perspective. We lose the all-important balance that is essential if our life is to have meaning and if we are to be happy! We are so busy chasing the all-mighty dollar that we have no time to cultivate relationships, no time to pursue leisure activities, no time to dedicate to our health, and we have surely put Mammon before God and sacrificed any hope of having a spiritual relationship with God. All we have is money, but ironically we don't even have money because we have already spent it before we have even earned it, so we are left with nothing, absolutely nothing.

It's very possible to be happy without being wealthy. But, is it possible to be wealthy if you're not happy? If in pursuit of riches you sacrifice your relationships with friends and family, violate your values and ethics, and have no time to enjoy the fruits of your labor, how can you possibly be happy? The truth be known, rather than having to choose between money and happiness wouldn't you rather have both? That is exactly what this book is about. **It's about having money without the money being a source of unhappiness!** It's about getting money "God's way instead of man's way."

The blessing of the Lord it maketh rich,
and he addeth no sorrow
(Proverbs 10:22)

The person who focuses single-mindedly on accumulating money may well get rich, but this will likely come at the expense of his happiness. In Charles Dickens' <u>A Christmas Carol,</u> Scrooge failed to understand that for the sake of money he had risked his very soul. All of us would agree that, that is too high a price to pay for riches. But the question still remains: How much are we willing to sacrifice for the sake of money? And, like Scrooge, do we even realize the sacrifices we are making?

Jesus Said, "Whoever can be trusted with very little
can also be trusted with much, and whoever is dishonest
with very little will also be dishonest with much."
(Luke 16:10)

What we really want is to have our cake and eat it too! Believe it or not, that is exactly what God's way of making money is all about. It's about having our cake and eating it too. It is really quite simple. When we live within our means, we are focused on meeting our needs, rather than our wants. We don't pay any attention to the Madison Avenue advertisers telling us that our wants are actually needs. We take control of our emotions and don't allow ourselves to feel unsuccessful if we don't live in a big house, drive an expensive sports car, or feel sexually unattractive if we can't fit into a size four dress. Whether we are male or female, young or old, the Madison Avenue crowd is out to trigger our emotions and in the process get us to spend our money so they can get rich and turn us into their slaves. If we are ever to be financially well off, we have to learn to associate **"pain"** with these types of messages. We have to remind ourselves that the way to become financially well off is to spend less than we make and save the difference. That is diametrically opposed to the messages coming from Madison Avenue. Remember that the Madison Avenue crowd spends billions to brainwash us into believing that our happiness is dependent on **"immediate material gratification."** Nothing could be further from the truth. Instead, our happiness is dependent on **deferring gratification.** They want us to consume our way into debt, which is just another word for **slavery.**

Happiness, not wealth should be our ultimate goal! We must shift gears and do something that is extraordinarily difficult. We must become content with less because the world can no longer support our excessive material consumption. **Ironically if we learn to live with less, to save our money and live within our means, we will ultimately end up not only being happy but also financially well off.** We will be able to go to bed at night without worrying what will happen to us if we lose our job, because we will have adequate cash reserves to weather economic adversity. We will no longer have to go to work at a job we hate just because it pays well. We will be able to do what we want for a living rather than what we have to. We will no longer be slaves to our possessions, because we will own them rather than them owning us. Our time will be ours to spend as we please, because we will not be slaves to our debts. We will be able to spend quality time with our family, our friends and ourselves. We will be in **"control of our lives."** Moreover, because of that, we will find true wealth and true happiness.

Despite current events, this is a great nation with vast resources. It can support us, but we must learn to spend less than we make and save the difference, pay cash for consumer items and reserve debt for leveraged investments that generate cash flow and make a profit. If we do these things, there should be no reason we cannot retire with financial freedom. **I define financial freedom as having enough money**

to live, whether we work or not. It's not about conspicuous consumption. It's about living within our means and investing what we don't spend so that we constantly increase our wealth.

From a **"worldly perspective"** the primary purpose of money is to give us control over our time, so that by virtue of having money we are able to achieve "balance."

From a **"Kingdom Perspective"** the primary purpose of having money is to allow us to be able to "sow into the Kingdom." Our giving allows God to multiply our seed and bless us by giving us dominion over man's materialistic economic system. He not only blesses us financially, but also makes us happy and adds no sorrow!

A generous man will prosper; he who refreshes
others will himself be refreshed.
(Proverbs 11:25)

To this end, we should strive to be as balanced as possible. A balanced life is one that focuses equal attention on health, relationships, career, finances, spirituality, and leisure time. If we are balanced the various aspects of our life are not in conflict; therefore, we feel in control. Hence we feel happy! In this instance our emotions are **"empowering."** They are contributing to our state of well-being and, as a result, we are experiencing pleasure. A common mistake that many people make is mistakenly believing that:

- **Money will make them happy.** By focusing too fixedly on money, we become indentured servants. We end up trading happiness for a pair of golden handcuffs.

- **A relationship will make them happy.** By focusing too fixedly on a relationship we actually end up damaging it, because we fail to allow adequate space for each person to develop as a person so we have our unique personalities to bring to the relationship.

- **A job will make them happy.** By focusing too fixedly on a job, we lose out on developing meaningful relationships and when we become disillusioned with our job we find out the hard way that we have not paid enough attention to friends and family.

- **Power will make them happy.** Power is an extremely dangerous aphrodisiac. Remember the old saying: "Power corrupts and absolute power corrupts absolutely." Power is a self-indulgent experience. It feels good, but it is bad for us and bad for others. Power can never be a basis of true happiness, because it is by nature abusive. What we really need to do is to focus on our relationship with God, because that is where ultimate power comes from!

So, this takes us full circle, and hopefully in the process gives us a better understanding that **balance** is the key to happiness. The pursuit of money is just one component of a balanced life. A balanced life is one that focuses equal attention on: **Health, Relationships, Career, Finances, Leisure Time and Spirituality!**

Achieving balance and happiness in your life depends on being in control of your time and money! To this end ask yourself the following questions:

- **Health:** Do you have time to focus on your health?

- **Career:** If you decided that you don't like what you do for a living, are you in a position to go elsewhere? Can you free yourself from the golden handcuffs?

- **Finance**: Are you in a position to be debt free or at least to live well within your means so that you are in control of the circumstances of your life instead of allowing your circumstances to control you?

- **Relationships:** Do you have enough free time to spend with family and friends or are you always busy working?

- **Spirituality:** Would you define yourself as being balanced, and do you have a higher purpose that goes beyond self gratification?

- **Leisure Time:** Do you have the time and money to enjoy leisure time either by yourself or with family and friends?

What did you decide? Is your life balanced and happy, or are you a victim of your excessive material pursuits?

Regardless of how you answered the above question; the state of your life is not the outcome of some random set of events that bless some and conspire to bring sorrow and misery to others. We are the architects of our lives. Our lives burst forth onto the screen of life like the brush strokes of the painter on the canvas. It is our passion, or compassion, joy, optimism, hope, zeal for life, clarity of vision, purpose and our spirituality that forge those moments that take our breath away and leave us speechless. Likewise, it is our procrastination, indecisiveness, lack of clarity and vision, fear, apathy, greed and lack of compassion that conspire against us to bring upon us our worst nightmare, a nightmare that we are all too familiar with, for it is of our own worst fears brought to life and visited upon us.

Do you choose a life of fear and desperation? If so you don't have to do anything. Just turn a blind eye to what is happening around you and man's greed will take care of the rest. If on the other hand you choose a life of hope and inspiration, you have to be willing to open your eyes and see what is going on around you. You have to be willing to make the conscious decision to make healthier, more responsible, better informed, more compassionate, more ethical, more spiritual decisions that subjugate your selfish, self-serving interest to the greater good of the masses of humanity who share this tinny, fragile sphere called earth with you.

It is we who decide whether we forfeit our dreams or if we make them a reality, but one thing is sure. **You have to have a PLAN if you want to win the game of life!** You have to take control of the circumstances of your life! You have to turn away from man's greed and pursue wealth God's way, which means you have to put the best interest of others before yours. You have to give that God may bless your giving:

> *...it shall be given unto you; good measure, pressed down, and shaken together. And running over, shall men give unto your bosom. For with the same measure that ye met withal it shall be measured to you again.*
> (Luke 6:30)

Do you choose to be **happy?** If so, you will need to cease your single-minded pursuit of materialism and choose instead to focus your life on a **balanced pursuit of health, relationships, carrier, finances, leisure time and spirituality, for it is from these that true happiness emanates!**

> *"Each and every one of us needs to learn to be responsible*
> *for our every action. We need to choose carefully what*
> *we want and we need a plan for how to get it!*
> *And mostimportantly we need to learn that balance*
> *not materialism is the key to happiness."*
> –Larry Ballard

> *"If you want to change something in your life ask yourself what will*
> *you no longer tolerate? What is your dream and what is your plan*
> *for attaining it? Is it in conflict with any other aspect of your life?*
> *Lastly, what do you have to **change in yourself** in order that what*
> *you want will be a source of happiness rather than unhappiness?"*
> –Larry Ballard

Even with the best intentions many of us fail to realize our dreams. Knowing why we fail is almost as important as knowing how to succeed, so before we turn our attention to how to succeed, let's examine:

Why Most People Fail At The Game of Life!

■ *Most people have no written plan:* They may have vague dreams, but when it comes down to it they have no idea how to get where they want to go. They allow the circumstances of their life to direct their course. In other words they **react to events rather than controlling events.** How can we be anything other than lost if we don't know where we are headed or how we plan to get there? All roads lead to a town called nowhere. Is that really where we want to go? Somehow, I doubt it!

> *"On our journey we must find out where we are*
> *before we can plan the first step."*
> –Kitty Bovinek

The following is a powerful example of exactly how important it is to have a plan, specifically how important it is to have a written plan. A survey was conducted at Yale University in 1953, in which students were asked if they had a **written plan** for their professional career. Only 3 percent responded that they had a written plan. Twenty years later in 1973 the same students were surveyed a second time. From a subjective point of view, the 3 percent who had written plans reported being happier, more excited about their lives and better adjusted than their peers who didn't have written plans. Subjective data certainly isn't scientific, but when it came to financial net worth the responses were anything but subjective. The 3 percent of the class who had written plans had a net worth greater than the other 97 percent combined. I can't overstate how important it is to have a written plan for your life, because if you don't, you will lack the focus necessary to win the game of life. Even if you are successful, you will still not realize your potential. How could you if you never knew where you were headed?

■ **Most people fail to execute, because they allow their fear to immobilize them.** They allow their circumstances to limit them, when instead they should choose to change their circumstances. They are overwhelmed before they even start because they focus on all the negatives: the problems, the obstacles, all the things they must do, and all the reasons they can't do them. They focus on the cost and sacrifices associated with achieving their dream and as a result they are the authors of their own self-defeating prophecy.

"People always blame their circumstances for being what they are. I don't believe in circumstances. The people who get along in this world are the people who get up and look for the circumstances they want, and if they can't find them make them."
                                                                –George Bernard Shaw

Instead, they should be focused on "the cost of not achieving their dream." Instead, they should focus on the end result. What is it they want? Why is it important to them? Why must they achieve it? They should see the end result as though it is already realized! They should bask in the pleasure of their accomplishments! They should reward themselves for their achievements. If we visualize our end result strongly enough, we will cease to be overwhelmed by all the negatives and the "HOW TO" will fall into place. We can always figure out how to do something if we are committed enough. So the key to success is to develop a strong enough reason for why we absolutely must be successful! For example, when America decided to put a man on the moon it had innumerable obstacles to overcome. If NASA had focused on the obstacles, America would never have put men on the moon. Instead, the focus was on what NASA had to do, step by step, to realize the objective. There was no thought of not achieving the goal. There was only resolve and the commitment to overcome obstacles as they arose.

- **Most people fail to surround themselves with supportive people.** It would be an understatement to call the environment at NASA supportive. It was an environment of total commitment, and every person there shared that commitment. Unfortunately, in life we often find ourselves in environments that are less than supportive. In fact they're down right negative. If we don't change our environment our failure is almost assured. Therefore, **failure to change a non-supportive environment (family, friends, co-workers, and peers) is a fatal error that almost assures failure in your endeavors.**

"There is nothing either good or bad, but thinking makes it so."
–William Shakespeare

- **Most People fail to properly prioritize.** As a result they get caught up in the detail and lose sight of the big picture. By contrast, NASA tackled the big problems first and by default many of the small problems were solved in the process.

"I have been given eyes to see and a mind to think,
and now I know a great secret of life for I perceive at last,
that all my problems, discouragements and heart aches are in truth
great opportunities in disguise."
–Og Mandino

■ **Most people fail to control Conflict.** If we have goals that are in conflict, our forward momentum is stifled. For example, if we have a situation in our lives that we would like to change and have not, it is because we associate more pain to changing than to not changing. We are in conflict because on the one hand we want to change and on the other we don't. Our forward progress is at a standstill until we resolve the conflict.

"No change occurs until we acknowledge the source of our pain, and seek to remove the pain by choice of a new course of action, a new direction. Then at that moment we are at a turning point from which a new outcome is possible."
–Larry Ballard

■ **Most people are too rigid.** They come to the table with a preconceived notion of how to do a thing and stubbornly refuse to learn from their mistakes and rigidly refuse to try different approaches. Growth and change are born out of the insight we gain from our mistakes. Failure is the great teacher.

"Nothing in the world can take the place of persistence. Talent will not; nothing is more common than unsuccessful men with talent. Genius will not; unrewarded genius is almost a proverb. Education alone will not; the world is full of educated derelicts. Persistence and determination alone are omnipresent."
–Calvin Coolidge

■ **Most people fail to reward themselves for the small incremental victories along the way.** As a result, they frequently get discouraged and give up prematurely. For example, every time NASA made a breakthrough, or for that matter had a failure, it either celebrated the accomplishment or analyzed the failure and then immediately turned its attention to the next challenge. This is the quintessential definition of constant change and constant growth. We could all learn from NASA's example and, if we do, we too can do the impossible, because, nothing is impossible if you have a strong enough reason why!

"Do what you love and the money will follow."
–Marcia Sinetar

You Win the Game of Life By Pursuing Constant Change and Growth!

To This End We Must Know:

What We Want?
This provides our.. GOAL

Why We Must Have It?
This provides our... MOTIVATION

How We Plan To Achieve It?
This provides our...ACTION PLAN

What Resources We Need?
This specifies the .... SKILLS/KNOWLEDGE

When It Must Be Done?
This gives us our .... TIMETABLE

Where to Get Help? This identifies needed .... RESOURCES
The sources of technical information, networking, role models,
mentors, team members, etc.

Our Negative Beliefs?
These are our .... SELF-IMPOSED LIMITATIONS

You Win the Game of Life by Having A Plan and Working It!
If you truly want to be happy and successful, make the decision to
be like the 3 percent of the class at Yale who had a written plan, and
as a result had a net worth greater than the other 97 percent combined.
Just think, if the 3 percent accomplished what they did by having a
written plan for only their careers; how much better might they have
done at the game of life if they had an integrated plan for every aspect
of their lives? *How much better off would they have been if they
were not only wealthy, but also good husbands, good fathers, good
neighbors and good stewards of God's wealth?* How much happier
would they have been if they were the picture of health and if they

regularly took time to do the things they loved with the ones they loved. How much happier would they have been if they had a spiritual purpose in life, one that went beyond self-serving interest, and instead served the greater good of society at large? How much happier, how much more joy would they have had, and equally important how much better off would mankind have been because they walked the earth in service to others? How much better off would we all have been if they lived *balanced lives* dedicated to pursuit of God's true wealth of happiness, which can be attained only by giving first and then letting Him show us just how loving and generous He is?

As soon as you finish this chapter, I encourage you to put this book down and take the time to develop a plan for every aspect of your life: **your career, finances, relationships, health, leisure time and spirituality.**

Carefully consider:

- What you want
- Why you must have it
- What sacrifices you are prepared to make
- How you plan to achieve it
- What resources you will need
- When it must be done
- Where to get any help you may need
- What negative beliefs you have that might stand in the way of turning your dreams into reality

How Do You Make Sure Your Goals Will Be A Source of Happiness?

It's entirely possible to realize our dreams or goals only to find out that they are a source of unhappiness. That is the ultimate definition of failure, because we put in all the work and actually get what we wanted only to find out that the very thing we wanted is a source of unhappiness: what a tragedy! So, how do we make sure we never find ourselves in these circumstances? Once you have completed the draft of your **"Life Plan - Success Plan"** you want to stop and ask yourself if there are any flaws in the plan that may cause you to not achieve your financial goals or that may contribute to making you unhappy. To this end, ask yourself the following questions:

- *Are any of my goals in conflict with one another?* Here we are not only focused on a particular goal, but also concerned about the six areas of our life that define our balance: career, finances, health, relationships, spirituality, and leisure time. Conflicts in these areas will lead to us being unhappy.

- *How should you prioritize your various goals in order to create balance?* We only have so much time and so many resources, so we need to prioritize our goals so that we optimize our resources and put the focus where it needs to be in order to maximize our efforts. Do the big things first and the small things will fall into place.

- *Does what you want do any harm?* If it does harm and we ignore it, we may well make money, but I guarantee you that in one way or another our decisions will eventually come back to haunt us.

- *Does what you want serve the greater good?* Nothing in the world feels better than helping others and nothing pays higher dividends. God multiplies what we give and returns it several times over.

CONCLUSIONS

By contemplating these questions you have an excellent chance of achieving your goals and along the way finding **balance, happiness and purpose!** One of the most important beliefs that we as citizens of a global community can adopt is a belief that in order to be successful we must find a purpose that fulfills us and makes us happy, while at the same time enriching society. If we enrich ourselves and diminish others we are a failure not a success. The end that we all seek whether we know it or not is to be happy; for a happy person is satisfied with his lot in life, at peace with himself, at peace with those around him, and is balanced and in harmony with his surroundings. We don't just wake up one day and find that all of our problems have dissolved and we are euphorically happy. We have to work at it day by day, and we have to have a plan for exactly what we want and how we plan to get it!

"Look well to this day, for yesterday is but a dream and tomorrow is a vision; but today, well lived, makes every yesterday a dream of happiness and every tomorrow a vision of hope."

– Unknown

So how do we "look well to this day?" The answer is by learning how to achieve **constant change and growth**. How we execute against that goal is to **develop a written plan for our life** in order to have a step-by-step plan for where we want to go and how to get there, and in order to be confident that when we get there we will find happiness and not sorrow! As you strive to implement your life plan, you will undoubtedly have to interact with a variety of people from a variety of different backgrounds and with a variety of different personalities. You could benefit from a set of tools that will allow you to effectively communicate with all of these different people. We are what we think, and others react to us based on how what we think determines how we act. If we want to communicate optimally, we need a set of tools that allow us to respond to people in a positive, upbeat, and non-threatening way. To coin a term, our goal is to enable communication. Therefore, I will provide you with a set of enabling tools so that you may be more effective in executing your life plan.

The tool kit consists of three parts.

1. ***Key Enabling Rules:*** To win the game of life, it helps if we have a set of rules that we can rely on to facilitate communication. The key enabling rules listed below are simply a summary of different principles that have been presented in various chapters of this book compiled into a master list for easy study and review. When it's all said and done, they create an open environment for communication that leads to execution of the various steps in your life plan. All forward motion begins with communication, and these principles make meaningful communication possible.

KEY ENABLING RULES

To be happy and win the game of life learn to incorporate these rules of conduct into your daily lives.

Design Your Life vs. Reacting to Circumstances

Accept Responsibility for Your Actions

Get Motivated (Cost of Not Achieving Your Goal?)

Spend Your TIME On What Makes You Happy

Focus on Balance and Happiness 1st and & Money 2nd

Make Sure Your Goals Aren't In Conflict

Be Flexible and Willing to Change

Become That Which You Pursue

Focus On Your Strengths vs. Your Weaknesses

Focus On The Pleasure You Want to Feel

Live in the Present

Take Action (Execute Your Life Plan)

Strive to Control Events vs. Responding to Them

See End Result and Set Priorities Accordingly

Reward Yourself Every Step of The Way

Be Grateful vs. Fearful (Key to Abundance)

Live within Your Means (Save First and Be Debt Free)

Spend Less Than You Make and Invest the Difference

Use Your Emotions To Facilitate Growth

Control What Things Mean to You (Your Rules)

Choose Your Words Carefully (Be Non-threatening)

Learn From Your Mistakes (Constant Growth)

Surround Yourself With Supportive People

Find Your Higher Purpose

2. ***Key Enabling Emotional/Traits:*** To win the game of life we need to have a core set of emotions that we can draw on in our interpersonal communications. These emotions are non-threatening and put the other party at ease, thus facilitating open communication. Far too often our interpersonal communication is geared toward getting our way or convincing the other party to agree with our perspective. This is a one-way communication style that—even though it may be cordial on the surface—it actually delivers a subliminal message that hinders productive communication. For years I sold multimillion dollar capital equipment. In that setting, I often dealt with committees of 20-30 people, all of which had a corporate agenda and even more important a personal agenda. In order to bring all of these diverse interests together, I learned that I needed to always ask myself ***"how to create a win-win environment where open communication could occur."*** What I found was that the less I sold the more effective I was. I became instead a ***"facilitator."*** I ask questions and listened to what people had to say. I then went away and compared my notes from all my individual meetings and looked for the common ground where I could allow the corporate agendas and the various personal agendas to have minimal conflict and optimal synergy. I then had a basis for meaningful discussion and negotiation. I had effectively found the middle ground, where compromise was possible and where agreement could occur, because everyone felt that even though they may not have gotten everything they wanted, at least a realistic compromise had been reached, which left all parties feeling that their interest had been represented to the fullest. The key thing I want you to get out of this section is that in order for this to occur, you first have to be viewed as a person who can be trusted to honestly represent people's best interests. This can only be done if you are able to create an atmosphere of trust. This requires that you become adept at conveying the key enabling emotions listed below.

KEY ENABLING EMOTIONS/TRAITS

"If you learn to routinely express these emotions in your communications with others you will substantially improve the quality of your interpersonal relationships and the quality of your life!"

Open-mindedness	Passion	Forgiving
Acceptance	Understanding	Sincerity
Flexibility	Caring	Confidence
Cheerfulness	Giving	Loving

3. ***Key Enabling Character Traits:*** To win the game of life, we need a core set of character traits that support constant growth and define who we are, how we conduct ourselves and how others respond to us. If we want to learn to be successful God's way as opposed to man's way it is imperative that we have absolute integrity and that we be viewed by others as a person who can be trusted and relied on to do what he says. We have to demonstrate that we are reliable, trustworthy and ethical, and we likewise have to demonstrate that our work is of the highest quality, can be depended on to be done on time, and that we always deliver what is expected and preferably even more than is expected. If you do these things, you will find that people will seek you out because you are conducting your business God's way not man's way. You are giving so that you may receive. You give first, trusting that what you give will come back to you multiplied. And why shouldn't it, if you constantly have the other person's best in interest at heart and if you constantly deliver more than expected? All of a sudden your business dealings are not just transactions; they become an opportunity to help another human being. Your business becomes less based on giving the best price and more on giving the best service, but even more it becomes about the other person knowing that they can trust you to always put their best interest forward. What price can you put on trust? Eventually, your business associates become your trusted friends, and friends do business differently than strangers. You find that your business is not stressful because even though you will still have problems you and the other party are honestly trying to work things out to everyone's mutual satisfaction. You also find out that you get a lot more joy out of work,

because every day you help someone and no good deed goes unrewarded. Those people will tell their friends that you are the only person to do business with. They will give you such a glowing recommendation that when referrals call you they will already be sold, because your friend and theirs told them that they could trust you. Trust me, this is a great way to run a business. Kingdom principles do work, and they bring with them not only prosperity, but also the personal satisfaction that comes from knowing that you have done your absolute best to help the other person and to truly represent their best interest. When you go home at night you can lay your head on the pillow, close your eyes and go to sleep feeling that you have done your best. It is a great feeling.

I came up with these key enabling character traits, which I like to call the "twelve great virtues," because, as a small boy growing up, my parents didn't provide much of a positive role model. When I became a young man I needed to find some role models to fashion my life after. I started by reading several autobiographies on men whose lives I felt were inspirational. I read about Thomas Edison, Abraham Lincoln, Albert Einstein, George Washington, and Theodore Roosevelt among others, and I found a lot of commonalities between the character traits of those men who society viewed as having been endowed with leadership skills. Though I found their lives to be inspirational, I didn't find the unifying thread that I was looking for. They each had their unique attributes, and they were each products of their environments. I needed something that was more constant and more timeless, and I found it in the Bible, the Talmud and the Koran. It would seem that even though mankind sees these religious doctrines to be in conflict, and in many ways they are, they all had a unifying theme. They all touted certain virtues as being desirable. Once I had found the unifying thread I was looking for, I went through the Bible and marked all the verses that espoused positive character traits and virtues. There were too many to be able to assimilate, so I culled them down to the twelve great virtues discussed here, which if taken in combination best define the human condition. I then wrote a definition of each of the virtues and set about to use them as a means to transform my life. At that time in my life I had a lot of anger and self doubt and

I didn't feel life had dealt me a fair hand of cards, but I somehow knew that wasn't true, and even if it was I could choose to create a new reality, one that was more socially acceptable, more positive, and one that would forge the golden key to the secret door behind which was the truth; the truth that would set me free. It can set you free if you will let it. The truth is that all is love; love is all there is. If you embrace love, you embrace God and in so doing all conflict ceases and all becomes harmony, because there is no conflict, fear, struggle, or strife in love, because they are diametrically opposing forces. The light and the dark cannot exist in the same place at the same time. The light of love obliterates the darkness once and for all. All that is left is the light, the illumination of God's ever present love!

How I incorporated the twelve great virtues into my life was that I took a different virtue each month, and for that month I endeavored to become the epitome of that virtue. The next month I went on to the next virtue and the next for an entire year. I found that as I expressed each virtue people reacted differently to me. For example, the month I spent focused on kindness I discovered that I had an amazing ability to put people at ease and to get them to respond to me in ways that had not happened in the past. This was because I was reaching out to them in kindness and they were simply responding back to me as a reflection of what I had extended to them. I was indeed able to forge a new reality not only for myself, but also for those with whom I had contact. The people I met were like mirrors, and what I projected was reflected back to me as the image of what I had projected. It truly was a new truth and it truly changed my life, and it can change yours too if you will but believe as a small child that you can create your own reality, a reality where you are in control of your destiny, where there is harmony and love and where fear does not exist.

"You shall know the truth and the truth shall set you free."

KEY ENABLING CHARACTER TRAITS NECESSARY FOR CONSTANT GROWTH

"These Character Traits define who we are, how we conduct ourselves and how others in tern respond to us"

Curiosity	Efficiency	Kindness
Discrimination	Courage	Charity
Patience	Tolerance	Devotion
Precision	Sincerity	Humility

PUTTING IT ALL TOGETHER

KEY ENABLING RULES

To be happy and win the game of life learn to incorporate these rules of conduct into your daily lives.

Design Your Life vs. Reacting to Circumstances

Accept Responsibility for Your Actions

Get Motivated (Cost of Not Achieving Your Goal?)

Spend Your TIME On What Makes You Happy

Focus on Balance and Happiness 1st and Money 2nd

Make Sure Your Goals Aren't In Conflict

Be Flexible and Willing to Change

Become That Which You Pursue

Focus On Your Strengths vs. Your Weaknesses

Focus On The Pleasure You Want to Feel

Live in the Present

Take Action (Execute Your Life Plan)

Strive to Control Events vs. Responding to Them

See End Result and Set Priorities Accordingly

Reward Yourself Every Step of The Way

Be Grateful vs. Fearful (Key to Abundance)

Live within Your Means (Save First and Be Debt Free)

Spend Less Than You Make and Invest the Difference

Use Your Emotions To Facilitate Growth

Control What Things Mean to You (Your Rules)

Choose Your Words Carefully (Be Non-threatening)

Learn From Your Mistakes (Constant Growth)

Surround Yourself with Supportive People

Find Your Higher Purpose

KEY ENABLING EMOTIONS/TRAITS

"If you learn to routinely express these emotions in your communications with others you will substantially improve the quality of your interpersonal relationships and improve the quality of your life!"

Open-mindedness	Passion	Forgiving
Acceptance	Understanding	Sincerity
Flexibility	Caring	Confidence
Cheerfulness	Giving	Loving

KEY ENABLING CHARACTER TRAITS NECESSARY FOR CONSTANT GROWTH

"These Character Traits define who we are, how we conduct "ourselves, and how others in tern respond to us."

Curiosity	Efficiency	Kindness
Discrimination	Courage	Charity
Patience	Tolerance	Devotion
Precision	Sincerity	Humility

WHICH WOULD YOU RATHER BE, A SCARED FIELD MOUSE OR A SOARING EAGLE?

It should come as no surprise that low achievers, average achievers and super achievers think and act very differently. Low achievers have a vocabulary and habits that support their need for safety and security and reflect their lack of confidence. They see failure as a negative rather than as a teacher. They lack the necessary self-esteem and will power to be leaders, doers and achievers. They are instead followers who fear failure and seek the security of their known non-threatening environment.

Average achievers have dreams and want to set goals and achieve them, but they somehow lack a connection between dreaming and achieving. Something makes them stop short of their goals and give up. Perhaps they lack the courage to take the necessary risks. Perhaps they lack the requisite skills to execute their plans. Perhaps they simply have too low of a goal, so that even if they achieve what they set out to accomplish they are still only average. They were unable to see the height of what was possible. They were unable to soar with the eagles. They were unable to believe strongly enough in themselves to allow themselves to have a lofty dream that they truly thought was achievable.

The good news here is that we programmed our brains and if we don't like the programming we can change it. The universe is ever-changing, and God gave us the ability to change, adapt and grow. So if you are currently a low or average achiever that doesn't mean you can't become a super achiever.

If you want to be a super achiever, all you have to do is learn to think and act like a super achiever; people will respond to your super-charged powerful brain, and you will attract like-minded people to you to help you achieve your dreams.

So how does a super achiever think and act? It starts with a super dream. They have lofty goals and dreams. They expand the boundaries of what is possible. They have detailed plans that they execute in small incremental, believable steps one by one. As the saying goes, they eat the elephant one bite at a time. In other words, they nibble away at the task at hand until eventually what once was a monumental task now seems truly achievable. They persist with courage, determination, conviction and faith until eventually they achieve their dreams.

The twelve great virtues are the most powerful set of values or habits in the world. If you apply them in your life until they are habitual and instinctual there will be no limit to what you will be able to achieve. One day you will look down from the clouds and realize that somehow mysteriously, while you weren't watching, you were transformed from a scared field mouse into an eagle soaring high above, surveying his domain and knowing that there is no limit to what you can achieve.

"Life evolves or life dies for there is no standing still.
If we don't grow we wither away and die a slow death of despair.
So to live is to grow and to grow is to change.
This is the key to finding happiness."
– Larry Ballard

Definition of "The Twelve Great Virtues" Necessary for Optimal Growth

- **Curiosity** is the desire to know. It is a natural inquisitiveness that leads us to explore our environment and experience growth.

- **Discrimination** is the process by which we learn to discern and distinguish how things in our environment interact, their similarities and differences and how they affect each other.

- **Patience** is necessary in order for us to learn to stay the course. Patience teaches us to be steadfast, despite obstacles, difficulties and adversity. For only through our continued efforts can we succeed.

- **Precision** teaches us to learn to distinguish differences and to discern the relevance of those differences. This is the basis of informed decision making and quality workmanship.

- **Efficiency** is the process by which we learn to efficiently optimize our time and available resources to achieve our desired goal.

- **Courage** is the ability to move beyond our fears. Without courage we would reach a point where obstacles, difficulties and opposition would eventually cause us to give up and simply quit. But with courage, we persist. With resolute determination, tenacity and stubborn persistence we continue unwilling to acknowledge defeat.

- **Tolerance** is the process by which we learn to consider opposing points of view, then to begrudgingly tolerate them and eventually to be open to the possibility of changing our own point of view.

- **Sincerity** is at the core of our self-worth. It is the faculty to be open, honest and free of hypocrisy; to be honest and genuine with our self and in our dealings with our fellow man.

- **Kindliness** requires that we consider the emotional needs of others. That we learn to be supportive, sympathetic, nurturing and caring, and that we extend ourselves to others.

- **Charity** is the process by which we become more benevolent. Charity denotes a genuine concern for others and the desire to help those less fortunate than us. It's an expression of care and giving that moves us further from an "I" orientation to an "other" orientation.

- **Devotion** is a spiritual commitment of faithfulness to an object of devotion that we hold above ourselves. Devotion represents our first step in truly giving ourselves to a cause or purpose that we hold higher than ourselves.

- **Humility** is the ability to look beyond ourselves. When we attain humility, we come to understand our role in the grand scheme of things. We become naturally unpretentious, grateful and finally capable of true love.

The twelve great virtues provide us the necessary skills for success in the material world and help us to develop our characters so that we are able to **continuously grow and evolve.** In addition, they provide us with a framework that we can use to **re-script our brains** so that, regardless of our early programming, we can realize our potential. If you look at truly successful people you have known or that society has revered, I believe you will find that they exhibited most if not all of these traits.

I urge you to take these virtues or character traits and develop them into habits. Once they have become habitual they will be your expression of reality: A reality that attracts positive events and people to you—a reality that ensures your success. If you learn to express these traits in your dealings with others you will be a supercharged magnet that will attract positive people and outcomes into your life. You will be capable of achieving greatness. In so doing, you will cease to be part of the problem. You will instead have become part of the solution, a solution that enriches your life and all those you come in contact with. These traits are in fact predominant habits of most truly successful and happy people.

I encourage you to take one of the twelve great virtues <u>each month</u> and spend the month applying it in your day-to-day activities. Do this for twelve months, and you will have converted all twelve virtues into personal habits. This process will go a long way toward reprogramming your brain by displacing any negative beliefs you may have with these powerful, ***empowering beliefs*** that are the keys to constant growth. Your brain can accept only one reality at a time. If you focus on the virtues, which are by nature positive, the negatives will be washed away into the shadow of oblivion.

> *"We are what we think; and what we think controls the emotions we feel. Therefore, the quality of our consistent beliefs defines the quality of our life!"*
> – Larry Ballard

As we close this chapter and the book, I would like to focus on our original premise, which is that there is going to be a second Great Depression. I would be remiss in my obligation to you if I didn't close by leaving you with an action plan for what you need to do to prepare yourself and your family to survive the economic hardships that will accompany the second Great Depression. So the question we must answer is:

WHAT CHANGES DO YOU NEED TO MAKE IN ORDER TO PREPARE FOR THE COMING SECOND GREAT DEPRESSION?

If we agree that money isn't the root of all evil, but rather a necessity, then the $64,000 question is how do we get the money we need without its pursuit making us unhappy? *Specifically, what do we do to cope with the inevitable changes that are being brought about by the second Great Depression?*

■   *We must learn to be less materialistic.* This means we have to stop saying "I Want That" and understand that wanting that, no buying that (on credit) is how we got in debt, and our debt is a major source of our current problems. The more savings we have, the more options we have and the less savings the fewer options. **It's that simple. Consumer debt is a yoke that enslaves us.**

According to the American Savings Education Council nearly half of all Americans have less than $25,000 in savings and nearly 60 million Americans, or one fifth of the population have no savings at all, absolutely none. There are nearly 75 million baby boomers nearing retirement and according to AARP the "typical boomer" has a scant $1000 in financial assets. Generally speaking the reason these people have so little savings isn't because they don't have good jobs. *It's because they consistently spent everything they made instead of spending less than they made and investing the difference.* You should pay cash for consumer items and reserve debt for leveraged investments that generate cash flow and make a profit. Instead these people lived high on the hog, paycheck to paycheck. I call them *penny millionaires,* because they look rich but in reality they don't have two pennies to rub together. Everything they have is leveraged to the hilt. They don't own anything. Instead their possessions own them. They are nothing more than indentured servants whose vanities are making the money lenders rich and them poor. In these times of economic uncertainty these penny millionaires live with one foot in the grave of economic ruin. If they are the victims of downsizing, outsourcing, mechanization, technological obsolescence, a merger or acquisition or any of a dozen other mishaps they will be facing financial ruin. Their cars will be repossessed, their home foreclosed and the bill collectors will be beating down their doors. This is the price they pay for letting the Madison Avenue advertising agencies brainwash them into believing that happiness and materialism are one in the same thing. In reality happiness depends on being in control of the circumstances of your life, so you have peace of mind and serenity, neither of which are possible when you are constantly worrying about how you are going to pay the bills. Worry and insecurity is the enemy of happiness. They cannot reside in the same house. Where one resides the other cannot survive.

■ *We must learn to live within our means.* This means we must learn to spend less than we make and to save and invest the difference, so when we are ready to retire we will be financially well off. The problem is that materialism is ingrained in the very fabric of the nation. We are constantly bombarded with a stream of advertisements designed to convince us that we need this product or that product because it is supposed to make us feel good, look good or be sexy. At every turn we are offered credit cards. They seem harmless, but they are the source of our poverty. For example, if you owed just $2,000 in credit card debt and paid just the minimum payment, it would take you eight years and nearly $5,000 to pay it off. By the way, the average American has over $10,000 in credit card debt. As I said earlier, our finances are driven by our emotions and our values. They define how we earn our money, how we spend it, how much (if any) we save, how we invest and ultimately if money will be a source of security, peace of mind and happiness, or if it will be a source of stress, conflict and unhappiness. If we live within our means not every unforeseen change of fortune is a catastrophe, so we are not unduly stressed out and it doesn't negatively impact the quality of our lives. *It's a fact of life that to be happy a person must feel that he has a reasonable level of security and control in his life.* If he does not, his life is governed by fear, and fear is a poison that robs us of happiness.

- ***We must become astute investors.*** This means we must take responsibility for our investments rather than turning control over to a stranger. That doesn't mean that you don't get help from experts. It means you get counsel, so that you can make informed decisions. I promise you, you will make mistakes, but the point is you can't learn from somebody else's mistakes. You can learn from your own mistakes. The other key thing to becoming an astute investor is learning to manage your risk, so that when you do make a mistake it will not be a catastrophe. Risk management boils down to greed management! Every time I feel I am tempted to violate my investment strategy, because I found a deal that was too good to pass up I remind myself of the following saying: ***"Pigs get fat and hogs get slaughtered."*** At that point, reason generally sets in, and I get out from under my emotions and let my reason take control. Remember you have a security bucket and a growth bucket for a reason and they serve different purposes.

- ***We must develop multiple sources of income.*** For most of us, our income comes from a single source: our jobs. We live with the fear that at any moment, owing to circumstances beyond our control, we could lose our jobs and since most of us have inadequate savings this is a serious concern. This leads to the paranoia and general insecurity that is the source of our unhappiness. According to the study a staggering 80 percent of us are unhappy at our jobs. So here is an interesting question. If so many of us are unhappy at our jobs why don't we leave? The answer is really quiet simple. We can't leave because we spend every penny we make and more! We are indentured servants. In exchange for immediate material gratification we have traded our financial freedom for a pair of golden handcuffs. We are slaves to materialism and, as a result, we live in fear, and where fear lives happiness cannot reside. You will remember from an earlier chapter that there are five distinct ways to make money and build wealth. They are: ***portfolio investments (paper assets); business (manufacturing, marketing, delivery of products and services); intellectual property (patents and copyrights); real estate investing and the Internet.*** I strongly urge you to learn about one or more of these five ways to make money and make the commitment to develop multiple revenue streams, so you can be self-sufficient and not have to rely on your employer, the government or anyone else for that matter.

■ *We must develop a recurring revenue stream.* In other words, we must put our money to work so our money works for us and we don't have to! The goal of our long-term retirement strategy is to allow our investments to accrue until they reach the point where we can live off the proceeds/cash flow of our investments without having to sell the assets. At this point our investments have reached a critical Mass, or the point at which the cash flow from our investments is adequate to cover all of our living expenses for the balance of our lives. By the way, based on current investment strategies, most Americans will not achieve this goal. Instead, they will retire on a downwardly declining annuity retirement program that will require them to systematically sell a portion of their assets each month in order to cover their living expenses. In essence, each month their net worth is reduced until they have nothing left. If they live longer than expected, they will live out the remainder of their lives in poverty. If you follow the advice given in this book, you can avoid this unpleasant outcome and be one of the 5 percenters who retire well off.

■ *We must accept the fact that balance not materialism is the key to happiness.* We must reject the Madison Avenue advertisers' brainwashing and no longer allow their appeals to our egos, self-esteem or sexuality to dictate what we buy. We must learn that our identity does not depend on what we have, but instead on who we are, the relationships we have, our values, our ability to work for the greater good and our desire to strive to contribute to society, rather than to take from it. These things are the basis of a balanced, full, rich abundant life. They, not materialism, will bring us happiness and true wealth! With this in mind, have you completed your life plan? Do you have a specific plan for your career, finances, relationships, health, leisure time and spirituality? Have you determined whether your life plan contains any conflicts that might cause you to either fail to achieve your goals or bring you unhappiness? In effect, do you have a plan for achieving the balance that is the requisite to achieving happiness? Have you taken

control of your life and are you headed to a town called somewhere, or are you still on the road to a town called nowhere?

WHAT CONSTITUTES A BALANCED LIFE?

> *"To be happy you must be balanced, and to be balanced*
> *you must be in control of your time and your finances.*
> *This allows you to choose how you spend that most valuable*
> *of all assets time, so that you may choose to spend it on those*
> *things that make you happy as opposed to having to spend*
> *disproportionate amounts of it on making a living.*
> *Lastly, in order to be in control of your finances you*
> *must live debt free or at least well within your means."*
>
> – Larry Ballard

- *It's time we focus on our health.* We have become a nation of
overweight, unhealthy people. Heart disease, diabetes and high
blood pressure have reached epidemic proportions, and they are
all directly related to obesity. Here too, the Madison Avenue
advertising agencies have played a role. They bombard us with
advertisements for junk food. McDonalds gets its hands on our
children and turns them into what they call **"users."** I guess this
is an appropriate term because, after all, food is addictive, especially food that contains fat and complex carbohydrates. When
was the last time you saw a commercial for broccoli, asparagus,
green beans or anything healthy for that matter? Try going to your
child's school and finding anything healthy on the lunch menu. At
the same time, there is no shortage of French fries, pizza and soda.
If you want McDonalds, Pizza Hut, Pepsi, Coke or any of several
equally unhealthy choices, no problem, — they are all there. As a
parent, wouldn't you like to see your child get a healthy, nutritious
meal at school? This is another example of materialism. The only
difference is that, in this instance, it isn't us overspending it's us
getting something that is clearly not good pushed on us because
it's profitable. Companies use advertising to brainwash us; they
convince us we can't live without their products.

- *It's time we focus on our relationships.* We have abandoned our neighbors, friends, and most importantly our families in pursuit of materialism. As a result, the national divorce rate has topped 50 percent and we are increasingly a nation of lonely, isolated people who don't know how to reach out to others in friendship. It's time we reclaimed these most precious relationships, because we can't be happy if we don't have anyone to share our lives with. You don't want to wake up one day and find out that your wife and children are strangers. That's a pretty high price to pay. It's like the lyrics to Tennessee Ernie Ford's signature song: "I load 16 tons of # 9 coal and all I get is another day older and deeper in debt. St. Peter don't you call me cause I can't go. I owe my soul to the company store." This is not a life; it is slavery. When we came from the farm to the city, we came for security. One hundred years later that security is an illusion. We need to take care of ourselves because the corporations and the government can't.

- *It's time we put our Careers and our Finances into perspective.* Let's face it our jobs are a major source of our insecurity, tension and stress. We can't depend on our jobs. They may disappear at any moment. Given this instability we are well advised to stop living from paycheck to paycheck and start saving for the future. We are well advised to get rid of the golden handcuffs by learning to live within our means and by avoiding consumer debt which breeds poverty. We are well advised to establish multiple sources of income, so if we lose our jobs we will have alternate income to live off. In this case, it is an inconvenience if we lose our job, but it is not a major catastrophe. The goal is to have enough residual income to be able to do what you want for a living, rather than having to stay at a job you hate just so you can pay the bills. That is not a living; it is a slow death.

- *It's time we focus on Leisure Time.* Remember the saying, "all work and no play makes Jack a dull boy"? I would go further and say that it makes him unhealthy; it ruins his relationships, negatively affects his job performance and generally reduces his sense of well-being. Believe it or not, you can simplify your life. The key to having leisure time is having financial security; and the key to having financial security is to spend less than you make and invest the difference. I would contend that we have let our pursuit of materialism make slaves of us. It's time we realized that time is our most valuable asset. If we cherish it and use it wisely, it is a major source of happiness. I seriously doubt that on our death beds many of us would wish for more time at work, but most of us would probably wish for more time with our loved ones. Why don't we take the time now while we still can?

■ *It's time we focus on spirituality:* We need to reclaim our values and spiritual beliefs and find a meaning and purpose that goes beyond materialism. It's time we learned that true happiness is based on giving, not taking. We have been a nation of takers for too long and look what it has gotten us. We are stressed out, burned out, disillusioned and generally unhappy. Giving to others is the greatest feeling in the world. Besides, God promises that whatever we give will return to us multiplied!

> *Whatsoever a man soweth, that shall he reap.*
> (Galatians 6:7 11)

> *God is able to do exceeding abundantly above all*
> *that we ask or think.*
> (Ephesians 3:20)

There can be little doubt we are headed for hard times. So the question is, if God were to come tomorrow would he judge that you had made money God's way or man's way?

God's way:
> *But seek first the kingdom of God and his righteousness:*
> *and all these things shall be added unto you.*
> (Matthew 6:33)

> *And it shall be given unto you; good measure, pressed down,*
> *and shaken together. And running over, shall men give unto*
> *your bosom. For with the same measure that ye met withal*
> *it shall be measured to you again.*
> (Luke 6:30)

Man's way:

*But they that will be rich fall into temptation and a snare, and into
many foolish and hurtful lusts, which drown men in destruction and
perdition. For the love of money is the root of all evil: which while
some coveted after, they have erred from the faith, and pierced
themselves through with many sorrows.*
(1 Timothy 6:9-10)

*No man can serve two masters, for either he will hate the one and
love the other, or else he will hold to the one, and despise the other.
Ye cannot serve God and mammon.*
(Matthew 6:24)

**If you are brutally honest, have you made your money man's way
or God's way? Who is your master, God or Mammon?**

The good news here is that God has made us a promise in his scriptures and God never lies. He is incapable of lying!

*If they obey and serve Him, they will spend the rest of their days in
prosperity and their years in contentment.*
(Job 36:11)

God also promised to reward us according to our deeds.

*"I the LORD search the heart and examine the mind,
to reward a man according to his conduct,
according to what his deeds deserve."*
(Jeremiah 17:10)

*The word of God is living and active. Sharper than any
double-edged sword, it penetrates even to dividing soul
and spirit, joints and marrow; it judges the thoughts and
attitudes of the heart.* (Hebrews 4:12)

I don't mean to be preaching, but I have seen God give, and I have
seen Him take away. I lost my family, because I made money man's

way, and I sincerely don't want any of you to have to learn the hard way, like I did. Now, I am on God's plan and believe me it is a better plan. He does keep His promises. So the really tough question is: If you are making money man's way, what are you prepared to do about it? Are you ready to change and receive God's blessings?

Every good and perfect gift is from above,
coming down from the Father of the heavenly lights,
who does not change like shifting shadows.
(James 1:17)

The LORD watches over all who love him,
but the wicked he will destroy.
(Psalms 145:20)

Now all has been heard; here is the conclusion of the matter: Fear
God and keep his commandments, for this is the whole duty of man.
(Ecclesiastes 12:13)

When the Second Great Depression comes and, heaven help us, when the end-of-time tribulations come on us, we will be rewarded *"...according to what our deeds deserve"* (Jeremiah 17:10). I don't know about you, but I want to be rewarded, not punished. I want God's blessings on me and mine, and I am writing this book because I believe God called me to gather the lost sheep like myself, so that we may receive His blessings and His protection. Please for your sake, take this message from God seriously!

P.S.

I have written this book in the sincere hope that I can help those who will listen and who will likewise be willing to take action and get their financial and spiritual house in order so that when the hard times come they will be spared from despair and destruction!

For other titles
or a free catalog
call 800-729-4131
or visit www.nohoax.com

Visit the author at
www.GeopoliticalAffairs.net
email: larryballard1@yahoo.com

Also by Larry Ballard:

*Modern Slavery
And the Fight For Freedom*

language); or we may use silence as a means of instigating turn-taking.

Grammatik Marker

My favorite use of silence is that of a Grammatik marker. When we read a passage from a piece of literature, we find marks of grammar that set one phrase or sentence apart from another… Such marks of grammar also indicate pause or silence:

1) Silence as Parenthesis: Parenthesis is used for information that does not follow the natural flow of your sentence, but that needs to be included anyway. Parentheses are often used to provide additional information that clarifies or supplements something already said. In writing, parenthesis is signified by the use of brackets, in speech, however, it is signified through the use of a short pause before and after the parenthesis.

2) Silence as Ellipse or Dash: An ellipse, in writing, is a set of three consecutive dots used to signify an extended pause. A dash has the same effect, but usually to a shorter degree. Dashes, however, generally unlike the ellipse, are often used before and after a phrase so as to set it apart from the rest of the sentence (possibly as emphasis).

3) Silence After Commas or Periods: A period signifies the end of a phrase or sentence, or otherwise the completion of a stream of thought. As it signifies an ending it is only natural that there should be a stop or pause after periods.

4) Silence After Exclamation: The exclamation mark is probably the most powerful marker in grammar. It signifies a rising of expression. An emotional surge. Excitement!

As another example: A husband and wife walk into a lady's fashion store... The wife says "Do you like this dress?", and the man doesn't answer. A response is given.

Requesting Response

Silence often terrifies people. In an interpersonal situation, where no one speaks and there is a sense of dead silence (a complete lack of noise), one person is bound to begin talking sooner or later. When a question is asked, and the listener does not respond, the same sense of dead silence can be felt. In such a case, the speaker often breaks the silence by continuing to speak, either by adding additional information and returning to request an answer, or possibly accepting no response and changing the subject to a different topic. What would happen though, if the speaker simply waited for a reply...? The listener would eventually say something!

Withholding Information

Silence can also be a means of withholding information. To plead the fifth, in the United States, means to say nothing. When somebody asks a question, you have the option of answering it in full; provide only a partial answer, or not answering at all. Depending on the context, you may have a strategic advantage in choosing one option over the other. The art of information manipulation, however, is a subject far too great for the likes of this book.

Emotive Language

Emotive language is the use of words that provoke some type of emotional response. If you really want to captivate people and pull their attention in towards you, you must aim to get them emotionally involved in the conversation.

Emotive language makes use of descriptive language as discussed above… With a special emphasis on adjectives that describe emotions (i.e. happy, sad, excited, lonely, etc.).

In the context of emotive language, all words can be thought of as divided into two main categories:

*1) **Denotation:*** The denotative meaning of a word is the actual or literary meaning of the word itself. This is fairly synonymous with the explicit meaning of words as discussed in chapter 4.

*2) **Connotation:*** The connotative meaning of a word is the essential idea that the word represents, generally in the view of the majority (of the people). This is similar to the implicit meaning of words as described in chapter 4.

Just to ensure understanding of this, let's look at a quick scenario: If I was to give a yellow rose to a friend, and say "I appreciate you", the yellow rose would signify good friendship; this is the connotation of a yellow rose as generally understood by the vast majority. If, however, the rose was red, the red rose would signify a stronger interpersonal relationship – Such as that between lovers.

In the use emotive language, we restructure our phrases so that the most emotionally implicit meaning of a word is used, instead of the explicit or denotative meaning. Consider the following:

"A house is just a structure; but a home is where you hang your hat".

The connotative meaning of words change the way in which the entire sentence is perceived through ideology (using words as ideas rather than the literal significance). It evokes an emotional response... The word "child" has a different meaning to most people, then the word "kid" (child relates to closeness and innocence, while "kid" simply refers to person who is not an adult, and could be of any age between 1 week and twenty years)... To elaborate on this, it is more likely that we would say call our own child "a child", and someone else's child "A kid" because the emotional involvement is greater with our own children, and significantly less with someone else's.

The word "woman" may refer to any female over the age of 20 years; while the word "lady" tends to refer to a woman of royal or similar class. The word "complete" simply refers to all pieces being accounted for; while the word "system" refers to a complete set that works together to provide specified results.

Learn to grow your vocabulary of synonyms, and reconsider the denotative and connotative meaning of words – Understand the impact of the words you use on your listeners. Use sentences that promote the connotative meaning when you want to excite an emotional response.

Figure of Speech

A figure of speech is a word, phrase or sentence that is designed to create an effect of some sort. Many figures of speech have become commonplace in day-to-day conversation, while others appear to be more confined to literature, and others yet are not often used at all. Below,

I've included only those that are commonly appropriate for spoken conversation.

Anaphora

Anaphora occurs when at the first part of a sentence is repeated in the second part of the same sentence. Sometimes, a word is changed so that it doesn't sound so much like a repetition. See the example below:

"Everybody likes winners, but nobody likes losers"

Cliché

A cliché is an expression that has been over-used, so that it has lost its expressive power. Examples include:

"Turn over a new leaf"

"A rose by any other name would still smell as sweet"

Hyperbole

This is the use of exaggerations for the purpose of amplifying a given statement. Most people use hyperbole naturally in day to day language. For example, if a task takes 5-6 hours to complete, we may say "It took the whole day" (did it really take the whole day?).

Hyperbole may be used to add humor to a conversation; or it may be used to add a sense of seriousness to the message.

Idiom

An idiom is a common expression that has come to mean something other than its literary meaning. Common Idioms include:

"It's raining cats and dogs"

"That cost me an arm and a leg"

Much like clichés, idioms have become common because of their over-use. Like clichés, idioms should be avoided.

Innuendo

Innuendo involves opinions, remarks or terminology that insinuates or provides subtle or indirect observation about a person or thing, usually of a salacious, critical, or wrongful nature. Examples of innuendo include: He was shooting his mouth off, and killed the conversation; or "He's not the smartest nail in the bunch".

Innuendo can be used to add humor to a conversation when speaking about events or inanimate objects. Innuendo should be avoided when referring to people to avoid future complications in relations.

Litote

This is a figure of speech in which an understatement is used for rhetorical effect, usually by using double negatives. Example: "He's not the most intelligent person in the world". (Meaning he's stupid).

Litotes may be commonly used amongst friends in a non-professional environment; but should be avoided in professional conversation as they devalue the subject of the conversation.

Metaphor

Metaphor is a very common figure of speech in where one word is equated to another or where one word is used to signify another, usually in an idealistic fashion. Metaphors often use comparative words to relate one thing to another. For example: the use of the phrase "broken heart" to suggest that a person is hurt and sad, however, the heart itself is not actually broken.

Because people often use comparisons to understand new ideas, metaphors can be used in explanation or to help reinforce a message (so others can comprehend the message better).

Metonymy

This occurs where one word is called by one of its associated words or ideas instead of calling it by its own name or instead of calling it what it really is.

A famous example of the use of metonymy is the phrase "The pen is mightier than the sword" ("pen" referring the writing skills, and "sword" referring to the use of force)

Another example is to say: "I need a **hand** with my suitcases" *("hand" refers to help)*. As another example: "Wall Street" is often used to refer to the U.S. financial sector; and "Hollywood" is used to refer to the U.S. major motion picture industry.

You can create your own metonymy, such that may be only understood between yourself and another person -The consistent use of which can help develop a relational bond. You can also use a commonly understood metonymy that is relevant to the conversation when you believe it would be understood by the listener, even if simply to change up your conversation .

Oxymoron

An oxymoron occurs when two terms are used together, that would ordinarily contradict each other.

Many oxymoron's are already a part of everyday speech or are commonly understood. Examples of oxymorons include: Clearly confused; act naturally; pretty ugly; alone together.

Because of their nature of including contradictory words, oxymoron may be used to add a hint of humor to the conversation. Place a stress or emphasis on the oxymoron when using them. Be careful, however, not to use oxymoron in a condescending manner.

Paradox

A paradox is a phrase or sentence that appears to contradict itself, but can be understood as not contradictory. Paradoxical statements often leave some room for debate.

A great example of a paradox, or paradoxical statement, would be to say "If this statement is true, then Santa Clause and the Tooth Fairy both exist". But the idea of Santa Clause and the Tooth Fairy exist, and to a child, a mother who exchanges a tooth under the pillow for money could essentially be considered "the tooth fairy"; and obviously the above statement exists, as you must have read it to understand my debate of the matter.

Paradoxical statements can be used to force someone to think deeper about a subject, think outside of the box of literary meaning, or otherwise to open intellectual debate about a conversation. Such statements should not be used otherwise.

Pun

A pun is a humorous comment that exploits words that have more than one meaning, or sometimes to exploit words that sound alike (homonyms and homophones).

An example of a pun would be "An elephant's opinion carries a lot of weight" (elephants also carry a lot of weight). Another example in response to the questions "Are you alright" may be "No, I'm half right, half left".

Puns can be used to add humor to a conversation. Before using puns, take note of the situational context, and the mood of the listener. Puns are best used when under a free-spirited and happy atmosphere.

Simile

A simile is a type of metaphor where two things are introduced as being similar (like the name says)… This is usually done using words such as "like", "as" or "its equivalent". In the movie 'Forrest Gump', Forrest uses a simile while sitting on the street bench talking to the old lady when he says "Life is like a box of chocolates, you never know what you'll get".

Like metaphors, similes can be effectively used in explanation or to help reinforce a message (so others can comprehend the message better).

Synecdoche

Synecdoche is a type of metonymy where a phrase or sentence uses words or terminologies that give a meaning similar or related to that which is literal in meaning, but is not meant exactly as is said. An example of synecdoche would be "Do you like my **wheels**?" (The word "wheels" refers to the entire vehicle).

> While synecdoche may be used to add a little spice to a conversation, it shouldn't be used too often, and may be considered a type of slang.

Tautology

In tautology, two or more words that are near-synonyms are placed together in context. For example: "Read the short summary about…", or "In my opinion, I think". In normal conversation, these figures of speech should not be used as they make conversation appear redundant, and lengthier than they need to be. Tautology can be created in two ways:

1) Successive Tautology: here, tautology is created when two words are used in succession, such as the examples above.

> Successive tautology does not add any apparent emphasis to a phrase and should generally be avoided because they make sentences appear too repetitive.

2) Non-Successive Tautology: Here, tautology is created using two similar words, but in two separate phrase. Take for example, to say "I am certain, and I do believe this is true."

Used effectively, this type of tautology can add emphasis and/or dramatic appeal to a sentence or phrase. Speak the tautology with an emphasis on the similar words. Do not use tautology too often.

Index Table

www.ingramcontent.com/pod-product-compliance
Lightning Source LLC
Chambersburg PA
CBHW060345200326
41519CB00011BA/2039